TRUST IN TOBACCO

The Anglo-American Struggle for Power

Maurice Corina

NEW YORK
ST. MARTIN'S PRESS

For SUSAN and JUDITH.

Neglected during the writing,
but not forgotten.

Contents

Contents

'I have acquired an Indian herb of marvellous and proved worth against the Noli me tangere and fistulas given up as incurable by the physicians. As soon as it gives its seeds, I will send some of them to your gardener at Marmoustier in a barrel with instructions for replanting and cultivating it.'

—JEAN NICOT, the French Ambassador at the Court of Portugal in a letter to Cardinal de Lorraine in 1560 on the curative powers of the plant later named in his honour Nicotiana

Introduction

The late Sir Compton Mackenzie smoked his first cigarette at the age of four, hand-rolled for him by an American cousin one summer day at Cromer, Norfolk. He moved through childhood secretly smoking the stubs of his father's cigars in a Petersen pipe. In later years, he was rarely without half a dozen favourite pipes, or a cigar, close to hand, and it was his annual resolution on New Year's Eve *not* to give up smoking in the New Year. The prolific Scottish author and broadcaster died in 1972, aged eighty-nine, having written some one hundred books. Among those works was *Sublime Tobacco*, published in 1957 'as a token of my gratitude for the immense benefit I have derived from tobacco and in complete certainty that I have not derived from it the slightest harm'. Such conviction is not, however, shared by the many thousands of families who have witnessed one or more of their number suffering the agonies of cancer of the lung. Sir Compton's study, a product of fine scholarship, is essentially the work of a romanticist, but his devoted description of tobacco's history to the turn of the century is not, of course, the full story.

There can be no argument about the romantic past of the fragrant weed, except by the tobacco antiquarians who still squabble over the details and each other's theories for the mistier years. Yet it is the rest of the story which is surely no less fascinating and certainly equally daunting in the telling.

This narrative sets out to describe the machine age of tobacco when an historic merchant trade, established between the New and Old World by the great adventurers of Europe, was fashioned into an industry of world significance and one upon which the United States can be said to be founded. The years which saw the introduction of mass-produced cigarettes and other tobacco products also spawned trusts and combinations, even the earliest multinational corporations, which fought for control of the burgeoning mass markets of Great Britain and the United States.

The giant personalities who sought to shape the industry's growth to their schemes of arrangement, and whose actions were not always creditable, have something of the boldness of all buccaneers, or pioneers. James Buchanan Duke, who features so strongly in these pages, and Lord Winterstoke, defender of Britannic markets against the invading Yankee trust, led by the 'plug chawing' Duke, were nonetheless very different men if endowed with more than their fair share of business acumen. They both became monopolists—the former by design, the latter by necessity—but differed in their exercise of market power. Both the American and Imperial Tobacco Companies were to come under the scrutiny of anti-trust authorities on each side of the Atlantic. The American corporation was emasculated and Duke barely escaped criminal prosecution, but Imperial, years later, survived official inquiry into its behaviour and, by its response to public disquiet over a shareholding in its main British rival, watched the wheel of history turn full cycle to bring back the American invader, precipitating something of a moral crisis in the City. There is much more to the story than this. The development of brand marketing, the board-room intrigues, the control of machinery, the great gift coupon wars, the mergers and take-overs effected long before anonymous executives assumed control of the modern corporations, and the response of vast enterprises (yielding huge profits for themselves and even greater revenues for their Governments) to the issue of smoking and health—all, and more, must be included in an account of the transatlantic tobacco industry since 'Buck' Duke once dreamed of world dominion.

What follows, the author earnestly hopes, is a clear and exciting narrative which, while necessarily selective in the events and personalities described, will contribute to public understanding and knowledge at a time when interest in the great corporations has never been so strong and before the big tobacco companies, now fast diversifying their interests, submerge into other industries.

It has been no easy task, so the help and encouragement that writers derive from other people need to be firmly acknowledged at the outset. In particular, I am greatly indebted to an old friend Peter Spearing, lately public relations manager of the Imperial Group, and his company colleague, Graeme McKelvie, for their patient help and initial encouragement. My appreciation must be recorded, too, to their counterparts in the other British and American tobacco groups, with a special mention for Gwynn Hargrove (British-American Tobacco) and Jack Prosser (Carreras) as well as the information executives of W. D. & H. O. Wills, John Player & Sons, and Gallaher. A separate sentence of praise must be devoted to the excellent archivists, whose painstaking research and maintenance of historic papers is taken for granted by the industry and deserves wider recognition for the help they give to historians and others.

My thanks must also go to the many people I have interviewed along the way, ranging from Lord Sinclair of Cleeve, President of Imperial, to the old age pensioners who remember so well the conditions and many of the events of the past. The help of Richard Spiegelberg on the pages dealing with the creation of Rothmans International is fully and gratefully acknowledged. Finally, I must thank the Editor of *The Times*, William Rees-Mogg, for permission, so readily given, to write this book and have access to the newspaper's own archives.

There are, of course, so many others whom one would wish to mention. They may not be listed here, but they are not forgotten. One person, of course, to whom single tribute must be paid is Mary H. Todd, an experienced amanuensis whose cheerful devotion to research, typing and correction has helped other and more distinguished authors and whose competence in steering this book to completion has been greatly valued.

Some may make different judgements or offer other versions of the people or events contained in these pages. There may be mistakes, even if honestly made. Antiquarians will no doubt continue their various arguments as high-speed machines disgorge cigarettes by the billion. Like the consumers of tobacco, their search is for some inner satisfaction. Sir Compton Mackenzie found his by writing a book to meet their demand while spending just as many pleasant hours pulling on his famous and favourite pipes while setting down his words. I can confess to deriving a dual satisfaction, too, though, in my case, it has been from contemporary machine-wrapped mild Panatellas, in trying to tell something of the no less remarkable story from where he chose to conclude.

MAURICE CORINA

TRUST IN TOBACCO

CHAPTER ONE

'Pro Bono Publico'

The large carrot-haired man replaced the telephone receiver on his New York desk. For the first time in his speaking life, James Buchanan Duke, one of the wealthiest and certainly one of the most controversial men in American industry, seemed lost for words. In the silence that followed the call—from Washington— he gazed round his office, eyes settling on a treasured sepia photograph of his father standing before the log cabin-cum-factory where as a shoeless, straw-hatted fourteen-year-old he had flailed out his first bale of bright leaf tobacco to be sold under the brand Pro Bono Publico in muslin bags at 30 cents a pound after tax.

It was little wonder that he took his time before speaking. Buck Duke switched his thoughts from those dusty days in Orange, later Durham County, North Carolina, to the present position. From that desk he controlled, by one means or other, virtually the entire tobacco industry in America and the American Tobacco Company combination in particular. The telephone that had jangled, and which had been pressed so anxiously to his ear, conveyed some astounding news. In the United States Supreme Court, Chief Justice White had just concluded a statement nearly ninety minutes long in a courtroom so crowded that even senators had to fight in the corridors to gain entry.

The Chief Justice handed down an appeal decision that held Duke and his combine guilty of violating the anti-trust laws in securing control of four-fifths of the total non-cigar manufactured tobacco industry. It was a bitter and damning ruling, bristling with censure for breaching the rules of fair competition by methods that went beyond reasonable exercise of ordinary rights to contract and trade. The direction was that the Circuit Court of Appeals in New York should arrange the dissolution of the Duke empire, and restore lawful competition between the constituent concerns. If the instruction could not be met in just six months, the lower court was authorised to put in receivers.

Duke's silence is reputed to have ended with his tearing up papers on his desk, letting the pieces flutter around him. Suddenly he growled: 'In England, if a fellow had built up a whale of a business outa that (pointing at the log cabin) he'd be knighted. Here they want to put him in jail.'

The tobacco tycoon's bitter comment that day, 29th May 1911, on one of the most momentous events in American business history, while obviously incorrect, was not without some irony. Some five years before, one Sir William Henry Wills Bt had been elevated to the Peerage as Lord Winterstoke, a real life tobacco baron. Nine years before Duke was born, the third child of Artelia and Washington Duke (and named James Buchanan in honour of a new Democratic President of the United States of America elected that autumn), the Lord Winterstoke had entered his family's business. At seventeen years old, he was to be equipped with a fifty-guinea horse of his own choosing and a four-wheeled dog cart, sent out to travel the United Kingdom from Bristol soliciting orders for Superfine shag pipe tobacco and cigars. Winterstoke died that year 1911 when the dishonoured Duke contrasted the English and American attitudes towards monopoly building.

Winterstoke, a one-time Liberal Member of Parliament, was the first chairman of the Imperial Tobacco Company (of Great Britain and Ireland) Ltd. The double irony was that Duke's counterpart came to head the English tobacco monopoly, if a lesser and more legitimate one. Further, Imperial was a lusty ten-year infant enterprise, whose birth had been painfully conceived against the wishes of England's gentlemen merchants, whose subsequent discreet, but by no means soft-headed, trading practices created a mighty corporation even bigger than Duke's interlocking pyramid, then standing on a net capitalisation of $315 million. The formation of Imperial was England's answer, as the century turned, to Duke, the plug-chewing business schemer (his cheeks were constantly distended by the addiction to mouldy tobacco that first afflicted him in his teens).

The giant Duke, stunned by Chief Justice White's opinion, the outcome of several years of fierce litigation and continuous investigation, realised well enough that nothing could be the same again. Would-be monopolists might like him learn some lessons and like Imperial avoid malpractice and restore everyone's shattered faith in the private enterprise system which would duly turn the United States into the richest and most powerful nation on earth by the development of mass production and marketing.

Contemporary historians tend to this day to overlook the actions of such powerful men as Duke. For them, the politicians and their administrations are still the dominant subjects for study and analysis. It is true that President Theodore Roosevelt's powerful presence stopped Duke's American Tobacco Trust in its tracks as it hurtled ever onwards. But to understand the reasons and the significance for corporate life of such dramatic action requires not just knowledge of Duke's almost unbelievable climb to business power but some assessment of his place in American history.

The years that followed the American Civil War spawned a generation of entrepreneurs whose role in creating the industrial machine that survived unparalleled depressions and even the collapse of Wall Street remains not fully explained. While the bright-eyed Carnegie revolutionised the steel trade in Pittsburgh, while Rockefeller in Cleveland was creating Standard Oil and while Frick, the king of Coke, dominated Connellsville, the Duke family was raising smoke of a more basic kind.

Buck Duke was born into a God-fearing farming family on 23rd December 1856, a lusty and big-boned infant who, as a twenty-month-old baby, was held over the coffin of his mother who died from typhoid fever at twenty-nine. For his father, Washington, it was the loss of a second wife and another of the regular tragedies that beset the families established in the Piedmont country of North Carolina. An aunt was to teach Buck to read and write, watched over by the severe Washington Duke who was to be conscripted into the Confederacy's militia to fight for a cause in which he had no heart. When Buck's father went to war leaving the homestead he had created out of pine wood, set in a three hundred acre farm, he could hardly foresee his eventual imprisonment.

The growing Buck was to be moved with Duke's other children into his grandfather's care in Alamance, unaware of the dramatic events taking place as a result of North Carolina's decision to throw in with ten southern states which seceded from the Union. Washington found himself in Libby prison, to be released after General Joseph E. Johnston, commander of the last remaining Confederate army east of the Mississippi, fought a desperate retreat before the forces of Federal General William Sherman near the Duke farm as they withdrew from Raleigh and Hillsboro. The two generals met to talk the terms of surrender, an event that assumed even more momentous dimensions as Sherman broke the news of President Lincoln's assassination.

For Washington, the military conventions that followed meant freedom. He was released, with a single cent piece, traded for a Confederate five-dollar note, and faced with a hundred and thirty-five mile walk back home. That weary journey ended with a grim sight. The family homestead had been looted of livestock. All that remained was a small hoard of tobacco in a log barn. Before the war broke out, Washington had become interested in the success of other farmers in producing bright tobacco leaf. Experimental crops were being grown and cured, derived from the seeds brought by colonial planters. Washington's small store of tobacco had been built up out of the need to have a crop that would easily turn into the kind of ready cash that all farmers need. There was always a demand for chewing plug and the products of Durham had attained quite a reputation.

That hoard was to prove an asset which laid the foundations for a corporate empire which established an unparalleled monopoly, incurring the wrath of a future President. With his family restored to Orange County, Washington was next to set out with his son Buck in the summer of 1865 on a mule-drawn pedlar's cart with the aim of selling the tobacco around North Carolina. The boy was to sit astride bags labelled 'Pro Bono Publico', helping to sell the plug for cash or in exchange for goods. It was during one of these trips that he had a fight with another, but better dressed, boy at Cary—one Walter Hines Page, who became American Ambassador to the United Kingdom and was to meet Duke again in London in 1914 when Buck was desperately trying to quit British shores.

Duke worked in the fields alongside his father, planting and transplanting, weeding and de-pesting. No one was prouder than the growing lad as each summer the starch turned to sugar, giving the leaves the yellow hue that indicated they were ready for curing. The leaves were plucked and hung in a special airtight barn, which was heated by a hand-fed furnace. After three days or so, the doors would be flung open to let in moisture and the leaf finally tested for quality and colour. A twenty by thirty foot log barn was constructed for granulation and packing. Later came a purpose-built factory where the leaf was turned into plug, or ground up into smoking tobacco. Between 1866 and 1872, output was raised from an annual rate of 15,000 to 125,000 lb and Buck went into his teens calling himself superintendent.

Meanwhile, a stepbrother, Brodie, had realised the potential of tobacco, too. As sheds and factories began springing up along the Bright Belt, Brodie rented premises at Durham's Station, marketing several smoking tobaccos, including 'Duke of Durham'. Durham's Station was to boom into the status of a bustling town, largely under the commercial leadership of William Blackwell and Julian Carr, who founded the famous tobacco business Bull Durham, borrowing the bull's head trade-mark of Colman's mustard products in Britain. Farmers came to Durham to sell their products, thus avoiding long journeys elsewhere and supporting the establishment of local auctions. Washington followed his stepson's progress with a close interest and soon they were jointly developing a family factory to process leaf with the help of machinery and planned workrooms.

Buck was to be despatched to a Quaker school, from which he quickly ran away. He reputedly stalked up to his father and said: 'Why those Quakers want to teach a fellow Latin and poetry and such like? What good'll that do me? I ain't going to be a preacher or a lawyer. I am going to be a businessman and make my pile.' Buck was subsequently to produce a prospectus for the Eastman National School of Business in New York. For the next six months he was to study book-keeping and accountancy with a fiendish devotion. When he returned, the now eighteen-year-old was allowed to set up new book-keeping systems at the family factory off Main Street. The books soon told him there were healthy profits to be made and, when he requested some capital to launch his own venture, his father took a snap decision to take him into partnership.

The next few years saw Buck mastering every facet of the business, buying tobacco, supervising, and working out new economies to raise profitability. Business was his sole concern, and when the enterprise became a formal partnership with an authorised capital of $70,000, as W. Duke Sons & Company, and with financial support from several outsiders, it was inevitable that he should shoulder greater responsibility. He understood figures and profit margins, even if he could not bear to write fine letters and find time for niceties. The rival Bull Durham Company was expanding faster and more vigorously than the Duke concern. There had to be an answer. And Buck found it. He recommended that they start making cigarettes.

The young embryo tycoon had heard that cigarettes were catching on in England, and that in New York a small firm, Bedrossian Brothers, was attempting to counter a small but rising demand for imported Turkish cigarettes by hand-rolling American mild bright tobacco into thin paper tubes on shop premises at 22 Wall Street. Buck's researches indicated that annual demand was over 230 million cigarettes, a rise of more than 100 per cent over a few years before, and without much active promotion. Buck cared little for the history of cigarettes.

Cigarettes were believed to have been introduced into Spain in the seventeenth century, called 'apeletes' and comprising reed tubes set alight at one end which 'slowly consumed themselves without giving forth a flame, the smoke being fragrant like an incense stick of Valencia'. The Spaniards were to substitute paper for the reed and the apeletes soon found their way into Italy, Portugal, the Levant and Russia, where they became well established before the cigarette arrived in France at the beginning of the nineteenth century. The first cigarettes to reach England came with visitors from the Continent, but it was not until after the Crimean War, when British troops became familiar with the cigarettes handed round by French and Turkish allies, that they gained a firm foothold in the English tobacco market.

The early English cigarettes Sweet Threes (ten for 6d) were made from strong Latakia tobacco dust, wrapped in straw-coloured paper, with cane or straw mouthpieces. Army officers smoked them in the clubs of London, giving them the stamp of respectability. It was appropriate that a Scottish ex-Paymaster to the Turkish forces, Robert Gloag, should have decided in 1856 to set up the first English cigarette factory, which at first employed foreigners skilled in hand manufacture and later well-trained women. He was eventually to blend in bright flue-cured leaf from America.

Gloag's venture was so successful that other merchants were to launch into cigarettes as a sideline. One London firm, Philip Morris, began turning out a brand of smoke-cured Turkish tobacco. Some American visitors to London were to take back supplies to impress their friends in fashionable New York circles. It was only a matter of time before Duke's attentive ear received word of the craze, but in the interim period some astute New York tobacco entrepreneurs were meeting the demand first with imports and then local manufacture. The Bedrossian Brothers employed the skilled hands of Russian and Polish emigrés, workmen who could turn out up to 2,500 cigarettes a day. What was important to Duke was that the emerging New York cigarette makers had begun blending Turkish leaf with American Bright. In Richmond a factory was to spring up to exploit demand for cigarettes made with the less expensive Virginia tobacco. It was the brainchild of F. S. Kinney, a New York manufacturer, who also used foreign labour from Europe. He and the others ignored the taunts that cigarettes were a passing fad, dependent for sales on effeminate men unable to appreciate a good pipe or a wad of chew in a distended cheek. Kimball's Peerless Tobacco Works in Rochester showed by skilled marketing that a rising demand could be stimulated, using romantic trade-marks such as Vanity Fair, Old Gold, Cloth of Gold, and Orientals. Down in Richmond the firm of Allen & Ginter were to give American smokers Napoleons, Opera Puffs and Bon Ton, while Marburg & Felgoer, of Baltimore, favoured High Life and Golden Age.

To Duke it seemed that any development that sold tobacco was important. It was apparent to him that, with the right labour and marketing, smokers' habits could be transformed and competitors such as Bull Durham caught wrong-footed. He decided to bring a foreman and a team of expert European hand rollers from New York to Durham.

The foreman was J. M. Siegel, a Russian emigré Jew who had gone to New York via the cigarette-making trade in London. Duke also hired Moses Gladstein, another expert hand roller, hired from the Kinney Brothers. Bull Durham's response was to take on Siegel's brother, David, to run a cigarette section as a precautionary sideline. Just as significant, however, was Duke's decision not just to run an efficient manufacturing unit but to find a salesman capable of selling the cigarettes to retail merchants. The man he hired for the task was Edward Featherstone Small, a good-looking ex-member of the Washington Grays, with an impeccable pedigree. Small was to transform the marketing methods of the tobacco industry with a series of advertising ideas that would enable W. Duke Sons & Company to sell over 740 million cigarettes in 1888 under such names as Pin Head, Cameo, Duke of Durham, and Cross Cut.

Small was a man of ideas. In Atlanta, Georgia, his eye caught sight of a photograph in a shop window of a French actress, Madame Rhea. He quickly obtained her consent to use her picture for advertising purposes. In a short time, helped by the endorsement, he had local orders for 800,000 on his books. Historical pictures were to be given away with cartons of cigarettes, and in St Louis he hired a sales lady—at that time unthinkable—a beautiful young widow whose sales pitch dealers found impossible to resist. Gifts were given to traders placing bulk orders.

But in 1883 came two developments destined to take Buck Duke and his family company into the industrial era. That March the United States Congress balloted to reduce revenue taxation on cigarettes to 50 cents per thousand from $1.75. The rate of levy had been determined during the Civil War. Duke's response was immediate. He slashed the price of his cigarettes and announced a big bonus to traders placing immediate orders on the understanding they would possibly be delivered some weeks ahead. There was an immediate flood of orders, requiring the building of a new factory and a rapid recruitment of new labour.

Meanwhile, the second crucial development was jelling. Three years before, the son of a Virginian plantation owner, James Bonsack, registered details of a new machine, the fruit of years of patient labour, which, he claimed, could make cigarettes on a continuous rod principle—an endless tube of wrapped tobacco that was sliced by a circular saw to produce 200 cigarettes a minute at a cost of 30 cents against 80 cents for hand-rolled products.

Duke had kept a wary eye on young Bonsack, just entering his twenties and eager to sell his machinery. But he was not the only interested party. Former Confederate Major Lewis Ginter, of Allen & Ginter, and his partner, John Allen, had also developed a sizeable production of cigarettes, starting six years before 1883. Ginter ordered a machine in 1880, but it was unfortunately destroyed by fire on its way from Salem to Richmond. The following year a new and improved machine had been built, with a complicated mechanism that had to be made in France, from where English interest was to be attracted. American tobacco firms were cautious, worried that customers would regard a machine-made cigarette as an inferior product after buying the hand-rolled brands for some years. Duke was deeply interested in machinery. The Durham works already boasted equipment for stamping out pasteboard containers for ten cigarettes, replacing the crush-prone paper wrappers. As Buck thought over the possibilities, in England Henry Herbert Wills, a qualified engineer and member of the famous tobacco merchants, W. D. & H. O. Wills, was evaluating two Bonsack machines with a view to acquiring the English patent, registered in 1881.

English interest in machinery was strong, if somewhat un-satisfied. The Paris Exhibition of 1867 had featured one much discussed invention, the Susini, and English manufacturers' agents had reported on several American machines in the 1870s, including the Hook and Emery models. H. H. Wills, known as Mr Harry, had been encouraged to study new ideas since joining the family firm in 1878 at one hundred and twenty-five pounds a year salary, prior to eventual partnership six years later, so he was well aware of James Bonsack's progress, and sped to Paris very early in 1883 when an agent reported that a machine was to be seen in operation at another international show. The result by the spring of that year was that Bonsack had erected a wooden demonstration model at the Wills Redcliffe works, and technical evaluation was under way. The machinery had its faults, but the engineering team and Harry's older brother, George, had looked at the Everitt, a rival machine not long introduced by the small London tobacco house Bettelheim. They were not impressed.

Negotiations opened in earnest with the Bonsack Machine Company on an offer of the assignment of patent, for £4,250. Harry Wills, by now in America, where he became even more aware of United States technical progress, sent cables to Bristol recommending a quick decision. In May 1883, terms were settled with Wills gaining the patent rights, which had been quietly and discreetly checked out, in the United Kingdom and her territories. Wary lawyer eyes were kept open for other machines—there were worries about the Emery—likely to be bought by rivals, but the second Bonsack, made with iron, would be installed by the end of the year, with further orders in hand. Some initial anxieties about possible patent infringements would keep surveillance of other machinery developments close and constant. Wills' technical interests did not stop here, they ranged from electrical generation and vending machines to factory humidifiers for controlling tobacco moisture, and even patent soldered half-pound tins for packing pipe tobacco.

Clearly the British were not lagging behind America in the race to develop, or encourage the development of, machinery. Thirty years before Wills' shrewd move, Robert Legg invented a continuously fed tobacco-cutting machine. And, in the same year, 1880, as Bonsack came forward with his continuous rod invention, a retail tobacconist in Gainsborough (Lincolnshire), William Rose, had risked his life savings making an appliance for wrapping 1-oz packs of tobacco—a machine that Wills was to buy. Wills found that the Bonsack machine's output of 200 cigarettes a minute compared with a hand-roller's output of 1,250 a day. By 1888, Wills would have eleven Bonsack machines in use at Bristol making 85,000 cigarettes a day.

Across the Atlantic, Duke and one of the family's new financial partners, R. H. Wright—he had once made his own smoking tobacco, Orange of Durham, then joined Buck when Washington Duke had withdrawn from active decision-taking—went to Bonsack's Station to see the Virginian inventor, who had hoped, through his company, to rent out his machine to American cigarette makers on a royalty basis. Bonsack's excursions to Europe were evidence of his impatience to win sales.

James Bonsack offered Duke the use of two of his machines on a trial basis, with the services of a top mechanic. A contract was quickly worked out. By late 1883 the machines arrived at Durham, but there were troubles from the complex mechanism. Weeks passed and Duke bullied the mechanic daily. On 30th April 1884, the machines went into action—and on their first ten-hour day gave no trouble.

For hours Duke toiled over the figures, and he concluded that it was not unreasonable to plan before long a daily output of 250,000 cigarettes, a staggering productivity improvement, taking costs down to levels beyond his wildest hopes. With a new revenue tax at 50 cents, and a prevailing tobacco price of 25 cents per pound, he calculated a production cost (including packing and forwarding) of $1.85 per 1,000 cigarettes. Since dealers would pay $4 per 1,000, with a 10 per cent discount on bulk orders, the profit margin was high and handsome.

The bargain with Bonsack, finally sealed in June 1885, was to use the machines on a royalty of 24 cents per 1,000, some 6 cents below the inventor's offer. Duke was careful to insert a clause that the royalty would always be a quarter less than the nominal rental sum.

But it was all very well to work out the figures. He had to sell the cigarettes on a scale that even the level of the tax cut could not match. There was no point turning out endless stocks. He moved swiftly, sending Wright on a year-long sales trip to open up export markets, and he took himself on $150 a month expenses to New York to face direct the full brunt of that great city's established hand-rolling industry.

A small attic in Chambers Street in East New York became his first office, and he found a furnished room. He canvassed hard for orders and, with four Bonsack machines in the loft, took the sales drive from the Southern and Western states to New York. Advertising bristled everywhere and dealers were inundated with offers of goods in return for orders. Duke made the New Yorkers ask for his cigarettes by name, and there was no more irresistible attraction to customers than his use of cigarette cards, with pictures of sportsmen, athletes, and actors, which came in numbered sets and sparked a collection on the scale of postage stamps. The promotions were inventive, and rewarding. Bulk cartons of cigarettes contained cash coupons, exchangeable for 50 cents. He offered payments to individuals who handed in the most empty packs, encouraging greater consumption. Chewing his favourite plug of mouldy tobacco (Buck never liked the cigarettes he sold so assiduously), he would stroll round the New York factory, which had soon expanded, finding fault and spurring everyone to frenetic efficiency.

As battle opened on the Eastern sales front, the Western market was not neglected. Small, the brilliant salesman, hired a roller-skating team, billed as the Cross Cuts, one of the new Duke brand names, to tour the towns and cities, where they made news and yielded free publicity in newspapers. Buck even had men stationed at immigration ports, presenting each batch of New Americans with his cigarettes, future customers who would journey across the nation.

By 1885, W. Duke Sons & Company was to be incorporated, with annual sales of $600,000 and a manufacturing output of one million cigarettes daily. It was on the brink of dramatic growth. Things were to be changed, too, when Wright, tired of selling tobacco overseas, wanted to go into business on his own account, and decided to sell out his shares. Later, stepbrother Brodie Duke was to give up his active interest as well leaving three Dukes and G. W. Watts (the partner who took a 20 per cent share in the original W. Duke Sons & Company in 1878).

Duke now steered the sturdy company hard towards Wall Street and its financiers. He began to arrange regular borrowings, developing a reputation for prompt repayments. Turning thirty, and aware that a young man needed a solid reputation with the money houses to exploit business talent, he saw in his pioneering of cigarettes the chance to undermine totally the then top four of the tobacco industry—Allen & Ginter, of Richmond (Virginia), William Kimball & Company, of Rochester, Kinney Tobacco Company, of New York City, and Goodwin & Company, of New York City.

In the next few years Duke, armed with his Bonsack machines and resorting to every means of promotion (not forgetting gifts for loyal dealers), was true to his belief for success in business: 'Hit your competitors in the pocket book, hit 'em hard. Then you either buy 'em out, or take 'em with you.'

The records show that by 1889 the United States consumption of new-fangled cigarettes was about 2,188 million and W. Duke Sons & Company was making 837 million. Much of the remaining trade was commanded by the Big Four, who desperately introduced machinery (such as the Allison and Emery models) to fight off the challenge from the upstart Buck. Not only did Buck understand industrialisation, he had an intuitive grasp of marketing techniques which to this day are copied along Madison Avenue. Men like Major Lewis Ginter rejected Duke as vulgar, and he was kept out of the tobacco trade's inner councils and annual dinners.

But time was running out and the financiers on Wall Street were getting restless with the so-called Big Four.

Before the end of 1889, Duke, by one means or other, had convened a meeting with his competitors in New York. He proposed a merger, taking care to lay figures on the table that could startle the opposition. Duke's sales were revealed as approaching $4.5 million a year, yielding a 10 per cent net profit on turnover. His latest advertising budget was set at double his annual profit (which anyway now totalled more than the four rivals put together).

Buck made no bones about his 'buy 'em out, or take 'em with you' business philosophy. He outlined his terms for an amalgamation. In essence, these were the formation of a new corporation, with a large capital stock, allotted to the five participants, according to their assets.

The bargaining was hard, but in the end agreement was reached to form the American Tobacco Company, to be registered in Virginia (but switched to New Jersey to take advantage of local corporation law).

There can be no doubt that Duke cast his spell over the ten delegates sent to the amalgamation talks. The shares were split into 300,000 common stock at $50, and 100,000 8 per cent non-cumulative preferred at $100. The allocation was

W. Duke Sons & Company	$7,500,000
Allen & Ginter	$7,500,000
Kinney Tobacco Company	$5,000,000
Kimball & Company	$2,500,000
Goodwin & Company	$2,500,000
Capitalisation	$25,000,000

Since valuation of assets came to around $3,175,000, clearly Duke had a golden tongue in promising to wring greater profits quickly to counter such excessive over-capitalisation. The value of the figures placed on the Duke family business of $7,500,000 compared with only $250,000 in 1885. It was even decided to make Buck, now thirty-three, the first president, with John Pope (of Allen & Ginter) and W. S. Kimball (of Kimball) as deputies, with the other companies providing the treasurer and secretary.

And so a monopoly was born, its birth formally registered on 31st January 1890, with the articles of incorporation charging the directors, worldwide, to cure leaf tobacco and to buy, manufacture, and sell tobacco in all its forms, to establish factories, agencies and depots for the sale and distribution thereof, and to transfer and cause the same to be transferred as an article of commerce, and 'to do all things incidental to the business of trading and manufacturing'.

CHAPTER TWO

The Virginians

It was the search for gold that had sent Europe's great adventurers to the New World. English colonists, who first settled in Jamestown, Virginia, in 1607, sought gold for the proprietors of their expedition, the London Virginia Company. They found only an inedible brown weed, *Nicotiana rustica*. The impoverished settlers, beset by famine and disease, had to wait for three years before someone touched by destiny would arrive to exploit a soil and climate capable of sustaining a mysterious leaf.

That man was to be John Rolfe, a young Englishman from Norfolk, who sailed into Jamestown in May 1610 on board one of two wooden boats reconstructed from the *Sea Venture*, wrecked in Bermuda after leaving London a year before. Life was so desperate in Jamestown that it was decided to move on, with the survivors of the original settlement, to Newfoundland. Fate intervened in the shape of Lord De La Warr whose craft the *Virginia* met the colonists in the James river. The incoming vessel was bringing new settlers and supplies. The courses of the outgoing craft, and history, were changed. Rolfe, a well-educated man, born into a prosperous family, was a smoker, used to the sweet and mild leaf *Nicotiana tabacum* increasingly imported and even grown in Europe.

Rolfe's acquisition of the habit of pipe smoking had a noble lineage in England, where even the earliest historians and adventurers had little idea of the origins of smoking. To this day tobacco antiquaries argue and pore over each other's researches. Their theories pass in and out of favour. It is a tricky task to pick

31

a middle path through the fact and fiction. But the romantic past could not have mattered less to Rolfe, running his fingers through the sandy Virginian soil and contemplating the small broad-leaved and shrub-like plant *Nicotiana rustica*, grown by the local Indians, but regarded as a useless weed by starving settlers concerned more with the belly than the lungs.

There was such a demand in Europe for tobacco that ships cluttered the harbour of Port of Spain in Trinidad, one English ship taking on board as much as 16,000 pounds a time. The Caribbean was a principal source and Spanish adventurers had secured a commanding grip on some of the most important sources. Not even the anti-smoking campaign of King James I could reduce English demand, with tobacco being landed from London to Cornwall. Like Buck Duke several centuries later, Rolfe was more concerned with practicalities and the present. Tobacco was a means of survival, a means of exchange. In 1611, Rolfe demonstrated his capacity for survival by marrying an Indian princess, Pocahontas, pleasing the indigenous Indians, whose skill at cultivating tobacco he admired and studied with care.

William Strachey, first recorder and secretary to the Virginia colony, wrote that the local *Nicotiana rustica* plant was 'poore and weake and of a byting tast'. Rolfe decided that the sweeter variety *Nicotiana tabacum* might be grown instead, and he arranged with a sea captain to bring some seeds from Trinidad. By 1613, Rolfe's first modest crop was ready and sailing for England on board the *Elizabeth*. He now blended into new plantings some seeds from Venezuela.

Ten years before that first shipment reached London's tobacco merchants, King James I had done his best to undermine the market place by ordering his High Treasurer, the Earl of Dorset, to raise the duty on imported leaf from two pence per pound to six shillings and eight pence. A weary war with the Spanish was over and he intended to stifle a resumption of smoking, which had still continued, in spite of a blockade, through smuggling, and the growth of English crops in the Cotswolds and elsewhere. It was ironic that Rolfe was helping to found the Virginia colony on tobacco, for King James had a hatred for Sir Walter Raleigh that was to be expressed in 1604 with an anonymous pamphlet (Royal authorship was confirmed in 1616) called *A Counterblaste to Tobacco*.

The document was a venomous attack on Raleigh for making fashionable in the Kingdom 'so vile and stinking a custom' derived from barbarous and unclean Indians. James said it was a miracle how the use of what he called a common herb that grew anywhere, 'springing from so vile a ground as godless Indians', and brought in 'by a father so generally hated', was still alive. It concluded:

> Have you not reason then to be ashamed, and to forbear this filthy novelty so basely grounded, so foolishly received and so grossly mistaken in the right to use thereof? In your abuse thereof sinning against God, harming yourselves both in persons and goods, and taking also thereby the marks and notes of vanity upon you: by the custom thereof making yourselves to be wondered at by all foreign civil Nations, and by all strangers that come among you, to be scorned and condemned. A custom loathsome to the eye, hateful to the nose, harmful to the brain, dangerous to the lungs, and in the black stinking fume thereof, nearest resembling the horrible Stygian smoke of the pit that is bottomless.

This was the start of Raleigh's long persecution, and thirteen years in the Tower of London, relieved by the writing of his *History of the World*. He had travelled the world more than most Englishmen as one of Elizabeth's merchant adventurers whose seafaring exploits still excite schoolboys and illuminate a turbulent period of European history permeated by great names and sea dogs. Raleigh had raised £40,000 and supervised in 1584 the founding of a colony near Roanoke Island situated on what is now the coast of North Carolina, giving the name Virginia to the new land in honour of his Queen, whom James I was to succeed. Two sea captains sent on the first expedition to Roanoke Island returned with three 'poor barbarous savages' to demonstrate the Indian practice of smoking. In 1585 a second expedition was sent across the high sea, led by Sir Richard Greville, with Ralph Lane as first Governor. Among the party was a young surveyor, Thomas Hariot, who had taught Raleigh mathematics. They landed at Wokoken Island, North Carolina, and soon ran into troubles with the local Indians, and suffered from food shortages. Sir Francis Drake was to pick them up a year later when returning from one of his Caribbean raids (carrying in his hold a stock of *Nicotiana tabacum* from Dominica and in his head the knowledge of its use in pipes).

Hariot was to write an account of the expedition, speaking of a herb known to the Indians as *Uppowoc* and to Spaniards as *Tabacco*. He described how the Indians dried and powdered the leaves before smoking the *Tabacco* in clay pipes.

The surveyor was to teach his friend Raleigh how to smoke one of the clay pipes brought back as an Indian curiosity. Others had tried smoking, too, including Sir John Hawkins, who had been to Florida some twenty years before. The sight of Raleigh smoking was the talk of Court circles and he even arranged for the planting of some seeds of *Nicotiana rustica* in Ireland; later a crop was to be grown at Winchcombe in Gloucestershire. Smoking quickly became fashionable, even ladies at Court were seen trying the pipes, while stories of Raleigh being extinguished by a horrified servant who thought him on fire became part of the folk lore that even had the majestic Elizabeth 'drawing smoke', leading to an attack of nausea and accusations of a poison plot.

The loose-tongued, mercurial Raleigh, who was to recognise the potential of potatoes and mahogany wood, and earn a reputation as an early scientist with an expert knowledge of metal assaying, was a doomed man when his Queen's throne passed to James VI of Scotland, James I of England. He was soon to be an outcast, stripped of influential office and finally charged with treason, for allegedly plotting, among other things, to make peace with Spain. A reprieve only sent him to the Bloody Tower in November 1603 for thirteen years where he conducted scientific experiments, wrote of the world he helped explore, and smoked tobacco. In 1616 Raleigh was released on the promise that he would lead an expedition to Guiana to bring back gold for the financially-pressed James I. A disastrous series of events followed, ending with his arrest by a turncoat friend, Sir Lewis Stukeley, Vice Admiral of Devon. Raleigh was to smoke a last pipe and stroll calmly to the chopping block on 29th October 1618, in Old Palace Yard, Westminster.

Thus one of the most famous of all England's merchant adventurers was to give to the world his writing, his discoveries, and the habit of smoking. More revengefully he wrote a will charging Stukeley with double dealing on Crown revenue for a certain stock of tobacco Raleigh said he had given him. Stukeley was to become an outcast, dying a lunatic's death two years later on Lundy Island, off the coast of the place which would become England's great tobacco manufacturing centre, Bristol.

Even as Raleigh prepared to lose his head, John Rolfe's plants in Jamestown were multiplying. The sweet-scented Virginia leaf was improved by cross-breeding, and the year of Raleigh's execution was to be marked with the export to England of 20,000 pounds. The ground in and around Jamestown was thick with the plant, which was endangering the church and other buildings. Exports were to reach a staggering 500,000 pounds within ten years of Rolfe's first planting, selling for up to eight shillings per pound.

The colonial trade flourished, helped at first by a decision by James, increasingly in need of money, in 1608, to cut his 6s 10d tax to one shilling. The heavy impost had been intended to discourage smoking, but a hard-up monarch had to live. Smuggling had reached uncontrollable levels. The King who despised tobacco and had imprisoned Virginia's famous founding father five years before Rolfe set sail for the New World next decided to take over, in 1613, all powers of importation of tobacco, barring any persons from dealing in tobacco who did not hold Letters Patent (holders were required to yield up half their profits to the Royal purse).

So James I, author of *Counterblaste* and the King who ordered Oxford University to arrange a debate in 1605 on the evils of tobacco, was to become Royal partner with two merchants, Edmund Peschell and Edward White. The partners were allowed to control those who would retail tobacco. Buck Duke was not the first to establish a monopoly. Two years later, the King raised his tobacco tax to two shillings a pound, satisfying his conscience and debtors.

The monopoly was by no means complete. Smuggling remained rife, so much so that by 1620 James decreed that all tobacco sold should bear a Government stamp. During these eventful years, Rolfe had returned to England, bringing his Indian princess to be presented with great success at Court, but she was to die at Gravesend from influenza in 1617 leaving her lonely husband to return to Jamestown without her. The King's interest in Virginia had been stirred, however, and when in 1620 the Virginia Company started to resist the introduction of Royal orders for a stamp on tobacco, he found himself agreeing to a duty of one shilling a pound, half the impost on the rival Spanish tobacco. He also took steps to limit growing of tobacco in England, so helping the colonial planters. Sent out, too, were one hundred white convicts to join the forced labour which consisted of Negro slaves bought at first from Europeans in exchange for tobacco.

By 1624, the monarch with a double-sided morality was formally to declare a Royal Tobacco Monopoly to protect his colonial suppliers, agreeing to give 'such prices to the Planters and Adventurers for the same as may give them reasonable satisfaction and encouragement'. He refused legal imports of any tobacco from other sources, though smuggling of Spanish and other leaf continued, and in England tobacco growers even used force to resist their King's embargo. James assuaged his conscience by trying to persuade the Virginia growers to take up other crops, such as wheat, and even had mulberries sent out to develop a silk industry. They carried on, however, planting tobacco in ever-increasing quantities.

The Virginia Company, which had a charter from James which agreed to run the colony with a council subject to Crown approval, had, because of growth, run into financial difficulty and found administration increasingly impossible from three thousand miles away. The King's Council had sent out a number of Governors who ruled the Colony with varying degrees of severity, but in 1619 came Sir George Yardley who admitted that it was impossible for one Governor to control the various boroughs and the proliferating plantations (London had sent out more people with farm experience). Sir George was instructed to set up a committee. Some twenty-two representatives of the boroughs of Virginia Colony met over six stiflingly hot days in Jamestown that midsummer. In spite of illness and the heat—one of their number even died—they created a code of laws and founded the House of Burgesses, the first self-governing body in America. They would meet only once a year and the idea was to copy English customs and legal practices.

It was not only apt but inevitable that there would be taxation of the inhabitants, who would elect the Burgessmen, but even more so that it should be decided that the levy was to be 10 lb of tobacco from every able-bodied male over sixteen years of age.

The pioneers were being given a taste of freedom, if limited. The introduction of self-rule provided them with the chance to break the dictatorial ways of previous Governors and exercise pressures on the London Virginia Company, now £75,000 in debt. It was ironic that James I allowed the Colony both a degree of democracy and economic preference, for the early farmers just kept on planting bigger acreages of the plant he once sought to ban. Even the lowliest settlers, for instance the servants of small-holders, could quickly pay off their contract passages out from England and move into ownership of huge plantations, eventually employing the slaves who were being shipped in by the 1680s at the rate of 10,000 a year.

James I died in 1625. His reign began with a vengeful assault on Elizabethan tobacco, only to end with thousands of pounds of Virginia leaf passing on his orders through the London Customs Quay (to the chagrin of Bristol whose mercantile marine and emerging trade in snuff, pipes—made at Winchester—and pipe tobacco were threatened).

Gloucestershire, Wiltshire, and Worcestershire had long fought the efforts to stifle home plantations. The growers found allies among provincial pipe makers who were resentful that the late King had granted a charter to London's Company of Pipe Makers, giving them exclusive rights of manufacture. Charles I lost little time in following his father's efforts to prosecute domestic growers, giving magistrates instructions to act against English cultivation. The West Country had no sympathy for the continued discrimination in favour of London and Virginia. Plymouth, the base for famous Elizabethan sea dogs, shared Bristol's anger. Demand for Virginia leaf kept rising, and imports by 1629 reached an annual rate of 1,500,000 lb.

In order to maintain control, King Charles then introduced licensing for retailers, which had the added advantage of bringing in new revenues. His next move came in 1638 with a decision to rescind the import monopoly of London and allow other ports, including Bristol and Plymouth, to share the trade. This had the effect of breaking the alliance of the West Country port authorities with local English growers, whose petition to Parliament on their plight went unheeded.

Meanwhile, the Virginian colonists were causing new difficulties. The arrival of Dutch merchants wishing to exchange stores and goods for tobacco had begun to direct leaf to the wider European market. The spreading cultivation of tobacco to Carolina, Maryland, and elsewhere was requiring a bigger market too. The English Privy Council tried to dissuade the colonists, and finally in 1639 the Assembly of Virginia came more into line by imposing a large extra levy on tobacco exported elsewhere than to England. Although there was always the need to stop the alternative supply of Spanish leaf, the Virginian growers knew well enough the importance of the English market, whatever their trenchant views on some of the high retail prices which they felt unnecessarily limited growth of demand.

The pioneer English growers—Francis Bacon had written years before that their product was 'dull and earthy'—sought the sympathy of the 2,000 or more licensed tobacco dealers, and others, to meet the favoured competition. They had some success, for Bristol and London's Virginia importers in 1650 were worried about the policy of the Protectorate of Cromwell which seemed ambivalent after the defeat of Charles I. The importers in 1650 petitioned Parliament against the home growers and their inferior product. A year later came the Navigation Act, ordering that tobacco must be carried only in English or colonial ships, landing in England first whatever the final destination. Initially, Cromwell, who recognised well enough the importance of the colonial tobacco trade, was not keen to displease the home growers, many of them concentrated in Worcester, Gloucester, and West Country regions, and potential recruits to the Royalist cause. But the pressures intensified, and in 1652 Parliament was to pass an Act that prohibited the growing of tobacco in England. This legislation introduced a fine on every pole of land planted with the leaf, half to go to the Commonwealth and the rest to the informers. It empowered anyone to 'grub, cut up, destroy, and utterly consume all and every such tobaccos'. Riots ensued in the tobacco-growing areas, and Cromwell was forced to allow, temporarily, the planting and curing for one year only, from September 1653, in return for an Excise levy of three pence a pound. The following year the English crop was a record. The Virginia importers of Bristol and London raised hails of counter-protest. Overstocked with Virginia leaf, they seethed with indignation.

Petitions were sent to the Privy Council and MPs briefed to have the 1652 Act enforced. An Order in Council was drafted for all home tobacco to be destroyed forthwith. Cromwell acted with caution. He was not anxious to advance Loyalist sympathies for Charles II among the planters, and his hesitation encouraged growers at Winchcombe and elsewhere to plead that their latest crops be harvested, promising to conform to regulations thereafter.

They won another year's reprieve. And they were to plant again in the following years.

The pressures on Cromwell remained intense. Half the shipping trade of Bristol was engaged in Virginia importation. Importers, who should have been placated by the appointment of Special Commissioners empowered to enforce the ban on home cultivation, remained incensed. Consumers who went to Gloucester, Hereford, Devon, Somerset, and Worcester met resistance. Even soldiers ran into armed guards round the tobacco fields. Local magistrates made little secret of their opposition to the Commissioners.

With the Restoration came a wave of new planting, spreading into Monmouthshire, Oxfordshire and even Yorkshire and Essex. It was still contrary to the law. Indeed in 1661 a Privy Council Act banned the growing of tobacco in Ireland as well as England, imposing bigger fines. The Governor of Virginia furiously sought tougher enforcement, and his views were well received by Charles II since Customs revenues were falling dramatically with the increasing sale of home-grown leaves. Fines were raised again, dividing the penalties three ways, between the King, the poor of parishes, and informers. Extra fines were allowed for resistance and Sheriffs of each county were ordered to do their duty by destroying crops. Troops were sent to help (one hundred and twenty Life Guards went to Winchcombe, the hottest bed of tobacco planting). The action was ineffective, partly because rewards for information about plantings were rarely paid and the unity of farmers remained strong, supported by local populations.

The fight against smoking was not confined to England. James I and Cromwell, shifted by events into a reluctant policy of Imperial Preference, knew the habit had taken grip elsewhere. Louis XIII had prohibited the sale of tobacco in France, except on prescription by a physician, while in some Eastern regions torture and death dogged smokers, who sucked their pipes of smuggled or illicitly grown leaf in secret.

King Charles II found events against him, too. Young blades patronised the tobacco shops and in London coffee houses were burgeoning, the meeting place of gallants, intellectuals, and merchants, who found a pipe conducive to relaxed discussion. Poorer sections of the population bought tobacco from many unlicensed premises, such as ale houses, ships' chandlers and grocers. The popularity of tobacco and snuff was well rooted by the time of the Great Plague in 1665, when it was commonly believed smoking afforded protection from the dreaded disease (the boys at Eton College smoked daily during the Plague, under penalty of a housemaster's whip for non-compliance).

Planting spread from county to county. When tobacco was destroyed in Nottinghamshire, Warwickshire and Yorkshire, it increased in Shropshire and Flintshire. Even the Duke of Monmouth, leading mounted horse troops, was to have little success in disrupting planting and harvesting in Gloucestershire. Injunctions, Crown letters to Lord Lieutenants and High Sheriffs, military action, and appeals, did not succeed.

While the struggle went on in England, shrewd Scottish merchants had worked alongside Dutch counterparts in establishing a buoyant demand and an alternative market for colonial leaf. Indeed, Scottish merchants offered good prices to Virginian growers and even supplied badly needed barter goods. Scottish ports were busy with tobacco ships, and Customs men sought with difficulty to keep control. In 1660, home growing of tobacco in Scotland was banned.

Protection of the colonial plantations was to be further complicated in 1685 with a proposal to add threepence per pound to the duty compared with a sixpence per pound levy on Spanish imports. There were new protests from importers. Some two hundred sailing ships were now engaged in the Virginia trade, yielding £130,000 in Customs levies for the Exchequer. Parliament was warned that plantations would be encouraged in Germany, France, Holland and Ireland. This was an important point. England had inadvertently helped the Spanish to teach Europe to smoke and take snuff for pleasure on a wide scale, even though *Nicotiana* had arrived on the Continent long before.

Archivists and historians of the Imperial Tobacco Company have patiently sifted the evidence. They explain, succinctly:

Commercial trading in tobacco on an international scale began about 400 years ago, for it was about the middle of the 16th Century that a demand for it, through the practice of tobacco smoking, began to be created in several different parts of the world from Spain to China.

To trace the *origins* of tobacco smoking, however, more especially the ritualistic burning of tobacco leaves and the inhalation of tobacco smoke, we must go back very much further—to the 1st Century B.C. at least and to the Maya civilisation of Central America. Later the Aztecs, another and more advanced civilisation dwelling in Mexico, are known to have had smoke inhalation in their religious ritual and further south the Arawak Indians of the Amazon valley observed a similar procedure. It was the Arawaks who subsequently colonised the Antilles Islands where the finest tobacco is said to have grown.

The theory that the tobacco plant originated in Africa or in the Orient and that tobacco was introduced to America by African slaves has few supporters today. No mention of the tobacco plant is made in the journals of early explorers such as Marco Polo and Vasco da Gama who visited Africa and the Orient; and no reference to it is made in any of the ancient books. It is therefore reasonable to conclude that the tobacco plant originated in America and found its way to Europe in the last decade of the 15th Century.

Soon after the discovery of the West Indies and of the continent of America accounts were written of the peoples of the New World and their customs; and from these accounts we learn of the methods of smoking employed at that time. We find that tobacco was used not only for smoking, but for chewing and snuffing. Perhaps chewing and snuffing were even older practices than smoking as the plant required less elaborate preparation.

In the West Indies, Brazil and Central America, it was customary at the time of discovery for the natives to roll small leaves of tobacco and wrap them in a larger tobacco leaf or in a maize or palm leaf— the prototype of our cigar: in Mexico tubes made of tortoise-shell, silver, wood, reed, or clay were in evidence; while further north the pipe was the normal apparatus in use for smoking. These pipes were made in various shapes out of clay, wood, lobster claws, or marble. We can therefore see that our cigarette was first thought of by the Mexicans and our pipe by the American Indians.

In 1492, when Columbus landed on an island to which he gave the name San Salvador, the Arawaks offered him some dried leaves as a token of friendship. Two of his men subsequently saw natives of Cuba smoking leaves rolled up into something like the shape of a cigar.

The explorer, Amerigo Vespucci, from whom America obtained its name, claims to have found in 1499 a barbarous but friendly people on an island off the coast of Venezuela who steadily engaged in the strange habit of chewing green leaves.

Fernandez Oviedo, a Spaniard appointed in 1514 to supervise gold-smelting in the West Indies, devoted much of his time to studying the customs of the natives, and in a history published in 1526 he referred to the inhalation of smoke by the natives. The smoke was inhaled through a forked tube, the two prongs entering the nostrils, the end of the tube being inserted in smouldering tobacco leaves.

About 1518 the Spaniards found that in Mexico the cultivation of tobacco was an old agricultural art. Cortez noted that tobacco was cultivated there, whereas in the Antilles the plants were growing wild. It was the Spaniards who introduced tobacco into Peru and Chile. Spaniards and their negro slaves first used tobacco in the form of cigars, but later they packed it in tubes of reed or silver.

The Frenchman Cartier visited Hochelaga (Montreal) in 1535 and was interested in the smoking habits of the Iroquois. He wrote: *There groweth also a certain herb whereof in summer they make great provision for all the year—only men use it—and first they cause it to be dried in the sun, then wear it about their necks wrapped in a little beast's skin made like a little bag with a hollow piece of stone or wood like a pipe. Then, when they please, they make powder of it and then put it into one of the ends of the said cornet or pipe and laying a coal of fire upon it, at the other end suck so long that they fill their bodies full of smoke till that it cometh out of their mouth and nostrils even as out of a tunnel or chimney. They say that this doth keep them warm and in health. We ourselves have tried the same smoke and having put it in our mouths it seemed that they had filled it with pepper dust, it is so hot.*

It was the rapid growth of smoking in the West Indies and Mexico among the Spaniards themselves that first indicated the great potential economic value of tobacco; and it was not long before it became a commodity for trade.

It has been claimed that Rodrigo de Jerez, who was sent to Cuba by Columbus in 1492, first smoked tobacco in Europe. Both he and Ramon Pane, a monk who accompanied Columbus on his second voyage in 1493 and who probably brought back to Europe its first tobacco seeds, returned to Spain prior to the end of the 15th Century so that there is little doubt that the smoking habit first spread from American territories to Spain and then to Portugal. Apparently half a century elapsed before tobacco became known north of the Pyrenees. Apart from an isolated reference to cultivation by a Belgian physician in his garden in 1554, the records of André Thevet and Jean Nicot are the earliest evidence of the spread of the tobacco plant to other European countries.

André Thevet, a Protestant, fled from France to Brazil to avoid religious persecution. He founded a colony there but returned to

France in 1556 and planted seeds in his garden at Angouleme. In 1560 Jean Nicot, the French Ambassador at the Court of Portugal, became interested in the curative properties claimed for tobacco. He wrote to the Cardinal de Lorraine: *I have acquired an Indian herb of marvellous and proved worth against the Noli me tangere and fistulas given up as incurable by the physicians. As soon as it gives its seeds I will send some of them to your gardener at Marmoustier in a barrel with instructions for replanting and cultivating it.* Eventually the seeds were sown and the plants applied medicinally according to the ambassador's advice.

Those early cures were popular in French Court circles and so the plant was named *Nicotiana* in honour of Nicot. Until the end of the sixteenth century, physicians were to prescribe tobacco for medicinal reasons, frowning on its use for personal pleasure and relaxation. They distilled juice, compounded poultices, powdered it into ash, and distributed plugs for chewing. The plant flourished in the Royal gardens of Portugal and Spain.

Smoking for pleasure tended to be concentrated around sea ports, and the age of voyages of discovery spread such usage across the world. Tobacco became a universal commodity, if not always tolerated by authority. English troops spread the habit across Europe during the Thirty Years War. Popes forbade its use, some under threat of excommunication. Even as Virginia and Maryland were establishing their economies on the plant, other parts of the New World vainly tried to suppress its usage. Kings and spiritual leaders took several centuries to learn that the revenues derived from the leaf that was chewed, snuffed and puffed were more important than the physical or moral damage claimed for their subjects and flocks.

By 1685 the colonial plantations were enjoying new preferential duties compared with Spanish suppliers. Trade continued to rise year by year, matched by improvements in quality. In 1710 Virginia and Maryland sent 23,350,735 lb to England, by which time the tobacco fields of Gloucestershire and Worcestershire and elsewhere had virtually been returned to normal agricultural purposes. Improved curing processes, low prices, and better distribution were a bigger factor in the eventual demise of English tobacco than laws (English tobacco growing did not gain legal status until 1910). Over-production in Virginia, Carolina, and Maryland intensified competition in world markets, and there were years when colonial planters even had to cut or stop planting.

Although the War of Independence caused temporary disruption to the pattern of trade and supply, England was still taking half the American tobacco crop at the turn of the seventeenth century. There had been some profound changes, however, in levies as well as in smoking habits (snuff had become very fashionable alongside the pipe, and now cigars were becoming popular).

The economy of the American Colonies had been firmly based on the growing of tobacco and the commodity was universally recognised as one of the mainstays of English commerce involving as it did the shipping industry, the export trade, and the home manufacturers—not forgetting its increasing importance to the Government revenue.

The first hundred years of tobacco duty—to the end of the seventeenth century—demonstrated the financial advantages to be gained by the Government from the trade in tobacco.

Succeeding Governments used it as a useful source of funds and did their utmost to stamp out illicit smuggling. By the end of the reign of Queen Anne the duty on a pound of tobacco from the colonial plantations stood at 6½d, and this was increased by stages until, by the beginning of the Napoleonic Wars, the rate stood at 1s 3d per pound.

To help offset the drain on the Exchequer caused by these wars, an increase of 4d was announced in 1795. This was followed by seven small fluctuations in the duty rate (only one of which was a reduction) until it stood at about 1s 8½d in 1805. In the following year, 6d was added, in 1812 2d was added and in 1813 3¼d was added, bringing the colonial rate of duty to 2s 8¼d per pound. In 1815, the duty was increased by 6d to 3s 2d and in 1819 it was increased again to 4s per pound—over three times what it had been in 1795.

In 1821, the home manufacturer was encouraged when the Government increased the duty on imported manufactured tobacco to 18s per pound. (Previously it had been the same as the duty on unmanufactured tobacco.)

In 1825, the colonial duty was reduced to 3s per pound and in 1826 it was reduced again to 2s 9d where it stayed until 1840 when it was increased by just over 1½d. At this time the duty on all other foreign tobaccos stood at 3s 2d but in 1842 the dual classification of imported leaf was abandoned and both were charged at 3s 2d. It remained unchanged until 1878 when it was increased to 3s 6d per pound.

This imposition, however, caused great agitation in the trade. The public refused to pay the extra cost and manufacturers were forced to bear the cost themselves. In order to recoup the extra cost, manufacturers bought quantities of inferior leaf and resorted to adding water to the tobacco to increase the weight.

The strongest representations continued to be made to the Government by the trade. But it was not until 1887 that the then Chancellor announced the repeal of the 'obnoxious 4d' and admitted that its imposition had been a mistake. At the same time he introduced legislation to limit the moisture content of the manufactured product.

Much of the effectiveness of tobacco taxation was due to the English statesman Pitt, who also introduced income tax. His Tobacco Act of 1789 laid some very firm foundations for ensuring tobacco revenues were tightly controlled and the Exchequer did not lose monies owed. Instead of the duty being levied as a Customs import duty only, he arranged that part should be raised as an Excise impost and part as a traditional Customs duty. Under the Act, the duty overall remained unchanged at 1s 3d per pound on British or American plantation tobacco, and 3s 6d per pound on Spanish and Portuguese supplies. The duty was paid when the tobacco came to be removed from Customs bonded warehouses, which is the British practice today. Pitt also brought in stringent regulations to stamp out smuggling—tobacco could only be carried in certain ships, crew allowances of loose tobacco were cut, and vessels found 'hovering' within four leagues of the English coast when carrying over 100 lb of tobacco were subject to seizure.

Elaborate regulations were framed to control re-exports of tobacco and products, so stopping frauds (leaf casks had to be marked by the Customs men when imported). Very elaborate arrangements were made to cover manufacturing, and Excise officers had rights of entry to premises to see that the law was being observed.

Howls of protest went up from manufacturers and a Parliamentary Committee heard their objections. But Pitt's reforms were very successful in stopping revenue frauds, even if smuggling was not totally stopped or adulteration fully stamped out. By 1825, the Excise duty had been switched back to a total Customs duty, with various regulations maintained until the Tobacco Act of 1840.

This new legislation, sometimes called the Mixing Act, abolished some of the irksome provisions of Pitt's controls. While the blending of other plant leaves with tobacco was banned, restrictions on adulterants, such as sweeteners, were lifted. The effect was an immediate mixing with tobacco of large quantities of honey, treacle, sugar, molasses, liquorice and salts. So heavy was the usage of sweeteners that revenue receipts of tobacco duty actually started to decline. One Chancellor, in the Peel administration of 1841, found less tobacco being imported than for some time before and he was even paying out money to manufacturers in duty drawback claims. Hurriedly, the Pure Tobacco Act of 1842 was passed, allowing manufacturers only the use of water (and alkaline salts in the case of snuff, which could be scented, too). Some oil was permitted for producing roll tobaccos. Fines and seizure were imposed for adulteration, and Customs officers instructed to take regular samples. The manufacturers protested vigorously, saying it was impossible to detect additives, which anyway had been used for many years to colour and flavour their tobacco lines.

The answer from the Commissioners of Excise was the formation of the Inland Revenue Laboratory (now called the Government Laboratory). A rapid seizure of 30,000 lb of Yorkshire and Lancashire tobacco revealed adulteration with sugar, rhubarb, hops, and even oak leaves. In one snuff factory a ton of sand was discovered. There were many convictions of retailers who sold adulterated tobacco. Adulteration, however, continued and the trade now argued that a reduction of the duty was the only answer. So a Select Committee was appointed in March 1844 to study the trade. For five months they conducted their enquiries among Customs and Excise officers, chemists, and factory owners. But the Committee became so bogged down with its work and dissension that it had to be dissolved. The struggle against adulteration went on. Smuggling was certainly reduced when, in 1856, the Admiralty became responsible for the Coastguard service, previously operated by Customs men. Eventually the Board of Inland Revenue was reporting in 1860 that 'adulteration of tobacco is now seldom attempted'.

More changes came when the American Civil War began to reduce supplies of Virginia tobacco. Scents had to be used to mask the inferior substitute leaf brought in from China and Japan and other sources. Manufacturers were quick to complain that the prohibition on sweetening matter put them at a disadvantage against foreign competitors. To deal with this W. E. Gladstone, then Chancellor in the Palmerston Government, introduced the Tobacco Act of 1863. This allowed sweetened tobacco, called Cavendish and Negrohead, to be made in bonded factories.

These premises had warehouses for storing duty-free tobacco. Duty was paid when the manufactured products were distributed to retailers. The bonds were specially built to meet Customs and Excise regulations, and the tobacco companies gave their bonds to the Crown to cover losses by robbery or fraud. The bonded warehouses exist today, supervised by Revenue men, who also observe the manufacturing process; with the heavy rates of duty imposed by successive Governments all manufacturers impose the tightest security in ensuring no loss or wastage of the world's most valuable plant.

The early planters maintained their quality by sending supplies to public warehouses, where inspectors could order the burning of poor leaf. Leaf was currency. It helped pay soldiers, clergymen, and even bought foreign women from Europe. In the late eighteenth century, a good plantation owner could yield up over 1,600 lb of tobacco an acre, which negro labour would strip and press into hogsheads for sale to English merchants through local agents. One important planter was George Washington, who knew well the value of tobacco when commanding a militia in the six-year War of Independence (British soldiers, such as the Redcoats of Cornwallis, often destroyed tobacco to lower morale and reduce its currency).

Tobacco growing continued to spread, and the methods of Maryland and Virginia were to be improved elsewhere by new cropping techniques. Nevertheless Richmond was to become the main springboard for the leap towards industrialisation.

The buyer of leaf for France's tobacco monopoly, one James Thomas, began around 1830 to process leaf into chewing plug, supplying the prospectors in California. Another Richmond personality, Robert A. Mayo, was to supply the United States Navy with a brand of chewing plug called Navy Plug. From

Virginia, Maryland, Carolina, Louisiana, Tennessee, and Kentucky came a variety of tobaccos, under such names as Thick-Joint, Hudson, Shoestring, Thickset, Frederick, and Sweet-scented. They faced world-wide competition as European cultivation in the Levant, France, Italy, and Holland vied with such far-flung sources as Malta, Canada, Brazil, Columbia and Venezeuela.

Years of American experimentation with imported seed and new cropping methods were to be crowned by a significant change in curing techniques. European smokers demanded mild tobacco and connoisseurs argued over their preferences. The original Orinoco or Trinidad seeds, reared in the sandy loam of Yorktown and along the James river, yielded a leaf that was first cured by hanging it up in open barns for two months, letting nature ripen the leaf to suit mild palates. Later there came artificial heat curing, with wood fires producing smoke that turned the hanging leaf dark brown and gave it a strength suited to the most hardy pipe owners or chewers of tastier plugs.

Before the Civil War (1861–1865) ripped across the tobacco-rich lands first sown by Indians and then the Englishman John Rolfe, there came a dramatic development in curing that was to give bright leaf a mild, mellow yellow quality. The light, bright tobacco was cured by a young slave, Stephen, and his negligence. Four planter brothers—Abisha, Elias, William and Thomas Slade—tilled a ridge of sandy land at Caswell County, North Carolina, using damp wood fires in their curing barns. One night in 1839 the slave fell asleep while on duty in the barn and in his rush, on awakening to find the fire nearly out, grabbed some charcoal from the nearby smithy pit to revive the dying embers. As the barn filled with fresh heat the leaf turned yellower than anything before. It was to sell at up to four times normal quotation prices. The Slades told others of their discovery. Charcoal provided the more balanced and smoke-free heat for which planters had long searched.

Some twenty-one years later charcoal was to be displaced by a better system, called flue curing, whereby an outside furnace supplied heat from steel fluted floors to the leaf hanging above. During this period, from 1839 to 1860, many farmers were to ape the success of the Slades and others in their curing and planting techniques. Two years before North Carolina seceded with ten other southern states from the Union, Washington Duke, father of Buck, had grown his first trial crop and had stored the leaf when the Civil War conscripted him, at thirty days' notice, into the Confederate army.

The growth and development of America gave the tobacco states a lusty home market to exploit, as well as the chance to plant new crops, such as cotton. Tobacco factories sprang up in profusion. By 1840, in Virginia and North Carolina there were around three hundred and fifty, and Richmond alone had about fifty; they permeated Lynchburg, Petersburg, and Darville, while far away in New York plug processing units extended the base of supply, even moving into cigar manufacturing, challenging the emerging expertise of New England where Cuban leaf was processed into Havana cigars and made fashionable by, among others, John Quincy Adams.

Snuff, cigars, and plug were sold under such brand names as Daniel Webster and The People's Choice. Northern producers were gaining a grip on the trade through their practice of buying leaf, processing it, and shipping their products out to wholesalers across the land (during the 1857 financial crisis southern suppliers got into serious difficulties because bills were not paid by northern customers).

Tobacco was a much demanded product both during and after the Civil War. Buck Duke could not have been born at a better time. The cultivation of leaf might have spread far and wide, but northern manufacturers still beat a path to Virginia and North Carolina's Piedmont regions to haggle for bright leaf. Competition came from the white and red Burley tobaccos of South Ohio and Kentucky, though they were increasingly used as filler for chewing plug that might have a bright leaf Piedmont wrapper. But the Union expanded the home market for all kinds of product, and the richest pickings would go to the best organised. That meant industrialisation and a wider scale of marketing.

It was the reason why James Buck Duke, who knew none of this history, annexed most of the competition on 31st January 1890, and found himself, aged 33, controlling the American Tobacco Company, capitalised at $25 million.

CHAPTER THREE

A Trust is Spawned

News of the formation of an American tobacco monopoly soon reached England, but few of the five hundred manufacturers seemed unduly perturbed. The largest, W. D. & H. O. Wills, founded in the eighteenth century, had been wise enough to secure the English Bonsack patent seven years before and the potential market for cigarettes had been steadily, if slowly, exploited since the 1850s. Indeed, Robert Peacock Gloag was in 1890 giving an interview to the trade journal *Tobacco* about his historic decision in 1856 to open a factory to make cigarettes for Gloag & Company at Walworth.

As paymaster to the Turkish allied forces in the Crimean War, Gloag had watched British troops take to hand-formed Russian and Turkish smoking tubes. The first products were both large and clumsy. Gloag explained in the interview: 'The tobacco used was Latakia dust and the paper yellow tissue . . . the mouthpiece was of cane. The mode of manufacture was first to make the canes, into which the tobacco had been pressed. In order to keep the dust tobacco from escaping, the ends were turned in. The size of the cigarettes was that which is now known as an Oxford, and they were put up in bundles of ten, to be retailed at 6d.'*

Some years later came Don Alphonso Spanish whiffs, at twenty-five for one shilling.

Wills, then led by William Henry Wills, created a Baronet in 1893 and elevated to the Peerage in 1906 as Lord Winterstoke, was among the first tobacco concerns to follow Gloag into cigarette

* *Tobacco*, 1st November 1890.

production (with the brand Bristol) with hand-rolling teams set to work in 1871. The business had been founded by Henry Overton Wills in 1786 centred in Bristol, and the famous W. D. & H. O. Wills company was to spring up from the initials of the founder's two sons who had taken over in 1826. The Wills family were to realise that the development of the American bright tobacco leaf meant the production of milder and more popular cigarettes. Through middlemen, they were soon buying the leaf from Virginia and Carolina.

Four years before Duke created his American Tobacco Company, Wills had outgrown its original premises at Mary-le-Port Street and Redcliff Street in Bristol and moved to a new factory, lit with electric lights, at Bedminster. Unknown to everyone, the age of a fragmented British tobacco trade was drawing to a close with the advent of industrialisation.

It was typical of the paternalistic streak in Wills management that a high tea was arranged on 27th March 1886 to mark the opening of the new factory. After a meal that included York hams, rhubarb tart, blancmanges, pigeon pies, and tea, Henry Herbert Wills, son of H. O. Wills, the third, rose to his feet and sang a solo. He was in fine voice and mood. It was his foresight that had helped to secure the Bonsack machine patent and reduced the price of the early Wills cigarettes. There were to be eleven machines in the new factory, each able to make from 80,000 to 100,000 a day. And soon he was to be married to the sister of his assistant, Sir Hugo Cunliffe-Owen (first secretary and later chairman of British-American Tobacco).

Three years before the factory's opening, the Wills company had launched Gold Flake cigarettes, using all-Virginia tobacco, which would sell alongside Best Bird's-Eye (exported to France). Cost figures showed they were 7s per 1,000 cheaper to make than the hand-rolled brands Bristol (1871), Passing Clouds (1874), and Three Castles (1878). Among the earliest producers of handmade cigarettes who faced the Wills challenge was Philip Morris, a London tobacco merchant house which twenty years before the first Bonsack machine arrived at Wills had used smoke-cured Turkish tobacco to make crude cigarettes. That the output was insignificant in total terms can be established from estimates given by a Parliamentary Select Committee on the Tobacco Trade in 1844, which estimated the division of the

British tobacco market as Shags 56 per cent, Roll 28 per cent, Snuff 12 per cent, cigars 2 per cent, leaving 2 per cent to be accounted for by cigarettes and other experimental products.

Lambert and Butler, founded 1834, which used a horse in the mornings to work a tobacco-cutting machine in a revolving shaft (in the afternoons the animal did deliveries), brought out a hand-made cigarette called Straight Cut, the London slang phrase meaning 'a respectable woman'.

Not all processors were interested in cigarettes. Thomas Gallaher, the eighteen-year-old son of a Derry farmer who founded Gallaher in Londonderry in 1857 making Irish roll pipe tobaccos, had moved to Belfast in 1870, and was interested at first only in hard tobaccos, but by 1885 was producing handmade cigarettes. Gallaher was sceptical of the Wills makes and promoted his cigarettes as superior by virtue of their manual production. He was soon to change his mind.

More apprehensive about the developments at Wills and in America were two young brothers, John Dane and William Good-acre Player. Their father John, son of a Saffron Walden solicitor, had died a year after Wills had bought the Bonsack English patent. At twenty and eighteen years of age respectively, they inherited a thriving business, John Player & Sons, which was nevertheless vulnerable to new developments. In 1861 their father had moved to Nottingham's Beastmarket Hill, trading as a seedsman before he bought a small tobacco manufacturing business (Wright & Son) at Broadmarsh. Three years before his death he had established the famous Castle Tobacco factory at Radford, Nottingham (opened in three blocks, two of which were leased out to lace makers pending future expansion).

The young Player brothers were courteous and never jealous of competitors, even if worried by their own sudden accession to responsibility. They were both to live long, John Dane to eighty-five and William Goodacre to ninety-three. They responded to the emerging challenge of cigarette manufacture by promoting hard the first brands introduced by their late father only a year before his death—Our Heroes, Our Charming Belles, and the Castle. The brothers greeted Wills' opening of a machine-equipped factory by introducing in 1886 Player's Gold Leaf Navy Cut cigarettes. Like Wills (Gold Flake, 1883) they saw the symbolism of the word 'gold'. The 900 lb hogsheads of bright Piedmont leaf in the factories looked like gold. It was gold, as all the merchant adventurers whose names thread through the antiquities of tobacco, the eternal weed, realised century by century.

Each Victorian manufacturer sought to distinguish his products with trade-marks. John Player's first mark was a drawing of Nottingham Castle registered in 1877. But six years later, not long before his death, he commissioned an artist to draw one of the world's most famous trade-marks—the head of a bearded sailor wearing Royal Navy uniform, with a cap erroneously name-banded Hero (omitting the letters HMS). The head was to be circled in 1888 with a lifebuoy, with the brand title Player's Navy Cut superimposed (two ships were added in 1901).

There was a long English tradition for tobacco trade-marks. In the late seventeenth century engraved paper wrappers were used by merchants to pack their customers' favourite smoking tobacco or snuff. Often shops had carved or cast figures in their windows or doorways, trade mascots and figureheads. A wooden figure of a fully-dressed Highlander was the traditional sign of a good snuff merchant.

Today the first wrappers, such as Black Boys, Virginia Men, Virginia Planters, Highlanders or Tobacco Rolls, are prized by collectors, as are cigarette cards. In 1887, as the young Player brothers were improving their father's original Navy Cut trade-mark, the Wills family was introducing an illustrated printing on the cards used to stiffen the crush-prone paper packs containing their new machine-made cigarettes. It was a coloured advertisement for the nine-year-old Three Castles brand, depicting a serving girl knocking on a door. Overleaf was a list of the other Wills brands.

American brands had begun appearing on the English market, the packs stiffened by colourful cards portraying famous actresses. Marketing development was curiously similar each side of the Atlantic. Indeed, United States retailers also had wooden figures, often on wheels, outside on the sidewalk. These were usually mysterious American Indians, or turbanned orientals, which symbolised tobacco's romantic history; in London, these were Jacobite Highland figures or wooden Negro boys in carved skirts of tobacco leaves, with outstretched hands on long clay pipes.

By the 1890s, pictorial cigarette cards began to appear regularly in England, supplanting the first advertisement stiffeners. They were to be collected with enthusiasm, a source of encyclopedia-type information. The Player brothers issued series of naval and army heroes and castles and abbeys. The cards were to be as informative as they were eyecatching. Music hall artistes, authors, wild animals, political propaganda—nothing was to be missed. In 1899 Ogden (Guinea Gold, 3d for ten) started a series of Actresses, Prominent People and Subjects of General Interest that was to last eleven years, during which time 20,000 different sets of cards were issued to smokers.

When the Ipswich-based W. A. & A. C. Churchman, founded in 1790, produced a series called Beauties to match Player's Gallery of Beauties and Wills' Actresses, outraged Victorian readers wrote to *The Times*. 'Placing licensed sex on a pedestal,' said one. Another said they were 'a form of sexual excitement to induce moral degeneration in the male'.

Today, 50,000 serious cartophilists* can chart great periods of history with the cards that proliferated through to the Boer and First World Wars, into the 1930s and into the Second World War, when paper and board shortages forced their end. One of the biggest printers of cards, Mardon Son & Hall, had one order in the 1930s for 350 million for just one series.

Machine-made Virginia cigarettes required romantic names for advertising purposes. The machine age might need a mass market, but the product had to give the discerning smoker an aura to his individual purchase. Wills, whose first brand in 1871 had been called Bristol, in November 1888 told its trade customers of two more brands—Cinderella and Wild Woodbine, both to sell at five for one old penny. Romantic names were needed to counter the appeal of the Turkish, Greek and Egyptian hand-rolled cigarettes that Robert Gloag and others had established on the market. In America, progressive blending of Virginia with aromatic imported leaf had hastened the downfall of exotic brands that had been made fashionable under high society's leadership.

Wills' Woodbine was to be a winner. It was well-named and keenly priced, thanks to the early Bonsack machines. The price was to stay at one penny until September 1915, when tobacco duty forced the addition of a farthing. During this period, it was to outstrip the sales of any other cigarette, England's first truly mass market brand. The rival Player's Navy Cut was priced at

* An auction of 250,000 cards in September 1971 raised £2,000.

2½d for ten. Ogden later responded to the Woodbine with Tabs, also at one penny for five—and it was the kind of daring that James Buchanan Duke appreciated. Across the Atlantic, he received reports on the English tobacco scene, even if he seemed preoccupied with planning other take-overs, such as Pfingst, Doerhoefer & Company, of Louisville, Kentucky.

Duke invited Basil Doerhoefer to New York, and told him he wanted to buy the business, which supplied dark Burley chewing plug under such names as Battle Ax, and Newsboy. Doerhoefer was overwhelmed by Duke's vision of a mass plug-making enterprise. He was told his present earnings represented 'peanut money'. No one could withstand Duke's persuasive sales talk and on 1st January the small town company was turned into a $400,000 corporation styled the National Tobacco Works.

Within months Duke's American Tobacco had bought the Old Virginia Cheroots firm of Whitlock of Richmond—extracting from the owner a promise not to become a competitor for twenty years—and several Baltimore companies, Marburg Brothers and Gail & Ax. It all cost over $6 million in cash and American Tobacco stock, for which the Duke empire raised its capitalisation to $35 million. No one was to regret the deals, for some of the owners became American Tobacco directors and the stock they gained took them into the millionaire class. The group's profits swept up to $5 million in 1893, largely due to the growth of demand for paper-wrapped cigarettes.

Not even a steadily rising wave of resentment to Duke and what was now called his Trust could deter his onward march towards real monopoly. His God-fearing father Washington began wishing that his son 'hadn't gotten us into this combination'. He was embarrassed by preachers, doctors and feminists who crusaded against the evils of smoking. The Duke family was a prime target. Sadly, Washington was to comment: 'You know, there are three things I just can't seem to understand: ee-lec-tricity, the Holy Ghost, and my son Buck.'

Son Buck was to grin over that now famous remark, carrying on his wave of buying by swallowing three concerns that made miniature cigars, Consolidated Cigarette of New York, Thomas H. Hall, also of New York, and Herman Ellis of Baltimore. He had in mind that if any laws were passed to ban paper-wrapped cigarettes, then he would be ready to market small cigars by mass methods. Consolidated had a machine which interested Duke much more than its brands.

There seemed to be no stopping the bull-necked redhead, who by now was engaged in a serious love affair with an attractive divorcee whose call on a telephone could bring him racing out of important board meetings. And some of those board meetings were turning into critical affairs.

The policy of new acquisitions did not win outright support from his fellow directors. Indeed, some of his original partners, W. H. Butler and Major Ginter, were plotting Duke's downfall with Colonel Oliver Payne, of Standard Oil, whom they persuaded to buy up large tranches of American Tobacco stock for a show-down at a stockholders' meeting. The plotters objected to Duke's strategy of diversification away from cigarettes, which were the obvious profit-makers and upon which the group ought to concentrate. By chance, Duke heard at the eleventh hour and managed to see Payne, a complete stranger though with a reputa-tion to shake any hardened businessman. Buck did not mince his words, as he tossed down a written resignation. When Payne asked what he would do if he quit, the angry Duke said he would im-mediately open a tobacco factory and expand on his own.

It was a master stroke. Payne knew Duke's record well enough from the figures and was a judge of an obvious profit-maker. Soon Payne had switched sides and was ready to support Duke. It was a formidable alliance and before long Major Ginter and W. H. Butler, as well as a few others, were selling their shares and quitting the board room.

At the root of the row over diversification had been Duke's ideas for mounting a well-prepared onslaught on the chewing plug market. America was, even after five years of American Tobacco's marketing of machine cigarettes, still the land of the moving jaw. The output returns for 1897 show more than 182 million lb of plug and twist being produced compared with 91 million lb of smoking tobacco.

The task was not an easy one, and it is easy to understand the concern of Ginter and Butler at their president's apparently mad scheme to fight the established plug makers, many of whom had been banded together into a protective association since 1884 to stamp out price cutting and unfair competition. Duke was spoiling for a fight, even if Virginian and North Carolinian leaf was less attractive for chewers (it sold mainly in Eastern markets) than the moist and well-flavoured Burley plug based on Western American markets.

Chewing his own mouldy plug, Duke had convinced his new backer, Colonel Payne, of Standard Oil fame, that he could break up the cosy ring of leading suppliers before they themselves had grander ideas. There was already talk of a possible merger of the biggest plug producers, perhaps Liggett & Myers (Star), the Drummond Tobacco Company (Horseshoe), and P. Lorillard Company (Climax). The first two were St Louis-based concerns and Lorillard was centred on Jersey City. There were other important suppliers, though these three in 1894 had a combined output of over 61 million lb, six times the production of Duke's three-year-old National Tobacco Works built out of Pfingst, Doerhoefer & Company. These others included P. J. Sorg, of Ohio, J. Finzer & Brothers of Louisville, and J. G. Butler, also of Kentucky. It was on the last named that Duke's eyes settled for the first take-over victim.

Butler's was bought for around $500,000 in the autumn of 1895 and dovetailed into Duke's existing Louisville manufacturing and selling operation. Now he set out to soften up the enemy. National Tobacco's Newsboy plug was already swamping Missouri markets, supported by heavy promotion. Now Duke fired his first shots in what the tobacco trade in America remembers as the Great Plug War. One-pound bars of Battle Ax plug were reduced from the long-standing fifty cents in progressive cuts to thirteen cents. The rivals were stunned, for the duty was six cents a pound. Free giveaways, massive advertising, and compulsory stocking by cigarette dealers were to push Duke's plug sales up from 8.9 million lb in 1894 to about 22 million lb two years later, reaching 38 million lb by 1897 to give him a fifth of the national market for plug. It was a bitter and costly campaign, for American Tobacco's net profits plunged through the losses sustained in unnerving the competitors.

Those competitors, unused to such tactics, made a half-hearted and abortive attempt to merge. Something had to be done, nevertheless, and they decided to hit back by making cigarettes, which they did in such quantity that Kentucky producers were turning out perhaps 15 per cent of the nation's cigarettes by 1897, when Duke's profitability was starting to worry him. But not for long. American Tobacco's leaf buyers were soon squeezing farmers on the prices paid for their crops. So savage were some of the fluctuations in prices that the North Carolina newspaper editors openly attacked Duke, and even his father, as vicious monopolists.

It was only a matter of time before white flags would appear. First Duke bought Drummond, and then Brown Brothers, to consolidate his St Louis armoury, promptly slashing the prices of their brands. The bright, high-living Pierre Lorillard resisted Duke's pleading and offers for his P. Lorillard & Company, one of the biggest plug makers, until the price reached $6 million, plus a promise to be allowed to run the business in exchange for the $3 million shares. In swift succession, others sold out to Duke— J. Finzer Brothers, J. Wright & Company, P. H. Mayo & Brother, P. J. Sorg (a particularly stubborn rival), and D. Scotten.

The new plug combination now spanned the United States. On 10th December 1898, Duke, with Colonel Payne's support, registered in New Jersey the Continental Tobacco Company to mastermind the operation of ten manufacturing plants turning out 106 million lb of tobacco, including 84 million lb of plug. This new enterprise had a $75 million authorised share capital, issuing $62 million (with $30 million going to Payne, Duke and colleagues for American Tobacco's plug interests). Duke became Continental's president.

Preoccupied as he was with the plug negotiations, Duke found himself suddenly threatened by a Wall Street syndicate of financiers and stock market manipulators. W. H. Butler, who had led the board-room rebellion which originally involved Colonel Payne's purchase of American Tobacco shares, had not been content to depart quietly. He had bought, as agent for the syndicate in 1896 when Duke was in the thick of the plug war, the National Cigarette & Tobacco Company, a small enterprise worth only $800,000. The threat was due to the powerful combination of names behind Butler. The acquisition had, of course, not escaped Duke's attention, for National Cigarette had tried some months before the take-over to indict Duke in New York County for conspiracy to restrict competition by secret payments to wholesalers for their loyalty.

The troublesome National Cigarette survived because it was holding rights to several cigarette machines, including those of Bernhard Baron, who a year before Butler's take-over had gone to

England to build and sell his machines in the wake of Bonsack, whom Duke had assisted in the earlier days.

That Duke had good cause for worry cannot be doubted. The syndicate was powerful and well heeled, led by one of Wall Street's most daring figures. He was Thomas Ryan, born to poor Irish-Scottish parents in Virginia and given the fateful middle name Fortune. A friend of Charles Schwab, first president of United Steel and subsequently Bethlehem Steel, Ryan had begun his business career as a dry goods clerk in Baltimore, but by 1886 had risen to become a protégé of the equally famed William C. Whitney. These two, Whitney and Ryan, were to take over and consolidate New York City's public transport system, starting with horse car services, and eventually owning the Interborough Rapid Transit Company. A Grand Jury was to allege in 1908 that their manipulating of stock and franchises was 'dishonest and probably criminal', but by that time Ryan was worth $50 million and had moved on to even bigger things.

Ryan was described by Whitney before the latter's death in 1904 as 'the most adroit, suave, and noiseless man that American finance has ever known'. He was destined to hold a Stock Exchange seat and to buy his way into the banking, railways, insurance, oil, precious stones, rubber, coal, power and typewriter industries, increasing his personal fortune to $100 million, and by 1924 was one of the nation's largest individual income-tax payers. He was to be a major benefactor of the Catholic Church, the Democratic Party, and own a Fifth Avenue home that included a private chapel, and art gallery (containing many busts of himself, including three sculpted by Rodin).

He was, as John Brooks, the brilliant American business writer, has described him, a 'classical capitalist buccaneer'. New York newspapermen referred to Ryan as 'the great opportunist', a man who only twice in his life made a public statement on his wheeling and dealing.

Clearly Duke had cause for concern to find such a man, backed by other associates besides the great Whitney, trying to horn in on American Tobacco's patch. Not that he had much warning, for the first Ryan deals were effected through Duke's old board-room adversary Butler, whose knowledge of the tobacco industry and contacts were essential to throw together, in only a matter of weeks, a serious challenge to the Trust.

While Duke's attention was somewhat diverted by his plug activities, Ryan and Butler pulled off their next coup—the purchase of the Durham Tobacco Company, which had grown alongside the original W. Duke Sons & Company and, indeed, whose Bull Durham brand of smoking tobacco even now outsold Duke's Mixture. Durham Tobacco was no infant, but a powerful trader and run by a new Harvard-educated manager called Percival Smith Hill, whose son George Washington Hill was to be trained in years to come at Duke's knee as a devastatingly successful marketeer extraordinary.

Durham Tobacco and National Cigarette were placed under a new $22 million holding corporation, the Union Tobacco Company of America. Clearly Ryan had watched and admired the Duke strategy of combinations. Indeed, Ryan, with Butler's help, now boldly approached Liggett & Myers, one of the few plug companies which resisted Duke's wooing. Butler, on Ryan's behalf, used as his sales pitch the need to fight the Duke Trust. It was a message with appeal, and Ryan gained an option to buy Liggett & Myers for $11 million.

Now came a stunning blow. Ryan let Duke know in 1899 that American Tobacco faced a dose of its own medicine, and Butler must have been beside himself with glee at his business enemy's shock. After the first flush of fury, Duke's shrewd mind steadied to a more even keel. Something had to be done. American Tobacco and its sister Continental Tobacco Company had to be protected at all cost. The cost was a spectacular realignment of corporate structure under which Ryan and his associates netted a cool $20 million or so profit on their original investments.

By a complex interchanging of stock and cash, American Tobacco bought Ryan's newly formed Union Tobacco group, and the associated Continental, which paid Duke a $50,000 a year salary as president, acquired Liggett & Myers. Boards were reconstructed with Ryan going on both boards of the enlarged sister companies.

There was a slight skirmish with a group of dissident small shareholders in Durham Tobacco who had refused to sell out to Ryan and now tried to stop the American Tobacco merger (Union Tobacco was to vanish under the arrangements). Duke, as the new controlling shareholder through American Tobacco, put in a receiver and liquidated Durham's assets to pay the troublemakers off. There seemed no sentiment in Duke. He coldly shut down the famous producer of Bull Durham, ignoring appeals to his ambivalent pride in his North Carolinian ancestry. Rather than retain the original and historic company, he now registered a new Durham Tobacco Company in New Jersey, earmarking it as a shell corporation to effect further take-overs that might cross his mind.

Not valued in the Durham books were the talents of Percival Hill, the general manager, or Rufus Patterson, a twenty-seven-year-old engineering wizard with a skill for making and improving machinery. Duke quickly spotted their worth and they were soon both vice-presidents of American Tobacco—Hill was given total charge of sales, and Patterson handed control of machinery supply, developments, and patents.

The bitter and profitable stock market lesson handed out to Duke by Ryan seemed to spark off new power. He now needed to complete his monopolistic design fast before any other of the emerging Wall Street manipulators got similar ideas. There was still some competition to mop up, notably the newly formed Atlantic Snuff Company, registered in 1898 by a group of small concerns. A threat of full-blooded Duke-style assault in the market soon had the big snuff rival in the Trust, under the wing of a new $25 million holding corporation called American Snuff, taking in Delaware's W. E. Garrett & Sons (among others) which then absorbed G. W. Helme, of New Jersey.

Now Duke could turn his full, covetous attention on one of the few remaining plums—R. J. Reynolds, producer of such brands of plug as Red Apple, Hill Billy, Early Bird and Brown's Mule. The Reynolds business had always been thought to be forbidden fruit by everyone other than Duke, who had long nursed a personal grudge and wanted to outsmart a long-standing competitor. The prey was now a company running a large factory at Winston, North Carolina, with an output of over 5 million lb of plug. It was controlled by Richard Joshua Reynolds, who, like Duke, had peddled tobacco after the Civil War and some ten years later had set up his plant to use bright leaf by mass processing techniques that gained him much admiration in the trade. Reynolds was a constant critic of Duke and his methods, and indeed sympathised openly with the planters in their mounting opposition to American Tobacco's ruthless domination of leaf pricing.

Like Duke, Richard Reynolds had broken away from a partnership with his father in tobacco farming, in Critz, Virginia, to set up at the age of twenty-four in Winston. He invested $2,400 in a small factory at Chestnut Street, employing two full-time workers and seasonal labour to make chewing tobaccos during the harvest, selling them on horseback during the rest of the year.

The tough-talking Reynolds had always thought himself a match for Duke, and enjoyed a big reputation for his aggressive statements. He is reported to have told friends: 'If Buck Duke tries to swallow me, he'll get the bellyache of his life.' Duke tried, and the 'bellyache' began years later when Reynolds, freed from the Tobacco Trust, proved his marketing skill by launching in 1913 the famous Camel brand of Burley cigarettes.

Above all, Reynolds knew the facts of business life and when Duke 'came a-calling' the proposal he heard had to be accepted. It was that Reynolds could choose between an outright price struggle, or a merger with Continental. The choice was sweetened by $10 million of shares and an assurance he could retain a reasonable degree of independence as the manager. And so R. J. Reynolds joined Duke's lengthy list of acquisitions, and not an equally formidable but fast fading roll of liquidated or lamed enterprises. Each company under the Trust's umbrella spawned others, dominating suppliers and customers alike.

The conquering Duke was still far from satisfied, even if he and his associates now controlled an organisation that produced more than 90 per cent of America's cigarettes, and 80 per cent, 62 per cent and 60 per cent of snuff, plug, and pipe tobacco respectively. There was still a profitable if somewhat small, by Duke yardsticks, trade in Turkish cigarettes. So the Trust now put its finger deeper into imported tobacco by the purchase of Anargyros of New York, whose Turkish Trophies and Egyptian Deities competed against Lorillard's Turkish brands as well as others from the Trust's many branches. Most of the cigarettes imported into American society in the 1870s and '80s were produced from Levant tobacco. As the Egyptian tobacco trade declined, it was more than supported by Turkish leaf made available by Greek merchants. The growth of demand in New York brought S. Anargyros to the City in 1891 to make cigarettes on the spot, cutting costs and raising profits. Indeed, the aromatic leaf was something of a growing problem for Duke, since, unlike English smokers used to Virginia smoking tobacco and now taking to Burley cigarettes, there was a touch of high fashion about the foreign brands. So much so that imported leaf was mixed with home-grown leaf.

The advent of the Bonsack machine had initially pushed up cigarette sales, but Duke had begun to worry whether his conviction that the market would keep expanding was still valid. Indeed, overall cigarette sales now paused long enough for him to propose substantial diversification not just into the Turkish market but into the developing cigar business, where the Trust was weakest.

The cigar was a product with as noble a lineage as snuff or pipe tobacco. It somehow was the obvious symbol for late nineteenth-century Americans anxious to demonstrate their success. The larger and darker the cigar, the more assured and authoritative felt the smoker. They were pleasant to consume amid aromatic clouds of smoke, an aid to full relaxation or an accessory to demonstrate the no-nonsense American virility which Europeans cartooned. Production of Cuban and Caribbean cigars was close to art, and customers were appreciative of the finest or roughest rolls. Everywhere successful men gathered in America or Europe, cigars came out, but it was in America that the common man aspired to afford them in the competitive and industrialised society which hard-working immigrants chose to establish.

The demand for cigars was to be acknowledged later with the famous remark of Thomas R. Marshall: 'What this country needs is a good five-cent cigar.' To which Will Rogers was to reply: 'Our country has plenty of good five-cent cigars, but the trouble is they charge fifteen cents for them.'

Production of cigars in the late 1890s attained around 5,000 million—and Duke was not getting what he considered his inevitable due, the lion's share. The turn of the century was to be marked by a tidy $20 million deal that linked American Tobacco with a leading cigar maker, Powell, Smith & Company, into yet another new corporation—the American Cigar Company, which was naturally registered in New Jersey. A series of take-overs was to follow, including the Havana-American Company with sales of 100 million cigars made from Cuban leaf in ten factories and largely based in Florida. It was the start of a heavy drive that secured a large slice of the market, involving acquisitions of Cuban and Puerto Rican plantations as well as distributors.

The time when Duke would experience his first major failure

was now fast approaching. Yet it was inconceivable that this patently successful man could make a serious mistake. He had an attractive mistress, Lillian McCredy, a huge and enlarging fortune, a close-knit team of executive accomplices, a large farm, Fifth Avenue home and offices, and, above all, power of decision-taking over a Trust with $125 million a year sales and around 100,000 workers. In his rather shapely frock coat, he worked long hours, usually six days a week.

He liked to brag that he made mistakes, yet they were very few in number. Duke once said: 'I've made mistakes all my life. And if there is one thing that's helped me, it's the fact that when I make a mistake I never stop to talk about it—I just go ahead and make some more.'

That he made a bad mistake in 1901 is for history still to judge. He decided to extend his covetous activities across the Atlantic Ocean.

James Buchanan Duke booked a passage for Liverpool and told his bankers and directors to stand by for 'some goddam action'. He took with him a banker's facility to spend £6 million.

CHAPTER FOUR

'Hello Boys, I'm Duke from New York'

'Hello boys, I'm Duke from New York come to buy your business.'

With these horrific words, the president of the American Tobacco Company greeted the brothers John Dane and William Goodacre Player. He was, using the words of a Player's historian, 'politely, but firmly, shown the door'. The blunt tycoon was nonplussed. He told Welsh-born W. R. Harris, his fastidious auditor, and Caleb Dula, two country-boy executives who came with the Drummond Tobacco Company take-over: 'Well, it kinda looks as if we've gotta slug it out.' The three had landed at Liverpool early in September 1901, refreshed by Atlantic breezes after some hectic months of stock manipulation which is still regarded with awe by students of American business in one of its most turbulent periods.

Here he was in England watching and hearing company doors slamming in his face, but not before he had placed one of his large flat feet into one—and penetrated the board room as the new owner. British tobacco manufacturers were in a phase of confident expansion. Wills now had twenty-two Bonsack machines in operation and, with the others, supplied no less than 350,000 retail outlets in Britain. Heavy duties had been maintained on imports of manufactured tobacco products and Duke's only hope of breaking into a lucrative market, where cigarettes were gaining rapid acceptance among smokers, was for his Trust to buy, or to set up, a plant to produce its brands on a local basis.

What bothered everyone in the English industry was the specific knowledge, relayed from its leaf-buying and other agents in the

United States, that Duke had more than sufficient resources to buy his way in by acquisition. The money came from some wheeling and dealing that began in the midsummer with circulars to shareholders in both American Tobacco and its allied Continental Tobacco. Duke and a number of his millionaire directors, such as W. C. Whitney and Thomas Fortune Ryan, were forming a new holding company, Consolidated Tobacco, to ensure their absolute control of the Trust. They put $40 million of their cash into the deal, under which shareholders eagerly exchanged their existing shares for bonds offered on a two-for-one common stock basis. What few could know was that the Finance Committee of the United States Senate was contemplating a reduction in tobacco taxation (it had been raised to pay for the war with Spain in 1898 and had remained at a high level). There was more than a tax cut on the way. Some favourable amendments to revenue law such as lifting restrictions on pack sizes would help big price-cutting manufacturers to slash 52 to 54 cents off cigarette levy.

A holder of $1 million of tobacco shares was one Senator Nelson W. Aldrich, father of Mrs John D. Rockefeller Jr. Senator Aldrich was chairman of the Finance Committee, and a friend of Ryan and Whitney.

The formation from the over-capitalised American and Continental shareholdings of the master Consolidated Corporation gave Duke and his backers the lion's holding of the controlling stock. Whereas they were a force among shareholders in American and Continental, and a power in management affairs, they now gained outright control. As shareholders switched into Consolidated bonds, reassured by the investment of up to $40 million in the new holding company to raise dividends, Duke and his partners acquired $102 million of the operating subsidiary voting common stock for Consolidated. In the event, the cut in taxes was a bonanza for the operating subsidiaries, control of whose stock now fell into the Duke circle's hands. During its short existence of a little over three years, the new holding company was to pay out $6 million in dividends, invest a surplus of $17 million and have access to additional $7 million surpluses tucked away in the American and Continental companies. At the same time, the operational subsidiaries contributed $30 million profit to Consolidated on the original $40 million cash investment that lured common stockholders to take fixed rate bonds.

Clearly, then, Duke was not short of dollars to make his trip to England very rewarding. And it was just as well that he was out of the country for a while as people began to realise the extent of the Trust's manipulation. Just before departure he had bought the United Cigar Stores, through the Havana-America Company, and set in train an invasion of tobacco retailing that spawned 500,000 United retail shops across the nation in the next five years.

No sooner had Duke and his two assistants, Harris and Dula, arrived than they were seeking an interview with R. H. Walters, the chairman of Ogden Ltd, of Liverpool. After several days of secret negotiations, there came an announcement which merited only a long paragraph in *The Times* (17th September 1901) but would eventually set off a chain of events that would transform in a matter of weeks the whole structure and destiny of the British tobacco industry. The report said: 'The American Tobacco Company and Messrs Ogden (Limited): negotiations have been going on for some days past for the acquisition by the American Tobacco Company, which, with its allied concerns, controls a capital of about £50 million sterling, of the business of Messrs Ogden (Limited), tobacco and cigarette manufacturers, of Liverpool. It is reported that at an interview yesterday between the representatives of the tobacco company and the directors of Messrs Ogden (Limited) and their advisers, a definite offer was made to Messrs Ogden (Limited) to obtain controlling interest in their business. This offer, which will be submitted to the shareholders at once, is said to be a good one, and likely to be accepted by the holders of Debenture stock and the shareholders, being a considerable advance upon the issue or quotation price. The capital of Messrs Ogden (Limited) is £500,000 of which 200,000 $5\frac{1}{2}$ per cent Preference and 200,000 Ordinary shares, all of £1 each, have been issued, together with £60,000 of $4\frac{1}{2}$ per cent Debenture stock. The present price of the shares is about 22 shillings for the Preference and 32s 6d for the Ordinary shares.'

It was the next day that Ogden shareholders received a circular offering £1 5s for the Preference stock, £2 10s per Ordinary share and £111 10s per £100 of Debentures. If holders of 75 per cent of the shares and stock did not assent, then American Tobacco reserved the right to buy what was available, but were not bound so to do. Since the directors were ready to sell out, shareholders had little choice but to follow suit. By the time a meeting of share-holders and debenture holders was convened in Liverpool on 20th September, the Trust had gained its controlling stake, with more acceptances coming in by each post. A solitary shareholder who objected to what he described as 'the smallness of the amount being offered' was overwhelmed with explanations of the board's decision to sell out on Duke's terms.

The Ogden business had been founded forty-one years before as a small retail shop run by Thomas Ogden. He set up other shops around Liverpool and eventually opened a factory, to be followed by five others before manufacturing of Guinea Gold and Tabs was eventually concentrated on one big factory, built at Boundary Lane, Liverpool, two years prior to Duke's intrusion into Ogden's affairs.

Walters, the Ogden chairman, did not mince words in justifying the sale of the growing business. He explained: 'The American company make no secret of the fact that they desire to acquire a large share of the tobacco trade in England and the Continent, and Ogden's had either to make a good bargain or regard with anxiety American competition.' He had looked at the serious disparity in the capital of the American Trust and their own, so he thought the decision was a wise one. Ogden's issued capital was £460,000, while American Tobacco's was £50 million.

'The business will not be wound up, but it will be carried on upon other methods,' Walters declared. It was this remark that sent shivers down the board tables of the apprehensive English tobacco manufacturers. The Players brothers knew well enough what they were letting themselves in for as Duke was turned away when he called at their Nottingham offices, convinced by the successful Ogden negotiations that others must follow.

Duke, who in 1901 also bought a controlling stake in one of Germany's largest cigarette makers, Jasmatzi, of Dresden, saw the English market as crucial to his recent dreams of world domina-tion. The Trust was already exporting 1,300 million cigarettes annually, and companies were set up in Australasia, Canada, Continental Europe, China and Japan (he was ejected from the Japanese market by a state monopoly formed in 1904). He had run into English export competition in more than a few markets, including the Far East, where Wills had established a more than useful seaport-based trade. And for several years prior to sailing for England, American Tobacco's exports to Britain had been halved as the home manufacturers entered the cigarette trade and obtained acceptance. Importers could not fully compete against low cost domestic output that did not bear the discriminatory import levy on manufactured tobacco, dating from 1823.

Imports of United States cigarettes had started around the 1870s through agents acting for both W. Duke Sons & Company and Allen & Ginter. Ginter's Richmond Straight Cuts and Richmond Gems sold alongside the burgeoning English brands, which did not deter Duke from shipping over such brands as Cameos and Kinneys Sweet Caporal. These imports, plus the switch of home manufacturers to the still improving Virginia leaf, steadily eroded the divided preference of smokers between Turkish cigarettes, made by such as Robert Gloag of Walworth, and the Virginia products from the new machines of Wills or the handrollers employed by others, such as Philip Morris of Bond Street, impressed by Bright Burley.

What Duke saw was a base for widespread expansion across Europe. The English had begun to develop his kind of mass marketing methods for cigarettes, which now held only one-eighth of the British market, compared with four-fifths for pipe tobaccos, such as Ogden's St Julien and St Bruno. Many retailers still made up their own blends of pipe tobacco from manufacturers' supplies.

Ogden's chairman, Walters, as we have seen, was clearly under no illusions. He told shareholders: 'It will not be a matter of great concern to the American Tobacco Company whether the Ogden business pays a dividend for three, four or five years to come because they may in increasing their interest go to such expense as may swamp the profits for that period with the intention of reaping their reward in the future.' But that statement, on 20th September, was being well heeded. A few days before, rooms had been booked at the Queen's Hotel in Birmingham for thirteen of the other main tobacco manufacturers to hold discussions on the threat from Duke. Even as Walters spoke, those talks had been in progress for twenty-four hours, and would last another four days.

The secret conclave had been convened at the suggestion of the Wills family, who had heard of the experience of John Dane Player and his brother, William, in meeting Duke, who was obviously not going to have his appetite satisfied by the Ogden acquisition. Charles Edward Lambert and Walter Butler, who came from a famous Drury Lane, London, tobacco firm founded in 1834 by their fathers (when barely in their twenties), were called into the preliminary consultations that prepared an agenda for the Birmingham conference. Walter Butler warned the Wills family that Duke would not be frightened off his task, for he had first-hand experience of the American industry, having been sent to Kentucky to learn the leaf-buying trade in 1875, and followed Duke's progress with apprehension.

There was general agreement in the preliminary round of consultations that strength against the 'Yankee wolf' lay in numbers. A federation ought to be created to meet the common enemy, but 'only efficient firms of good financial stability' should be invited to join an appropriate defensive alliance. Fears of American industry were firmly rooted in the British business community and no one doubted that an appeal to patriotism might convince the more hesitant. The era of British political power seemed to be passing—Queen Victoria had died twenty-two days into 1901 (Wills put a black border round its Transvaal series of cigarette cards), and the failing Prime Minister, Lord Salisbury, would hand over to Balfour in 1902. The United States was banging on all the doors of world trade and her industry was surpassing that of Victoria's machine based on coal, ships and patriotic wars. Upstart American cousins were still figures of fun in British business circles, but the enlightened few knew that America's growing railroads, telegraph system, mass production methods, and steel-making capacity, were symbols of the world's new leading industrial power. Through Liverpool were passing annually over 120,000 steerage emigrants (Britain had 675,000 paupers in 1901) as the new century began, whole families setting out from Europe to seek their fortunes. Anglo-American relations had been somewhat shaky since 1895 when President Cleveland intervened in Britain's boundary dispute with Venezuela, which prompted international arbitration to cool a serious crisis. Anti-American letters were still appearing in the correspondence columns of *The Times* in 1901, several pointedly criticising the quality of United States goods.

One man skilled in both politics and business was ready to appeal to the tobacco industry's sense of patriotism. He was Sir William Henry Wills, Bt, who in 1880 was elected Liberal MP for Coventry, which he represented for the next six years. On his election he returned to the family firm's Redcliff Street, Bristol, factory where cheering employees thronged galleries in the entrance hall.

In 1886 the Wills company opened its big new manufacturing establishment and headquarters at Bedminster, Bristol. For the next nine years Sir William was to help build up the company into Britain's biggest tobacco enterprise, worth about £6 million at the end of the century. The Mill Hill- and London University-educated son of William Day Wills went into Parliament again as Liberal Member for East Bristol in 1895 until 1900, having been recently honoured.

Not long before Duke's arrival, the ageing Sir William—he was seventy in 1900—had begun to hand over his business power to other members of the family and favoured executives. He had indeed made a generous arrangement to surrender some of his interests in the enterprise 'in consideration of the recognition of his right to a greater freedom from the ties of business'. The portly, wing-collared ex-MP was looking forward to a retirement of breeding shorthorns and shire horses on his Blagdon estate. It was not to be.

A director of the Great Western Railway Company and a member of the Reform Club, which saw as much of him as the staff at his London home at 25 Hyde Park Gardens (he also had another house at Thanet), the doughty Sir William was, as a keen sailor of the Royal Squadron, more interested in Sir Thomas Lipton's efforts in the autumn of 1901 to amend the rules for the America Cup than business affairs, when one of the new Atlantic steamers disgorged Buck Duke onto a Liverpool quay, bound for Ogden's front door as one port of call.

Sir William agreed with his family's concern for Wills' future and felt a patriotic urge to send the upstart Duke packing. This pleased his young and somewhat strait-laced cousin, George Alfred Wills, who knew that Sir William had the qualities and contacts necessary to negotiate a 'defensive scheme of arrangement' with competitors. There were some strong and turbulent characters in the British industry who would seek to strike hard bargains before surrendering their individual authority for a common purpose.

In the few years prior to 1901, Ogden had developed into one of Wills' strongest competitors. The new Tabs at 1d for five was proving a strong rival to Woodbine and Cinderella cigarettes, for it was promoted well and its cigarette cards were well produced. It was this competitive challenge that led to indecision within Wills on enforcement of list prices, and that indecision was only just beginning to resolve itself as Duke strode into the Ogden board room. All tobacco manufacturers were trying to achieve a sense of orderly marketing and price control, even if Wills was not always cooperative when it came to taking firm decisions.

The Wills family had long trembled when the name of Duke was raised in conversation. Indeed, for some years there had been discussion on how Wills should react should his ambitions take him more directly into the British market place. And for some time American Tobacco had been a disruptive force in export markets. At first, the worries concerned the security of leaf supplies from the United States, and George Wills foresaw possible difficulties that had even prompted a board meeting in 1895. This meeting examined two lines of action—the possible amalgamation with leading British tobacco companies, or the more drastic course of a merger with Duke's American Tobacco Company. Both ideas were rejected.

Not for another three years did the subject merit further formal examination. Later, in 1898, the board resolved its support in principle for an amalgamation with a number of competitors, such as John Player, Lambert & Butler, and, perhaps, Stephen Mitchell & Son. The Wills financial and legal advisers pored over the complexities of a merger, such as valuations, and the consequential problems to be overcome. While the exploratory work went on, under conditions of great secrecy, representatives of Hignett, whose Richmond Cavendish export business was already in battle with American Tobacco, visited Wills at Bedminster to tell of their growing fears of an American invasion. Approaches came, too, early in 1900, from J. & F. Bell, of Scotland. The jockeying between the potential constituents of a manufacturing alliance continued throughout 1900, not reaching any conclusion because of the size of Wills and the problems of valuing the various enterprises, necessary for any practical agreement.

Clearly, Duke had not taken the leading tobacco companies by surprise even if his generosity in buying Ogden somewhat stunned them. In the spring, before Duke sailed for Liverpool, the Wills board had talked over an urgent plan, put up by the machinery inventor and entrepreneur Bernhard Baron, that Wills buy Ogden to avert a possible sell-out. Baron wanted to promote an amalgamation that included Ogden, but his motives were distrusted by the Wills family. Talks took place with Ogden but foundered in the summer because of suspicions that an auction was under way. Too late, Wills sent emissaries, after a board meeting on 13th September 1901, to investigate the Ogden intentions, but Duke had already disembarked, intent on buying tobacco businesses.

When the tobacco trade heard of Duke's purchase, there was uproar. Inevitably, many turned to Wills for leadership, not knowing that the Bristol company was partly to blame for its prevarication. Fortunately, Wills and other manufacturers had been well on the way to an understanding that might be quickly progressed by an intensive round of negotiations.

The negotiations, when they started at the Queen's Hotel in Birmingham, were to prove complex and less than straightforward. Broadly, the idea was, in view of the urgency of establishing a formidable alliance, that the thirteen well-chosen concerns be merged into the British Tobacco Company. It took five weary days to reach agreement—embodied in a signed memorandum not to sell out to Duke—on setting up a master enterprise with a federal structure that allowed the contributing owners of individual companies involved in the constitution freedom to run their businesses, consulting only on the most major policy issues. There was general approval for the idea that Sir William Wills should be the first chairman, because of his known skills as an arbitrator and politician, as well as long experience of the industry. Various parties to the talks argued that other British companies had to be brought in, too (there were five hundred in Britain) and here Sir William's presence would provide reassurance as well as negotiating ability.

In great secrecy, contracts to sell out to common unity were initialled on 3rd October 1901 by an Organising Committee, meeting in London, and arrangements put in hand to draft a prospectus to obtain a Stock Exchange quotation, and, of course, to register a name—The Imperial Tobacco Company (of Great Britain and Ireland) Ltd, of East Street, Bedminster, Bristol. A group of bankers, the National Provincial, Samuel Smith of Nottingham, and the British Linen of Glasgow, were set to work with teams of solicitors and brokers.

The tobacco trade was, by now, alive with wild rumours that Wills and Players were plotting a stout defence against Ogden, which had begun to cut the retail price of its cigarettes, first to 2½d per packet. On 20th October, wholesalers and retailers gathered for an emergency meeting of the United Kingdom Tobacconists' Alliance, fearful that a British combination said to be in the making would be no better than Duke's Trust. These were fragile days for small traders (in the week ending 19th October there had been 163 company failures, mostly small men). Not everyone enjoyed the wealth of one Max Schubach, late owner of the Klingenstein cigar importing firm, whose will published three days earlier showed a £159,125 fortune, of which he left just £50 to the Tobacco Trade Benevolent Institution.

Trafalgar Day, 20th October, was no less historic in 1901. In London the Lord Mayor was appealing for tobacco and pipes to be sent to the Boer War troops. And an official announcement had been drafted after the Buller affair of a reconstruction of the War Office. In New York, an athlete called Flanagan established a new world record for weight putting at 36 feet 9½ inches. In Parliament, politicians were awaiting the imminent return of Lord Salisbury from holiday, much concerned with the War Office crisis. But they did talk also about a report from Washington that President Theodore Roosevelt had entertained a negro, Booker T. Washington, to dinner (of which the *Memphis Scimitar* said: 'The most damnable outrage which has ever been perpetrated by a citizen of the United States was committed by the President when he invited a nigger to dine with him at the White House.')

Amid these and other events, a reporter from *The Times* found time to write a short note that he understood that an enterprise known as the Imperial Tobacco Company of Great Britain and Ireland was proposing 'to take over each of the thirteen firms entering the combination on a footing of ten years' purchase of the average profits of the past three years for goodwill'. Other assets were to be paid for separately.

It was to be a little while before tobacco traders could scrutinise the prospectus. Ten days before, the thirteen founder companies had the Imperial Tobacco Company's name officially registered, and one of the reasons for the delay since the 19th–23rd September conclave in Birmingham had been the shock discovery that Buck Duke had cheekily registered their original British Tobacco

74

Company name for himself. On 20th October, Duke was busy in Belfast trying to buy the flour mills of Barnard Hughes to convert the premises into a factory as a base for taking over the Irish trade.

This in itself was a belligerent new challenge, especially to one leading manufacturer who had not joined the Birmingham war talks—Thomas Gallaher, the Ulster farmer's son whose tobacco and snuff business had grown and even gained Royal interest from King Edward VII. Gallaher had formed a £1 million limited company in 1896 and was doing well in the English market (he opened a factory at Clerkenwell, London, in 1889), even paying in 1900 for two hundred retail tobacconists from the Midlands and northern counties of England to visit his big York Street factory in Belfast, completed in 1897 and using yellow Burley leaf which he helped to buy on personal trips to Kentucky, North Carolina, Virginia and Missouri. Gallaher was a man to be reckoned with, and Duke's interest in a Belfast base sent him into immediate talks with machinery suppliers about tooling up with equipment to provide the machine-made cigarettes he had originally despised. The brand that resulted was Park Drive, a flourishing brand to this day.

There were to be other responses. The Philip Morris tobacco house which had a growing reputation for its cigarettes (as well as cigars and pipe tobaccos first supplied in 1850) had talks with its sole American agent, one Gustave Eckmeyer, of Broad Street, New York, and it was decided to push English brands harder in the United States market, behind Duke's back. In 1902, the first Philip Morris Corporation* was formed in New York, listing among its principal assets a brand sold in London called Marlboro and destined to become one of the world's largest selling cigarettes.

It was clear that the new machinery for making cigarettes and processing and packaging tobaccos would be among the principal weapons of cut-price warfare. Fortunately, Wills was already well equipped and more than a few manufacturers had ordered, or studied with care, an impressive display of equipment mounted four years before at the Tobacco Trades Exhibition at the Agricultural Hall in London's Islington district. No one was then left in any doubt that the days of hand-rolling cigarettes were numbered.

* Seven years later the British owners of Philip Morris re-incorporated, and in 1919 a new concern, Philip Morris & Company, was formed in Virginia.

As if sensing the mood, the exhibition organisers had run a competition to find the most expert manual cigarette makers, with a member of the pioneer manufacturing family, Frederick Gloag, among the judges. With great dexterity, one Miss Lillie Lavender was judged the most expert of the contestants, turning out 162 near perfect cigarettes in thirty minutes. It was a task that James A. Bonsack's one-ton $\frac{1}{2}$ h.p. machine had performed sixteen years earlier in 44 seconds, and now, after improvements, could match in ten seconds or so.

The craft of cigarette making by hand would not vanish overnight, but the substitution of capital equipment for skilled labour would receive great impetus from the cost effective scale of competition that lay ahead as Duke made his battle plans, drawing on his United States experience. For years teams of women, first trained by foreign men from romantic places, had sat in rows at desks, receiving numbered boxes of tobacco from wheeled trolleys. The tobacco was recorded against the name of the cigarette maker, who balanced the debit by the number of cigarettes they made. One contemporary record for 1893 shows an average balance of pay of 15s per week for two hundred girls. 'She takes a pinch of tobacco, wraps it in her dainty bit of rice paper, and with a stick of starch paste, imprisons the yellow weed, and by her side gradually grows a pile of cigarettes, each the same size, each the same weight to a mere sprig.' Nor were these skills the sole preserve of the cigarette-making floor of the early factories. The women who stripped leaf for processing into an appropriate form for filling cigarettes worked no less fast or skilfully. Mrs F. Harknett, one of Carreras' oldest pensioners, recalls the 'Millionaires Gangway' where pay packets could be fattened by fast work. The characters included Rocking 'Orse Winnie, whose chair would rock rhythmically as she stripped tobacco for 1d per lb, wearing a mask and with fingers stained yellow.

By the early 1890s, at least nine different cigarette makers had come into use, functioning with varying success. The Susini machine, exhibited in Paris in 1867, had at one time been ridiculed for its maker's claim to a production of 3,600 cigarettes per hour. This, together with the rival Hook, and Emery equipment, had come before the Bonsack, first used by Wills in 1883. The French tobacco monopoly was among the customers in 1895 for the Decoulfe, with a capacity of 20,000 to 25,000 cigarettes in ten hours promised by the manufacturer, A. E. Decoulfe of Rue Roger, Paris. Other French engineers, Allagnon (Père et Fils) of Vitry-sur-Seine, matched this with their Allagno.

In an advertisement, Allagnon said: 'It is by purely mechanical means that the tobacco is taken from the bulk, combed, and distributed in the paper in a continuous, perfectly homogeneous filler, which will cause the cigarettes to smoke easily and pleasantly, the smoke arriving in the mouth regularly filtered. The cigarettes are closed lengthways without the aid of any sticking material of whatever kind, and are ornamented with two pretty longitudinal seams obtained by various means of goffering.'

The Islington show was used, without advance warning, by the British American Machinery Company to demonstrate the new Venners, named after its New York inventor, J. H. Venners, who arrived unexpectedly in London and proved speeds of 480 cigarettes a minute while he claimed over 630 in United States operations. Among those on the many exhibitors' stands were two men destined to make a big impact on machinery development and utilisation—Bernhard Baron, and J. S. Molins.

Baron had arrived in England in 1895 from the United States, bringing a machine to make 400 cigarettes a minute and featuring a single colour, or with metallic ink printing unit. His claim compared well with a figure of 300 cigarettes per minute for an American machine, the Briggs-Winston, which was a big competitor to the Bonsack. The agent in England for the Briggs-Winston was J. S. Molins, who with two sons Walter and Harold was soon to set up J. S. Molins & Sons to import machinery and make cigarettes.

The elder Molins was an experienced tobacco merchant, and had arrived in London, via America and Cuba, to continue making cigars and tobacco products, but also developing the Briggs agency he had first negotiated in 1893. He was to sell a number of Briggs models (he introduced the first machines to Spain) before selling his agency to the United Cigarette Machine Company of America, which made the United. Under the deal, Molins was allowed the free use of three Briggs machines to make cigarettes for trade customers supplying their own tobacco in addition to producing several of his own brands. Meanwhile, the two sons concentrated on developing machinery for the manufacture of packets, with variations for cardboard matchbox-like 'hull and slide' packets. These packs were to displace, in due course, the early open-ended paper cups and the newer sealed paper packets offered to British smokers.

Baron was to have more immediate success than Molins in creating a machinery business of some importance, even if the latter's family was subsequently to found an enormous British manufacturing enterprise offering a high speed system capable of 4,000 cigarettes a minute. Some of his machines were to be made by Robert Legg,* the first British manufacturer of tobacco machinery. Legg said at that time they were 'easily the best of the somewhat crude cigarette-making machines which were available'.

It was to Baron that the Player brothers turned for their earliest machines, unable to obtain the Bonsack, on which Wills had sole British rights. But the Wills patents would not exclude them for much longer. W. & F. Faulkner, of London, installed an American Luddington in 1897, whose makers were to invite Wills to join it, Baron, and the Briggs interests represented by J. S. Molins, in a new British company called the United Cigarette Machine Company (registered two years later).

Events now piled one on top of the other. Retailers and wholesalers had formed protective trade associations, which then entered into an alliance for consultations. Five days after the Ogden takeover, Duke was offering a rebate of 3d per pound for Coolie Cut Plug on condition that with every 5 lb the trader took 2 lb of St Julien pipe tobacco in packs. With orders of 1,000 Guinea Gold or Tabs cigarettes an additional 200 would be supplied free, the first brand to sell at 2½d for ten and the other at 1d for five. By 20th October 1901, when the United Kingdom Tobacconists' Alliance met in Liverpool, fearful for their future profit margins and even the future ownership of their businesses, a plan had been evolved whereby the leading multiple, Salmon & Gluckstein,† which ran 180 shops and had a £500,000 capital, might supply a range of brands on advantageous terms in return for loyal anti-combination orders.

Salmon & Gluckstein had little respect for the leading manufacturers who had objected to it establishing a small factory at Dingley Road, London, now only running at 25 per cent of its capacity, and had imposed stringent conditions of sale for any of

* Now a subsidiary of the American Machine Foundry Company.
† Formed by the founders of J. Lyons & Company.

their brands sold in the chain's shops. The Alliance envisaged on 20th October a twenty-year deal to sell their rebel brands. The chain was anxious to lead a traders' rebellion, for it had received an approach from Duke to buy the business, and participants in the embryo Imperial organisation had also hinted of their interest. The experiment in self-help was not to be a success because retailers knew before very long there was developing a strong demand for cheap, well-advertised machine-made cigarettes as well as loyalty to existing smoking tobaccos. They would not risk their trade by not stocking the brands smokers would ask for in sharply rising numbers, and, in their hearts, they were opposed to Salmon & Gluckstein, whose growth could not be in their interests.

Salmon & Gluckstein were skilled at price cutting, and pushed the different brands of rival manufacturers according to the discounts they derived on bulk orders. So powerful did the chain become that in 1896 Wills had brought together a group of manufacturers to agree a common policy on resale price maintenance and trade discounts. It took many months of wrangling and broken pacts before agreement was reached. Even within Wills the line management, particularly at the Holborn factory in London, disagreed sharply with their Bristol colleagues, and at one stage Sir William Wills even threatened resignation over a too rigid system of price control that might upset smokers. Attempts at joint action by manufacturers suffered various setbacks.

The unity of manufacturers was by no means obvious. Ogden had been a founder member of a group that had formed in 1898 the National Association of Tobacco Manufacturers, under the chairmanship of Tom Gallaher. Wills stayed outside and formed its own Bristol & West of England Tobacco Manufacturers Association, which operated standard discounts on smoking tobacco. Wills also strongly involved itself in the development of a tobacco committee of the London Chamber of Commerce. But a sense of order on minimum pricing was to be delayed until 1899 when Wills issued its own full pricing schedules for retailers and wholsesalers. Match-makers were no less active.

Through the eighteenth century, smokers had progressed from tinder boxes and flint and steel to French sulphur spills, the Lorentz fire pistol and the Instantaneous Fire Box (pasteboard matches were lit by plunging them into a bottle of sulphuric acid). Then came the Austrian Dobereiner Lamp, a gas lighter that was to be overtaken by the friction match. One man who had been intrigued by explosive mixtures was John Walker who ran a bow-windowed chemist's shop at 59 High Street, Stockton-on-Tees. He was developing what he called friction lights, selling tins of fifty sticks coated with sulphur, gum and chlorate of potash for 1s. They would light on being struck on folded sandpaper. Walker was never to patent or to exploit his important invention (he stopped making them a few years after developing them).

The Liverpool meeting of traders heard many ringing speeches. Duke's was not the only American interest represented in that area. In 1895, the Diamond Match Company, equipped with new continuous match-making machines turning out the Puck, Swan Vestas, and Captain Webb brands, set up manufacturing at Litherland. But in 1901 the London firm of Bryant & May made a successful offer for the factory. It was no less interested in shutting out American interests. For forty years prior to 1901, the firm, founded by two business partners, William Bryant, from Plymouth, and Francis May, a Londoner, had been successfully supplying smokers with matches from their famous Fairfield Road, Bow, factory in London's East End. Match-making was a lucrative industry, and the growth of cigarette smoking was an important new cause of expanding demand.

Fortunately for smokers, who often used a dying ember from the hearth to avoid using the many fire contraptions, Samuel Jones, another chemist, of 201 Strand, London, had heard of Walker's work from Faraday at a Royal Institution lecture. He brought out similar products, which he called Lucifer and Pro-methean, and another Strand chemist, G. F. Watts, was to make the Watts chlorate match. Other match-makers were to come—Richard Bell of Broad Street, who even started a factory for wax Vestas, Charles Sauria, a poor Frenchman who failed to patent a phosphorous match that was to be exploited across Europe and to be produced in Britain as the Congreve, often sold by street hawkers.

Bryant & May brought out Vestas to strike anywhere and when John Lundstum, of Sweden, astounded the growing breed of match-makers with his sensational slow-burning safety match, they secured British rights and made the famous Brymay Special Safety Match, sold with the Ark emblem. Such brand names as Crown, Pearl, Ruby and Tiger were soon to follow.

While Bryant & May protected their growing monopoly, Wills and Players decided to enlist public sympathy by an advertising campaign to explain their motives in forming a combination. The basis of their appeal was patriotism. They felt that smokers might desist from buying Ogden if it was felt that such purposes would harm their country. There was sufficient anti-American sentiment to strike the right chord.

Duly the advertisement shown overleaf appeared.

There was more frantic activity when the shrewd Harry Wills hurried to France and forestalled a bid by the American Tobacco Company for the Braunstein Frères cigarette paper company by negotiating a restrictive three-year supply pact. An attempt by Duke to buy into a Swedish company supplying stiff cartridge papers, needed by Mardon Son & Hall for making cigarette packs, was headed off. Eyes were cast in the direction of the Salmon & Gluckstein chain, which publicly thought Duke's arrival was heaven sent to place cut-price cigarette retailing beyond the re-proof of the established manufacturers.

Another crowded meeting of the United Kingdom Tobacconists' Alliance, this time in Birmingham, heard on 22nd October from the president, Mr Hey, that 'two combines are in battle array and no one can doubt that sooner or later the sirens of war would give out on one side or another'. A *Times* writer examined the first advertisement and pronounced: 'An amalgamation formed not to secure the monopoly of a particular business but to resist a hostile invasion appeals a good deal to one's national instincts.'

This went some way, as an independent comment, towards providing some slight reassurance. And some traders were soon beginning to wonder if some intense competition might not be a bad thing not only for the volume of retail sales but even for profits if trade inducements were to become generous. Duke's next response to the as yet unincorporated Imperial Tobacco Company was to start offering free gifts.

By 10th December 1901, the parties to the formation of Imperial gathered at the Great Western Hotel, Paddington, and disclosed their innermost secrets—their profits. And it was clear that Wills would dominate the amalgamation. Only some expert diplomacy by Sir William Wills, backed by his young and far-sighted cousins George and Harry, stopped the eleventh-hour withdrawal of several parties. That day, the Imperial Tobacco Company was

formally incorporated, holding its first board meeting in Bristol on the following day. It is recorded that when the figures were submitted for the purchase by Imperial of the original thirteen, the dominance of Wills 'caused consternation among the other twelve, who thought that they might be jumping out of the frying pan into the fire'.

The original thirteen firms that formed The Imperial Tobacco Company, in order of the purchase price paid for them as shown in the Company's prospectus, were:

		Purchase Price
1	W. D. & H. O. Wills Ltd, Bristol	£6,992,221
2	Lambert & Butler Ltd, London	754,306
3	Stephen Mitchell & Son, Glasgow	701,000
4	John Player & Sons Ltd, Nottingham	601,456
5	F. & J. Smith, Glasgow	525,803
6	Hignett, Bros. & Co. Ltd, Liverpool	477,038
7	Franklyn, Davey & Co., Bristol	473,555
8	William Clarke & Son Ltd, Liverpool	403,582
9	Edwards, Ringer & Bigg Ltd, Bristol	372,603
10	Richmond Cavendish Co. Ltd, Liverpool	319,805
11	Adkin & Sons, London	146,497
12	D. & J. Macdonald, Glasgow	134,973
13	Hignett's Tobacco Co. Ltd, London	54,183
		£11,957,022

They were joined shortly afterwards by:

Mardon, Son & Hall Ltd, Bristol	1st January 1902
W. A. & A. C. Churchman, Ipswich	1st May 1902
W. T. Davies & Sons, Chester	1st May 1902
W. Williams & Co., Chester	1st May 1902
W. & F. Faulkner Ltd, London	1st May 1902

It was a powerful amalgamation even if for one reason or another some important manufacturers were left out of this combination. These included Gallaher, E. & W. Anstie, Godfrey Phillips, Cope, Carreras, Scotland's J. & F. Bell (Three Nuns), John Cotton and W. Dobie (Four Square), and the Co-operative Wholesale Society (which two years before had started making cigarettes for local retail co-operative societies). Of the founding thirteen, Richmond Cavendish and Hignett's Tobacco were affiliated to Hignett Brothers & Company. Scotland was still well represented by Stephen Mitchell, founded in Linlithgow in 1723 and very expert in leaf buying, as well as F. & J. Smith and D. & J. Macdonald (also noted for its leaf expertise). William Clarke had been founded at Cork in Ireland in 1830, but moved to Liverpool forty years later to compete against Hignett Brothers. The other Liverpool concern, Richmond Cavendish, was largely engaged in the export trade. London supplied Adkin & Sons, formed in 1775 at Ratcliffe Highway, as well as Hignett Tobacco (whose factory at Aldersgate Street was to be burnt down in 1902). Franklyn, Davey & Company was an old-established Bristol tobacco house, whereas Edwards, Ringer & Bigg was an amalgamation of four other local houses from the famous tobacco city.

One of the new group's first actions was to buy the Bristol packaging and printing concern Mardon, Son & Hall on 1st January 1902, which supplied many packs, labels and cigarette cards to the industry.

The problem of the dominance of Wills was resolved by Sir William's proposal at the first meeting that room should be made for some directors not shown in the original articles of association. He was shrewd enough to include, nevertheless, a few extra names from the Wills family to secure future control.

THE IMPERIAL TOBACCO COMPANY (OF GREAT BRITAIN AND IRELAND), LIMITED

First Directors named in the Articles of Association

William Henry Wills, Bt (W. D. & H. O. Wills)	First chairman. Created Baronet in 1893. Elevated to the Peerage in 1906 as Lord Winterstoke. Son of W. D. Wills and nephew of H. O. Wills, the second, the two brothers (sons of the founder of Wills, H. O. Wills, the first) from whom the title of the firm of W. D. & H. O. Wills was derived.
Henry Overton Wills (3rd)	Father of Sir George Wills, H. H. Wills, and W. Melville Wills.

Sir Edward Payson Wills, KCB	Father of Sir Ernest Salter Wills.
Sir Frederick Wills, Bt, MP	Father of first Lord Dulverton (Sir Gilbert Alan Hamilton Wills, Bt)
George Alfred Wills	Created Baronet in 1923. Son of H. O. Wills, the third. First deputy chairman, later chairman and then president.
Henry Herbert Wills	Son of H. O. Wills, the third.
Walter Melville Wills	Son of H. O. Wills, the third.
Charles Edward Lambert (Lambert & Butler)	Son of co-founder of Lambert & Butler.
William Nelson Mitchell (Stephen Mitchell & Son)	Succeeded George Alfred Wills as deputy chairman of the company in 1911.
Richard Davey (Franklyn, Davey & Company)	
John Dane Player (John Player & Sons)	Son of founder of John Player & Sons.
Arthur Walton Hignett (Hignett Brothers & Company)	
Edward Burnet James (Edwards, Ringer & Bigg)	Knighted in 1908. Twice Lord Mayor of Bristol. Son of Sir George Edwards, four times Mayor of Bristol, who was knighted by Queen Victoria at the Council House in 1887.
James Smith (F. & J. Smith)	
Samuel Crosby Hignett (Hignett Brothers & Company)	
Thomas Clarke (William Clarke & Son)	Father of W. R. Clarke and of C. S. Clarke, who was the father of R. S. W. Clarke (Imperial chairman 1959–1964).

Robert Adkin
(Adkin & Sons)

James Macdonald   Father of J. D. Macdonald and
(D. & J. Macdonald)   grandfather of D. B. Macdonald.

John Septimus Hignett
(Hignett's Tobacco Company
Limited)

Directors appointed at first board meeting, December 1921

William Ruddell Clarke   Appointed to replace his father,
(William Clarke & Son)   Thomas Clarke, who had resigned.
                              The board decided that W. R.
                              Clarke should be treated as if he had
                              been named an original director of
                              the company.

Walter Butler   Son of co-founder of Lambert &
(Lambert & Butler)   Butler.

Thomas Davey
(Franklyn, Davey & Company)

Stephen Mitchell
(Stephen Mitchell & Son)

William Goodacre Player   Son of John Player, founder of John
(John Player & Sons)   Player & Sons.

E. Chaning Wills   Eldest son of Sir Edward Payson
(W. D. & H. O. Wills)   Wills, Bt, who was a brother of H. O.
                              Wills, the third. Second Baronet.
                              Succeeded by his brother Sir Ernest
                              Salter Wills.

A. J. Hamilton Wills   Son of Sir Frederick Wills, Bt. Died
(W. D. & H. O. Wills)   in 1905 and did not succeed to his
                              father's title. Elder brother of the
                              first Lord Dulverton (Sir Gilbert
                              Alan Hamilton Wills, Bt).

The vital administrative post of secretary went to Henry W. Gunn, a cousin of G. A. Wills and also secretary of W. D. & H. O. Wills. Gunn was made deputy chairman from 1919 to 1928.

That Wills was dominant could not be doubted. The first intention had been that the number of directors should be proportionate to the profits earned by the individual companies at the time of incorporation of Imperial, so Sir William's tactical move was clearly an important concession. The share capital was to be held almost entirely by members of the great tobacco families, with the Wills family holding nearly 68 per cent of the issued ordinary shares (falling to 55 per cent ten years later).

Among the new-born combination's first decisions were to liquidate Richmond Cavendish, the exporters, and transfer the overseas trade with that of the John Player & Sons branch to Bristol. In return, William Goodacre Player was given the key job of advertising manager of Imperial, and a department was set up in Nottingham to coordinate promotional activity, an early indication that freedom of action by the branches would be limited even if they would manufacture and sell under their various trade names through established sales forces. The courteous Player brothers would prove a moderating influence, for Sir William Wills was leading a team of strong characters.

A brief forty-eight-page history of the period 1901–66 prepared by Imperial for internal use records that, while now seventy years of age, Sir William 'unhesitatingly came back to play a leading part in the fight against the American Tobacco Company. His long experience of men and affairs and his power of exercising authority were of immense value in the formative years of the Company in handling a strong, if sometimes turbulent team. The directors of the thirteen firms that formed The Imperial Tobacco Company had been used to running their own businesses without interference, and their attitude to the new Company was not unlike that of the thirteen States of America who, when the Federal Constitution was first adopted, wanted to give the Central Government as little authority as possible, and retain as much power as they could in their own hands.'

It was decided at the outset that the English combination would seek to avoid the worst features of its American challenger's structure. Many of the directors would become managers of their original businesses, with liaison effected through an executive committee and the board. Mr George Alfred Wills, later Sir George, Bt, was made deputy to Sir William, the first chairman. The founders' enterprises would be designated branches, and any obvious central administration would fall to the executive committee. The most urgent and pressing task was not just to define the policy for meeting Duke's immediate competitive actions, but also to study other likely threats and potential weaknesses in Imperial's federal structure.

The actions in 1902 would prove decisive, with profound consequences for both the British and American industries.

CHAPTER FIVE

Rule Britannia

> Rule Britannia! Britannia rules the waves!
> Britons to Yankee Trusts will ne'er be slaves!
> We'll not encourage Yankee Bluff
> We'll support John Bull with every puff!

So ran one of the patriotic advertisements flowing from the new promotional department set up at Nottingham by William Goodacre Player for Imperial. But the new British combine was not, nevertheless, anxious to reward the patriotic smokers of British brands with price cuts. Its management decided that, initially, the cultivation of loyalty among retailers would be crucial for protecting the factories, where more machinery was being installed. To this end, Imperial proposed, amid the flag waving, that wholesale and retail dealers should sign a Bonus Agreement. Under this plan, a proportion of the company's profit would be set aside for distribution to those trade customers who promoted Imperial brands and observed the group's conditions of sale.

Those brands had been strengthened by the addition in 1900 of Player's Medium to sell at 2½d for ten compared with the 1d for five price of Weights, or Wills' bestselling Woodbine. Sales of cigarettes in the British market in 1901 still only accounted for 12 per cent by weight of total tobacco trade. Across the span of the new combination there was a formidable list of products. Nevertheless a bonus scheme was still felt very necessary, given Duke's acknowledged marketing skills which, despite the restrictions and higher costs, had helped to lift imports of cigarettes and manufactured tobacco (other than cigars and snuff) to 3,632,000 lb in 1900 and 4,471,000 lb in 1901—a figure not to be matched again until the end of the 1914–18 war.

To qualify for the bonus, a distributor had to sign a written agreement to become a direct customer of Imperial's branches. They undertook to stock 'bonus bearing goods and display them prominently and effectively' in shop windows and to make 'all proper and reasonable efforts' to extend the sale of Imperial goods, conforming to price lists, terms and conditions of sale.

More to the point of this offensive weapon was a clause precluding the trader from stocking the goods of American Tobacco, or its associates. Under the agreement, Imperial was to distribute as bonus the equivalent of one-fifth (later two-fifths) of that part of the amount required for Imperial's dividend on ordinary stock arising from net profits on annual sales. The bonus would be determined at a percentage rate per net sales of bonus bearing goods.

Duke had not long received a copy of Imperial's prospectus offering a proportion of its £15 million share capital for subscription on the London Stock Exchange. It was a document full of revelations. The capital was divided into 5 million 5½ per cent Cumulative Preference shares of £1, 5 million Preferred Ordinary shares of £1, and 5 million Deferred Ordinary shares. The founder companies empowered their new combine to create mortgaged Debenture stock representing half the opening Cumulative Preference shares, and held by trustees, one of whom was Sir William Wills' old business crony, Earl Cawdor, chairman of the Great Western Railway Company.

City financiers and investors, like Duke, had pored over the prospectus filed with the Registrar of Joint Stock Companies ahead of three days of share buying from 17th February 1902. The vendor companies were offering the public £300,000 worth of Cumulative Preference shares and £1 million worth of Debenture stock. They took for themselves 1,500,000 Cumulative Preference, 4,259,049 Preferred, and 4,259,048 Deferred Ordinary. It all meant the founding fathers were taking the largest proportion of the share capital permitted by London Stock Exchange rules governing a quotation as part payment for their businesses.

Investors were contemplating the offer of this small allotment alongside that of another company choosing this moment to 'go public'—Shell Transport & Trading. The promoters of Imperial did not offer a high proportion of property assets. The £11.9 million purchase money due to thirteen companies in cash, shares, and debentures compared with a little over £3.4 million in land, buildings and stock-in-trade (£2 million). A sum of no less than £8,518,097 had been included in the acquisition prices for the thirteen companies to cover 'goodwill, trade-marks, licences, proprietary brands, etc.'

But the more eagle-eyed, like Duke, now back in New York, spotted that chartered accountants Deloitte, Dever, Griffiths & Company, had combed the accounts for the previous three years and, after all charges, pinpointed an average annual combined profit of £1,062,922. With their large individual share stakes, the first directors could hardly have bothered about their proposed £2,500 a year fees.

That Imperial was serious about its bonus scheme for retailers could not be doubted. The prospectus defined it as 'giving to the customers a direct interest in the prosperity of the company, by setting apart, for such as accept its provisions, a yearly sum regulated by the amount of home trade profits distributed as dividends upon the Ordinary shares, which will be apportioned amongst the participating customers by way of percentage upon their purchases of proprietary goods, as compared with the total amount of such goods sold by the company during the year'. As soon as Imperial received its legal certificate to start business, the bonus scheme would begin.

Duke could not be under any lingering illusion that Sir William Wills and his board were not serious about their provisional plans to reward loyal shopkeepers. He laid aside the prospectus and called in an aide to take dictated instructions, for transmission by cable, to his Ogden management in Liverpool. 'Commencing 2nd April 1902, we will, for the next four years, distribute to such of our customers in the United Kingdom as purchase direct from us our entire net profits on the goods sold by us in the United Kingdom. In addition to the above we will, commencing 2nd April 1902, for the next four years, distribute to such of our customers in the United Kingdom as purchase direct from us the sum of £200,000 per year. The distribution of net profits will be made as soon after 2nd April 1903, and annually thereafter, as the accounts can be audited and will be in proportion to the purchases made during the year. The distribution as to the £200,000 per year will be made every three months, the first distribution to take place as soon after 2nd July 1902 as accounts can be audited and will be in proportion to the purchases during the three-months' period. To participate in this offer, we do not ask you to boycott the goods of any other manufacturer.'

Since Imperial's bonus agreement included a restrictive clause regarding American Tobacco, Duke's instruction that traders were not asked to boycott his rivals' products made more than a few retailers reconsider their attitude towards the Yankee invader. Perhaps, they thought, he might offer the better deal if it meant less direct intervention in their sales policies. Duke's offer astounded the tobacco trade.

First there had been cut prices and heavy advertising, followed up with souvenirs and free gifts. Now he was giving away the whole of Ogden's net profits for four years, plus a sum of £200,000 per annum until 1906. Thomas Ryan backed up Duke's attempt to unnerve Imperial with a rare public statement that American Tobacco would firmly establish itself as the leading British manufacturer within four years 'or lose $5,000,000 in the attempt'. *The Times* commented: 'There is no parallel to this magnanimity, except perhaps in the case of that friend of country yokels who sells sovereigns for sixpences.'

The effect on Sir William Wills and his consortium of British tobacco barons was not immediately obvious. The Ogden bonus— destined to yield for Ogden a net £376,000 loss on sales of £1,850,000 in the period 1st December 1901 to 30th September 1902—served to progress more rapidly some important and as yet still secret negotiations between Imperial and four more tobacco companies, which by 1st May would join the original thirteen British concerns. They were W. A. & A. C. Churchman, of Ipswich, two Chester-based enterprises, W. T. Davies & Sons and W. Williams & Company, and from London, W. & F. Faulkner.

Churchmans was a hundred and two years old and run by the Ipswich founder's two grandsons, William and Arthur Churchman, who had succeeded to ownership in 1888 when twenty-three and twenty-one years old respectively. The former would become Sir William and the latter Lord Woodbridge (a director of British-American Tobacco between 1904 and 1923). Its inclusion in Imperial obviously widened the geographical grip of the new combine into East Anglia.

For some weeks, Sir William had difficulty persuading the twin Chester businesses of Davies and Williams to join. Davies was founded in Chester by William Twiston Davies, who for health reasons had been unable to implement his training as a missionary. He attributed his business acumen to a grounding in Latin, Greek and Hebrew, a view not shared by his great local rival in the tobacco business, William Williams, a fox-hunting, hard-living man. The two were to join forces and operate from the same premises before Imperial was formed. They might have joined the original founders of Imperial but for the ageing Twiston Davies, who refused to take Ordinary or Preference shares and wanted Debentures. In the words of Imperial's own records, 'he was literally forced by his sons to sign, and even then his sons had to take up his quota of Ordinary shares, as a result of which they became much richer than their father.' Faulkner's was a famous pipe tobacco house founded in the early nineteenth century near London's Blackfriars Bridge. Eventually, in 1954, this new Imperial branch would swallow Davies and Williams, before itself vanishing into Ogden in 1959.

Not all retailers, looking for guaranteed profits, were delighted with the patriotic bonus scheme. It looked too much like a monopolistic action worthy of Duke. The opposition was strong enough for Imperial's organising committee to start reconsidering the terms, but the angry reaction of Harry Wills,* who had helped draw up the bonus plans, preserved its main terms. But he had to grit his teeth and accept the committee's action of writing to retailers making some of the most restrictive clauses only operative on three months' notice.

Price maintenance was a strong plank of Imperial's policy and a marked increase in advertising was to strengthen brand choice by consumers, whose requirements no dealers could really ignore.

The enlargement of Imperial with the purchase of more manufacturers was not the only additional move to forestall and block Duke's every move. Before long, details were being disclosed of an important coup leading to more direct vertical integration.

Unknown to Duke, on 2nd January 1902, Isidore and Montague Gluckstein, Alfred Salmon, and other owners of the leading retail tobacco chain had signed a confidential agreement with Imperial.

* H. H. Wills almost resigned over the issue.

This envisaged the reconstruction of Salmon & Gluckstein's share capital to enable Imperial to take the controlling interest and 'the whole of the surplus profits'. The deal went through as Imperial's status changed to that of public corporation. Duke was now shut out, and Sir William declared: 'It is believed that this arrangement will tend largely to protect the interests of the customers of the Imperial Tobacco Company.'

Sir William and his co-directors had realised that Duke was always liable to buy the group to extend cut-price trading, for the chain had a history of keen pricing and had started to engage in manufacture for itself and other retailers.

Sir William was sensitive enough to heed the inevitable protests from retailers and wholesalers. To please the former, he announced that the number of outlets in the group's present trading area would be restricted to the existing 184, it would not hold an undue share of retail trade in any town, and would, if going to a new area away from London, acquire only established businesses, not open new outlets. The self-imposed limitations were extended to placate wholesalers with a provision that Salmon & Gluckstein would not engage in any wholesale trade. Retail outlets were also barred from selling confectionery or newspapers, and would not open on Sundays. These rules were to be bent slightly with the defensive purchases in 1902 of two other retail businesses, James Quinton and A. I. Jones & Company.

Smokers heard of each new development with keen interest. Ogden's cigarette cards were particularly popular, including a series of glamorous actresses which Imperial tried to counter with Mardon, Son & Hall's printing expertise and the 'Footballers' and 'Boer War' series, backed with text and the slogan 'British made by British labour with British capital'.

One patriotic claim which could not be made, however, was that the tobacco was British grown. American bright Burley and Perique leaf was now the staple tobacco. In 1902, out of a total 126,221,000 lb of unmanufactured tobacco, some 116,129,000 (92 per cent) came from the United States. The demand for Oriental and Latakia leaf had slumped to less than 10 per cent of total imports. The 352,243 tobacco dealers registered in 1902 knew well enough that the 502 licensed manufacturers logged on Customs and Excise books for duty (yielding over £12 million for the Exchequer on net home consumption receipts) were now heavily dependent on supplying the highly palatable American tobaccos. There was plenty of speculation that Imperial might have an Achilles heel if Duke and his Trust were to be tempted into rigging leaf markets even more in their favour. It was no idle chatter, for Imperial's board had despatched various experts to the United States to head off any notion by Duke's buying organisation to corner the Virginia crop of 1902.

A central leaf-buying committee had been established in November 1901 even before the formal incorporation of Imperial, under the leadership of Walter Butler, of Lambert & Butler, who had practical experience of American leaf purchasing. Virtually all the constituents of Imperial bought their requirements from British merchant importers or through other agents. One of the companies, William Clarke & Son, had a processing plant in Kentucky to handle their Dark Western tobacco requirement.

Experts sent to the United States consulted two leaf dealers—Wellford Clairborne Reed (dealing with Lambert & Butler) and Alsen F. Thomas (dealing with W. D. & H. O. Wills)—on how supplies of the 1902 crop might be secured and Imperial protected in the longer term. Reed had been a tobacco broker in Richmond, Virginia, since 1894 after serving with a number of companies in the bright tobacco belt. Thomas, of Lynchburg, who had quit school at fourteen but briefly became a schoolteacher after 'larning himself nights' while a store keeper, was a well-established export trader, selling the leaf as a middleman from Virginia and North Carolina.

Reed and Thomas knew the English market well and they agreed to come to Bristol to meet the leaf committee, to which they proposed that Imperial might set up a subsidiary leaf-buying organisation in the United States. The former wanted to buy leaf from well-known redrying plants, but Thomas urged the acquisition of factories in all major buying regions. The discussions went so well that Reed and Thomas were persuaded to become co-managers of the proposed new venture, working under an Imperial director—James Macdonald, of the Stephen Mitchell & Son branch, was picked for the job—handling general supervision of finance and administration. It was now March 1902.

Temporary offices for the embryo American Leaf Organisation were found at Richmond, which offered excellent banking and communication facilities.

The brief was a compromise of both Thomas's and Reed's views, but it clearly laid down that a procurement system 'be inaugurated at once and perfected as fast as circumstances will permit'. While the strategy was initially to follow Reed's advice of buying direct from planters' drying units, the written policy approved by Imperial included the statement: 'That the ultimate purchase or control of your own factories to be operated by your own servants for handling of your purchases in such markets as may be selected, so far as is feasible, be borne in mind from the beginning, and if any such arrangements can be made in time for the 1902 crop, a start in that direction be approved.'

The lean James Macdonald, sporting a walrus moustache and accompanied by his son, John Duncan, Imperial's assistant leaf manager under C. S. Clarke (brother of Imperial director William Ruddell Clarke) set up offices at the Dispatch Building, 904 East Main Street, Richmond, for the next three years before a $24,000 building was provided at Sixth and Canal Streets. Almost immediately buying agents were found and Reed quickly began negotiating for factories, somewhat sooner than most had anticipated. Within a year or so there would be four well-equipped factories and an older processing plant at Durham, with plans in hand for another two. With his parted, silvery hair, severely cut suits and military moustache, Wellford Reed insisted that the latest techniques be built into the factories. Order branches were set up to work with the roster of approved buyers and these agencies would employ over 4,000 within a year compared with around 2,600 factory hands. The balding, contemplative Thomas worked well with Reed, but the former had other ambitions that led to his resignation in 1903 and subsequent entry into politics as a State Senator, strongly interested in education. Reed, whose appreciation of horses was nearly equal to his knowledge of tobacco, and was a pillar of the local Holy Trinity Church, had only a few more years to live.

Reports of Imperial's rapid bid to secure its future leaf supplies were received by Duke in New York and the American tobacco tycoon felt they were a sign of panic rather than a serious threat. Anyway, he was still preoccupied with trying to force Imperial into a price war on his terms, irritated by the Englishmen's refusal to engage in loss leading which would drain their profits and make them vulnerable to his ideas of a monopoly of trade in the English-speaking world. Through the spring and into the summer, Imperial's buying committee scanned reports on progress. Meanwhile, a member of the Wills family decided to open peace feelers with a discreet letter, posted to Thomas Ryan, expressing hopes that the developing tobacco war might be ended by mutual agreement. Word was passed to Duke, who promptly misunderstood the offer as a sign of emerging weakness, and seemed temporarily preoccupied with tidying up the tricky details of his American Cigar Company's coup in taking control of Cuba's cigar industry, and planning a new home on his 2,200-acre Somerville farm.

Imperial's directors were in fact determined to negotiate from strength. To this end, a deputation was appointed—comprising John Dane Player, Ernest Gunn, and W. R. Clarke—to visit the new Richmond headquarters, letting it be known they were in the market to buy up any tobacco business still free of the Trust. The war was to be carried into Duke's territory. The American press responded with heavy coverage of the counter-invasion and reporters were handled with skill by the giant Gunn, a former manager of the *St James Gazette*, known for 'a splendid turn of phrase'. Duke was not a popular figure and the 'get up and go' attitude of the British tobacco industry which dared to challenge the mighty Trust delighted growers and the disgruntled alike. Not only would Imperial be fighting on the warehouse floors for leaf, but there was at last a direct possibility of Duke's menacing grip on leaf prices being loosened.

It was now the turn of Duke to worry. 'Just bluff,' he reassured colleagues, but soon doubts would creep into his repeated attempts to dismiss the threatened turning of the tables. On 1st July 1902, Imperial's board met to resolve which American businesses might be purchased to begin sales in Duke's home market. It was also the target date for formally opening the new American Leaf Organisation's operations, for which plans had been well laid, with factories plotted in Greenville and Kinston, North Carolina. To add to the ominous atmosphere, Imperial had booked passage to England for one Samuel Untermeyer, a famous American lawyer who would handle any take-over formalities alongside Imperial's wily Bristol lawyer, James Inskip.

Bluff or not, Duke could surely not take chances now. The upstart Limeys were proving too bold and too aggressive. Other directors and big shareholders were getting not a little nervous, and expected something other than Ogden's mounting losses on the original investment in Duke's dream of conquering Britain. The thought of the hog-tied United States market being disrupted was viewed in terms of the hard cash profits, which subsidised Ogden, being placed at unexpected risk.

Duke had been receiving various indirect approaches to suggest that peace might be negotiated. One of these involved Harry and George Wills sending Hugo Cunliffe-Owen* to see a French paper maker, who was on friendly terms with Duke and who agreed to whisper discreetly in the American's ear.

The net earnings of American and Continental Tobacco were now running at an annual rate of over $26 million, which would mean $16 million of cash dividends for the Consolidated holding company. Thomas Ryan and Colonel Payne kept a watchful eye on the accounts, too, and the former had taken the precaution, if seemingly casual, of dropping a note back to the Wills family, saying that he would like to meet Sir William, Imperial's chairman, but any business negotiations would have to be the affair of another, James Buchanan Duke. That message served to alert Imperial and to delay the appraisal of opportunities to start American sales. A cable was sent from Bristol asking Ryan to come over and meet Sir William. Duke agreed that Ryan should go and listen. By August, when Ryan sailed for England, Duke was impatient to learn whose hand was best. Ogden's losses, while acceptable at first, could not be carried for ever, and they were only the means of softening up the British for more spectacular conquests.

Received on several occasions by Sir William in August 1902 at his Hyde Park home in London, Ryan found himself victim to West Country charm, mixed with obvious business acumen. It was quickly evident to him that Duke might have misjudged the man at the top of Imperial. Both were old and very, very rich men. Sir William, now in his 72nd year, four years away from ennoblement as the First Baron Winterstoke of Blagdon, and first Freeman of the City of Bristol, was not overawed by the legendary Ryan. Besides his chairmanship of Imperial, the portly ex-M.P was now one of the trustees for the debenture stockholders and in a powerful position to speak for the British combine. As a politician,

* First secretary of British-American Tobacco, later chairman, and knighted, whose sister married Harry Wills in 1886.

he knew how to make friends and Ryan found himself being led gently into painless negotiation over the companies' differences. An initial meeting with some of Imperial's directors at the Paddington Hotel went well.

Sir William let it slip, neatly, that there need not necessarily be a war in the United States market, if reason prevailed. What was the point of reducing each other's profits? More to the point, what did Ryan think about selling Ogden and American Tobacco's British interests to Imperial on mutually agreed terms? Lunches and dinners were arranged to give Ryan a chance to see the opposition's directorial and managerial talent for himself. The jokes and increasing bonhomie of Sir William's hospitality seemed to sweeten the reasoning in a way that Ryan, America's legendary wheeler dealer and hard bargainer of 'the tramways gang', found increasingly irresistible. Within three weeks, he was cabling Duke in New York to 'please get over quick'. Negotiations took a far more serious turn when eventually Duke arrived to hassle, and Sir William took the precaution of including Imperial's lawyer, Inskip, in the first meeting.

The events that followed would be momentous for the future development of the Anglo-American tobacco industry, whose customers by the end of that decade would be smoking over 80,000 million manufactured cigarettes a year and consuming 812 million lb of tobacco by weight. Duke, whatever his faults, knew the sales potential and given his proven skill in monopoly practices had sailed a second time for England believing his dream of world dominion was near realisation. The accommodation of Imperial into an international trust with dimensions that no businessman had ever before dared to contemplate seemed possible, 'thanks to good ol' Tom Ryan' and the Ogden 'squeeze play'.

CHAPTER SIX

Arcadian Competition

Pall Mall, the heart of London's clubland, was alive with hansom cabs and carriages and pairs. Aristocrats, politicians, and City personalities thronged through the imposing portals of the clubs. Wealthy and fashionable people would stop by a shop at No. 5A, opened two years before by a thirty-three-year-old Russian refugee, Louis Rothman, to sell handmade cigarettes of high quality for the discerning smoker. Supplies were supposedly delivered with discretion to Buckingham Place, but Rothman made little secret of his Royal patronage to win the custom of the privileged.

The trade of Louis Rothman had been diligently cultivated over a period of twelve years, for he had arrived in London in 1887 as an eighteen-year-old, the emigré member of a Ukrainian family that had owned a tobacco factory. For three years he worked for British merchants who appreciated his skill in the hand-rolling of blends of Balkan, Crimean, Turkish and Oriental leaf. With a capital of only £40, he decided to go into the business on his own account, buying a lease on a tiny retail kiosk at 55A Fleet Street. This was a well-chosen site, for he made his cigarettes by day and night and canvassed sales among newspapermen, whom he knew would spread the news, whether in print or by their wide ranging personal contacts, of his products. Lords Rothermere and Northcliffe and Sir Arthur Pearson were among his regular customers, as well as the working journalists and printers they employed. Trade grew rapidly and his reputation was exploited further through two other shops, opened at 181 Queen Victoria Street and 33 Copthall Avenue, close to the City's Stock Exchange. Then he moved into Pall Mall.

The premises stood under the fashionable Carlton Hotel, where any guest would be pleased to be known to be in residence in its sumptuous and famous suites. And this was why one Jim Thomas, a tanned and well-travelled American tobacco sales executive, was proving an embarrassment at the reception desk. Thomas, in that summer of 1902, was insisting that James Buchanan Duke must be registered and the initially genuflecting, but now bristling, receptionist was declaring no knowledge of such a guest. The puzzled Thomas, who was Duke's Far Eastern manager, finally produced the cable summoning him to England and the Carlton Hotel. Messengers were summoned and before long Duke strode up, arranging to lunch with the visitor the next day. It was not to be, for in the early hours of the following morning Duke called Thomas at another hotel and ordered him to return immediately to New York with a bundle of important papers, where he would be given another batch of documents for return on the same ship.

James A. Thomas was too shrewd an aide to question his president's actions, and he would be back by 15th September. Around one-third of American Tobacco's cigarettes were exported, but increasingly local production facilities had been established in overseas markets. The onslaught on Britain, if abortive, had been part of the expansion plan. But there had been great success in the Far East, and Thomas's role had been critical. Son of a Bright Belt planter, Thomas had followed Duke to New York and studied at the Eastman National School of Business, Poughkeepsie, before peddling plug around the South Seas in competition with Wills salesmen from England. He went onto Duke's payroll after the take-over of Motley & Company and developed mainland and island sales throughout the Far East. Literate* and opportunist, he opened up the vast Chinese market, and his record drew the open admiration of Duke.

The reliability and loyalty of Thomas explained why that August of 1902 he had been hurriedly called to London, where Duke had arrived secretly three weeks after Ryan. Thomas was not the only one to follow the tobacco tycoon. Another arrival was Williamson Whitehead Fuller, the former Durham lawyer who had earned his spurs fixing up the legal side when the American Tobacco Company was incorporated in January 1890. It took twelve days from Jim Thomas's return with the documents to

* Years later Thomas was to write several books on his life.

negotiate the terms for ending the year-long Anglo-American tobacco war.

On 27th September 1902 the directors of Imperial entered into two historic agreements with Consolidated Tobacco and its twin pillars, American Tobacco and Continental.

The first of these agreements provided that Imperial should purchase (subject to certain conditions and with minor reservations) the business of American Tobacco's United Kingdom subsidiary, Ogden. The second agreement provided for the transfer of the export and overseas trade of both Imperial and American Tobacco to a new company to be formed in the United Kingdom, the British-American Tobacco Co. Ltd. As a result of these arrangements: (i) American Tobacco withdrew from the United Kingdom market and undertook not to re-enter it, and Imperial agreed not to enter the United States market; (ii) each of the two companies acquired the trading rights in the other's brands in its own home market, including the right to use the respective trade-marks; (iii) except as provided for in (ii) the two companies agreed not to engage in exports except through BAT, and BAT became entitled to purchase at a price not exceeding cost any export business afterwards acquired by either Imperial or American Tobacco, any shares in foreign companies which might be acquired by either, and the export business and the assets employed in such business of any company the direct or indirect control of which might be acquired by either Imperial or American Tobacco; (iv) Imperial was allotted one-third and American Tobacco two-thirds of BAT's equity capital. Both appointed directors to the board; (v) BAT was bound not to trade in the United Kingdom or United States markets; (vi) American Tobacco acquired (through the sale of Ogden) a substantial minority interest in Imperial and the right to nominate three directors to the board.

All was not sweetness and light. Duke raised objections to many provisions of a draft agreement prepared by Imperial's legal adviser, and at one stage in the talks nearly cancelled everything. He was not an easy man to deal with, given his record of normally dictating the terms in any hard bargaining. But the eventual agreement appealed to him for its essential simplicity for making the peace and creating a partnership that stopped short of outright amalgamation.

The ink was hardly dry on the heads of this agreement before Duke had sent off cables to his father, Washington, and Colonel Payne. The latter was told: 'Papers signed ensuring great deal for our companies—Duke'. It had indeed been a breathless, almost unbelievable, twelve years since American Tobacco was written into the corporate register of New Jersey. The transit entrepreneur William C. Whitney, founder of a business and political dynasty, seemed to sum it all up at a celebratory banquet where, under crossed Union Jacks and Stars and Stripes in the Charles II banquet room of the Carlton Hotel (Duke's presence in London was now revealed to a startled London Stock Exchange), Whitney placed a hand on Duke's shoulder and described him as 'the greatest merchant in the world'. It was indicative of Duke's powerful control over American Tobacco that such a momentous deal could be arranged so swiftly and without months of board meetings in New York.

The dream of world dominion seemed much nearer to Duke who now joined the board of Imperial Tobacco (on 16th October 1902), an appointment he held for the next nine and a half years. Moreover, he was elected first chairman of British-American Tobacco, with Henry Herbert Wills, second son of Henry Overton (the first Chancellor of Bristol University), as deputy chairman. H. H. Wills (knighted in 1923) had played a vital role in the negotiations for he managed the Wills' branch export business. A trained mechanical engineer and deer-stalking enthusiast who could also boast the ownership of one of the earliest motor cars, the forty-six-year-old H. H. Wills had come in for some criticism for not fighting hard enough for a better deal. Imperial's secretary, Gunn, was among the disappointed, arguing that the one-third interest was 'lacking in justice'. Wills, however, countered that the split, with a two-thirds share majority for American Tobacco, was based on the scale of export business of each shareholder. Anyway, the board representation was evenly split and what was of great importance was that BAT was registered in England and so was a British company. H. H. Wills resigned shortly afterwards 'for personal reasons', going into local politics as a County Alderman and eventually serving as High Sheriff of Somerset in 1910.

Above all, Sir William Wills was satisfied. The agreements looked watertight and the Anglo-American tobacco alliance would be a formidable profit-making machine unlikely to be disrupted by fierce competition. Most of the purchase price for Ogden was paid in Imperial shares, so American Tobacco now had a holding of 14 per cent in Imperial and was the largest individual owner of Deferred Ordinary except for the Wills family. From Sir William's viewpoint, registration of BAT in Britain would be very important if the company grew strongly and very profitably. That was a prophetic judgement. Meanwhile Imperial confidently lifted the Bonus Agreement clause that prevented loyal retailers from stocking any of American Tobacco's products.

When Imperial looked over Ogden's books they found a net loss of £376,000 on sales of £1,850,000 between 1st December 1901 and 30th September 1902. On 11th November 1902 the Imperial board raised the group's capital to £18 million from £15 million, divided equally into Preference, Preferred Ordinary and Deferred Ordinary, and the seventeen tobacco manufacturers in the organisation were now arranged into fifteen branches, excluding the paper and printing operations of Mardon, Son & Hall. Some thorny legal difficulties connected with Ogden deals done in the battle with Duke had to be cleared up in the courts.

There followed what became known to the legal profession as the Ogden Litigation. The 4,670 traders who had accepted Duke's bonus agreement and signed on the line for their share of promised income from Ogden in its war with Imperial grouped themselves into the Ogden Bonus Association. They began well over seven hundred actions for a total £700,000 of unpaid bonus and profits due to them. All were separate and this number was to be kept in progress in the courts and even in the House of Lords before a conference was held on 19th September 1906 and the terms of an amicable settlement agreed. During this massive legal onslaught on Imperial, some three hundred and fifty briefs were given to counsel plus more than two thousand other instructions for the various trials and applications. The traders' militant leader, one Henry Nathan, was rewarded by his grateful Ogden Bonus Association members with a handsome commemorative plaque, engraved with the story of their fight and the portraits of the judges, lawyers, and Law Lords involved in the complex courtroom struggles. Duke's six-month ownership of Ogden was proving a very costly affair, indeed.

There were now around 480 licences issued for tobacco manufacture in Britain and Ireland and 359,289 licensed dealers. So, given the exclusion of American Tobacco from the market place, all was set fair for sustained growth, and by 1905 Imperial would be selling 47.8 million lb of cigarettes and other tobacco products, more than doubling this total by 1920. The independent manufacturers were naturally apprehensive about the accord reached between Imperial and Duke, but they comforted themselves with the thought that Imperial was opposed to price wars and operated the competitive brand system. Louis Rothman turned his efforts to consolidating his trade with 'top people' while opening up export sales to South Africa, Holland, India and Australia. Tom Gallaher of Belfast was preparing to boost his overseas sales by winning prestigious gold medals at international tobacco exhibitions. The eight-year-old Ardath Tobacco Company also looked to sales growth overseas to widen its marketing base. The long-established family concern, Godfrey Phillips, founded in 1844 as a cigar business, felt sure its emerging sales of Best Dark Virginia pipe tobacco would be safe, for its customers seemed defiantly loyal to the BDV brand.

But one man who had misgivings was Bernhard Baron, the machinery inventor, now operating from Aldgate in London's East End. Unable to sell his machines to Imperial, he fell in with William Johnston Yapp, a Wardour Street tobacco and cigar importer who had been carrying on the business of José Joaquim Carreras, an expert in tobacco blending and cigar making who had been a founder committee member of the Tobacco Trade Benevolent Association.

Like Louis Rothman, José Carreras had sold special blends to 'the highest in the land'. The third Earl Craven had had a standing order in the early 1860s, and after his death it was sold to the public as Craven Mixture, attracting specific praise from Sir James Barrie, of Peter Pan fame, in his bestselling book, *My Lady Nicotine*, published in 1890. José Carreras produced smoking mixtures by the score and some of the best known were Guards, Hankey's, Philips and Mugge's. These sold alongside hundreds of brands of cigars and snuff. The son of a Spanish nobleman, Don José Carreras-y-Ferrer, who had fought under the Duke of Wellington in the Peninsular War and was later forced to seek political asylum in London in 1843, the younger Carreras had opened his first shop at 61 Princes Street (later renamed Wardour Street), Leicester Square, and in 1853 received a warrant to supply the Spanish Legation. Warrants came in due course from members of the Royal Family, the Duke of Saxe-Coburg-Gotha, and King Alphonso XII of Spain.

Yapp had taken control of the Carreras business just before the turn of the century and he was very much aware of the emerging demand for cigarettes. Baron and his machinery interested him. If an association could be formed, Carreras might turn itself into a public company and raise development capital to survive the era of machine competition. In February 1903, Yapp agreed to sell Carreras to John Crowle, a Kensington-based financier (he was chairman of Slaters Ltd) for £100,000 on the basis of Crowle promoting and reselling the company for £160,000 in cash and shares on public offer. Baron was brought into the deal, along with a mineral water manufacturer, Frank Durrant, as a director.

There was an obvious marketing skill within the company. Yapp had made his name with a striking advertisement for Craven Mixture that carried an endorsement from Barrie whose *My Lady Nicotine* was mainly devoted to the merits of a fictional pipe tobacco called Arcadia. Barrie was a regular customer at Carreras' original shop, and he had raised no objection in 1897 when Yapp asked him if he might use in advertising his written confirmation: 'What I call the Arcadia in *My Lady Nicotine* is the "Craven" mixture and no other.' This endorsement was to be exploited for the next forty years.

The prospectus, eventually issued on 16th June 1903, attracted widespread City criticism. Prospective investors did not like offers which declared 'it is not deemed expedient to publish a statement of the profits realized in the past'. Nor could they like the small print on the contracts which showed that Crowle 'should be at liberty to retain and dispose of as he might think fit the sole right to manufacture cigarettes to be known as Craven Mixture, Hankey's Mixture, Guards Mixture, Sid Philips Mixture, Clarence Mixture, and Mugge's Special'. Another worrying feature was a proposal to allot shares in all cases where practicable to retail tobacco dealers. This offer saved the promoters from undersubscription, for a number of prominent traders foresaw the potential of Carreras and knew well enough the talents of Baron. The shares were fully taken up in the face of the criticisms of other investors.

Formation of Carreras helped Imperial to point to new competition when accusations were levelled that it was a monopoly trading with, and now seeking to emulate, the notorious Trust of Duke. The directors at Bristol also referred critics to Gallaher, now turning out its new Park Drive machine cigarettes in increasing quantities. Baron had no doubts that Imperial would view his association with Carreras with hostility. Already Imperial was insisting that all branches should use Bonsack machines, now able to make 600 cigarettes a minute, and so Baron lost his original custom with John Player & Son. Imperial was also closely controlling supplies of other machinery being introduced into tobacco processing, often to its own design and specifications.

But there was new competition rearing its head, lower down the ladder. Julius Wix was in his second year of creating an enterprise that would one day bring American Tobacco back to Britain. And, in 1902, the then seventeen-year-old cigar partnership, Cope Brothers, bought Richard Lloyd, independent tobacco manufacturers, founded in 1785. For some years Cope had been a leading manufacturer in terms of size.

By now, the United Kingdom tobacco industry was a source of considerable revenue for Whitehall's coffers. Customs and Excise duties in 1903 brought in well over £12 million (net receipts). The standard rate of tobacco duty on unmanufactured tobacco, which had been reduced in stages to 2s 8d per lb in 1898, was raised to 3s per lb in 1900 to help pay the heavy costs of the Boer War and would remain at this level for some nine years when it was raised to 3s 8d.

Business was good for the match-makers Bryant & May, who in January 1903 incorporated as a public company. Their prospectus disclosed that it had formed a working pact with the Diamond Match Company of Illinois (who had sold their Liverpool factory to the Bow-based concern in July 1901). Besides covenants on international trading practices, the two concerns had just concluded special arrangements to buy jointly large tracts of timber-yielding land in California, starting with 65,000 acres, worth over £100,000 at that time.

The year 1903 was largely spent by all parties to the historic 1902 agreement consolidating and arranging the administration systems. Buck Duke set to recruiting young men to BAT to exploit Imperial's brand names in world markets alongside his American efforts. In February 1903, Imperial took its American leaf-buying operations a stage further by incorporating the

Imperial Tobacco Company of Kentucky, which annexed the William Clarke branch's local subsidiary and bought itself a processing factory.

So preoccupied were Imperial's directors with the new détente with the United States industry that few were fully aware that thousands of miles away something called the Rhodesian Cigar and Tobacco Syndicate was being founded and one of its members, Dr Sketchley, would that same year build a brick barn for air-curing tobacco which a number of pioneer planters had grown for some years (in 1900 the Rhodesian Scientific Association had been shown Virginian seed that would be harvested in March of the following year). Earl Grey of the British South Africa Company was encouraging the development of agriculture and had suggested tobacco as a possible crop. Even as Imperial began raising its investment in American leaf-buying, the United States Department of Agriculture was somewhat naïvely, if unselfishly, analysing, free of charge, soil samples and tobacco sent from Rhodesia.

It would be another three years before Imperial would take the Rhodesian efforts to grow and sell leaf into account and send an expert to assess buying prospects in Nyasaland, no doubt worried by the growing militancy of American tobacco farmers towards the big manufacturing combines.

So pleased were Imperial with progress that Sir William Wills proposed a resolution at a board meeting on 15th December 1903 thanking the new American Leaf Organisation for one and a half years' steady progress. A copy was cabled to Richmond to James Macdonald, now installed as resident director, who would stay on for another seventeen months. Two days after the board resolution was passed with acclaim, the brothers Wilbur and Orville Wright made North Carolina world famous for something other than tobacco cultivation by making their successful first aeroplane flight at Kitty Hawk beach.

CHAPTER SEVEN

'The Trust is a Hog'

The advent of the machine age had spawned the monopolists and manipulators of money and markets. The tobacco combinations of Britain and the United States begat the British-American Tobacco Company, and by 1904 were seeking world dominion. In this eventful year, a young man who would one day use his comic genius to satirise machines and his political convictions to attack the emerging trusts was dismissed from the packing department of the London tobacco firm of Pritchard & Burton.* Charlie Chaplin, sacked by a foreman for the constant sabotage by clowning of the packaging machinery, designed for submissive automatons, would one day become more famous and world renowned than the tycoon Buck Duke—and, ironically, portrayed on millions of cigarette cards.

Another famous name, and one now constantly on Duke's mind (vying with Mrs Lillian McCredy whom he would marry shortly before his forty-eighth birthday) was Theodore Roosevelt, who had succeeded Duke's hero William McKinley† to the Presidency. From the White House, Roosevelt viewed with suspicion the emerging combines and declining reputation of the Wall Street stock market which produced such problems as the great corner of Northern Pacific Railroad shares three years before, when the powerful house of J. P. Morgan & Company fought Kuhn, Loeb in a series of titanic financial struggles. Early in 1904, the United States Supreme Court decided that J. Pierpont Morgan's Northern

---

* Now part of Philip Morris.
† Duke had a statue of McKinley at his Somerville estate.

Securities (the holding company for Northern Pacific and Great Northern by virtue of its ownership of a majority shareholding in each) was unlawful. Roosevelt's trust-busting teams were delighted. Duke was alarmed.

The Consolidated Tobacco Corporation, formed a little over three years before and now paying out a dividend of $16 million, through its control of American Tobacco and Continental, bore a marked structural resemblance to the now illegal Northern Securities. And Duke was shrewd enough to sense the public disquiet over the inside dealers who were his collaborators. To forestall Roosevelt, he had his lawyers and accountants draft a switch-round of the trading assets to create one master corporation, to be the original American Tobacco Company. After some abortive legal action by one small shareholder of Consolidated bonds, the amalgamation was to be approved in October 1904, with a capital of $255 million and book assets put at $274 million (but generally thought to be around double the capital, if allowance was properly made for investments in subsidiaries and affiliates).

Several factories, at Durham and Rochester, were put into the BAT export organisation, which recruited single men and expanded sales with strict performance targets.

The Trust's tentacles spread across two hundred and fifty companies controlling four-fifths of the United States tobacco output, including 82 per cent of cigarette production. Advertising cost $10 million annually. It bought 400 million lb a year of leaf, mainly within the United States.

Naturally, the second biggest customer for the leaf was Imperial, which in 1904 decided to build itself prestige offices at Richmond on Sixth and Canal Streets to coordinate the American leaf operations, based now on half a dozen processing plants. Just as important was the 'head-hunting' of rival Gallaher's Virginia and North Carolina manager to expand buying of Dark Western tobacco for the pipe requirements still dominant in Britain, in spite of the rapidly growing sale of cigarettes which was now holding around 26 per cent of the United Kingdom tobacco market.

Under the pact with Duke, the Imperial management was now developing with assurance. An executive committee was controlling finance, ensuring uniform leaf grading, and coordinating spending policies for a group with about 66 per cent of the British manufactured tobacco output. As if to remind its competitors of its obvious power, the trade-marks of J. & F. Bell, of Glasgow, were acquired and the home trade of Bell brands, including the re-nowned Three Nuns tobacco, was handed over to the Stephen Mitchell & Son branch. The Dingley Road tobacco factory in London, once owned by Salmon & Gluckstein, now in the Imperial fold, was fully annexed and turned into the headquarters of the Adkin & Sons branch and a cigar-making unit.

Individual members of the Wills family continued to make news in 1904. Sir William Wills, still two years from his peerage and the title Lord Winterstoke, became the first Bristolian to be made a Freeman of the City, to which he and other members of the family were to give several millions of pounds from their fortunes, like Duke in Durham, to found a university. Harry Wills, who had gone to British-American Tobacco as deputy chairman (the Wills export business had gone with him), decided to retire, devoting himself to charitable work with the help of a fortune that still totalled £2.7 million when he died eighteen years later. A. C. Churchman, later Lord Woodbridge, joined BAT's board under Duke. Meanwhile, Melville Wills had taken the W. D. & H. O. Wills branch firmly under his personal management, pushing ahead on mechanisation and cigarette advertising. The Wills branch now supplied close on 48 per cent of British cigarette consumption and dominated the Imperial sales effort, selling six times the cigarettes by weight made by the John Player branch, and twelve times the production of Ogden. Within three years, the Wills branch would celebrate the annual sale of 5,000 million Wild Woodbines alone.

It was quite clear to Imperial's remaining competitors that the combine could only be attacked by cultivating customer loyalty with quality, blends, or new methods of marketing. Someone who decided to challenge Imperial and its Bonsack cigarette machines was Bernhard Baron, who had tried to involve Imperial in the purchase of Ogden to forestall Duke. Carreras, the company he helped form in 1903, now set up an allied concern called Carreras & Marcianus Ltd, operating from St James's Place, Aldgate, the former works of Baron's Machine Company.

The idea was to test in the cigarette market Baron's machinery skill against the Bonsacks and other machines of Imperial, whose patents and operational experience would seem to make any new competitive venture a foolhardy affair. In the last six months of

1904, however, Carreras & Marcianus launched three brands, of which Black Cat was the most important. Smokers took to Black Cat cigarettes liking the lucky-sounding name; they were heavily advertised with an appropriate feline trade-mark.

The Black Cat name was rooted in Carreras' past. A cat was kept at the original Wardour Street premises and smokers began to refer so constantly to the 'Black Cat shop' that the son of the founder put a picture of the animal on some labels.

Further Carreras brands would follow, notably Chick, Jetty and Sweet Kiss. But what was important to Imperial was that the up-start Carreras in 1905 began to market Baron's machine-made cigarettes with the aid of special offer coupons and numerous competitions for prizes. Trade bounded so much that the following year extra manufacturing facilities had to be found in the East End and even more brands, such as Ovals and Seven Up, were to follow. At the more select end of the market, Louis Rothman was developing an international prestige, with orders flowing in from South Africa, India and Australia, where expatriates who knew his shops readily spread the word about his select mixtures and often specified such brands as Pall Mall and Royal Favourites. Tom Gallaher, now sixty-four, with factories in Belfast, London and Dublin, continued to introduce machinery, encouraged by the growing demand for Park Drive cigarettes. The export trade of Gallaher was assisted by the winning in 1904 of gold medals at the American World Fair and the New Zealand Exhibition. And he drew criticism of himself from the House of Commons for some forthright remarks on the high rate of tax on imported leaf. While Gallaher greatly encouraged the growing of Irish tobacco, he was a regular visitor to the United States, supervising leaf purchases, bidding against Imperial and American Tobacco at the auctions.

In the course of those American travels, Tom Gallaher was becoming very aware of the hostility felt within the tobacco-growing regions towards the Trust and always stressed his independence. The Irishman acknowledged Duke's ambition and grit, but remained openly distrustful of his business methods, especially when farmers, journalists, politicians and others drew attention to American Tobacco's power, without always making clear that not all manufacturers operated by the criteria of the biggest. As far as the United States was concerned, he felt its rapidly expanding population ought to support far more manufacturers and even importers.

That American Tobacco had its enemies cannot be doubted, even Roosevelt's motives were not solely of a political nature as the President nursed a personal grudge against Duke for attempting to influence the Republican Party against his nomination in 1904. Early in 1905, newly married to a woman who was deceiving him through her love for another, even on their honeymoon, Duke was to contract a painful foot disease, during which time his eighty-five-year-old father, Washington Duke, fractured his hip and later died. In the summer, he went to London, returning to file suit for divorce from his bride of less than a year. Lillian Duke and her lover, Frank Huntoon, wealthy president of a mineral water company, communicated with each other when apart by cables and personal newspaper advertisements. These appropriately described Duke as 'Octopus'.

The New Jersey divorce action of April and May 1906 ended successfully for Duke, but the sensational disclosures, transmitted round the land by newspapers, only served to intensify the hostility of his critics. They included Colonel John Webster, owner of *Webster's Weekly*, and Josephus Daniels, of the *News and Observer*, of Raleigh, whose passionate editorials on and investigations into Duke's tobacco combine increasingly found favour in the tobacco-growing regions where every difficulty, even mildew on crops, was being blamed on American Tobacco and its associates.

Wholesalers in tobacco products were drawing special payments for favouring Duke's products and the Trust had begun buying shares in jobbing enterprises. So much secrecy surrounded American Tobacco's shares, patenting, licensing and general dealings that many within the combine were unaware that they served not one octopus, but many. Duke encouraged trusted aides to conceal American Tobacco's ownership or control of certain firms, often thought to be competitors. Even the International Tobacco Workers Union could not find out which were Trust companies. Consumers did not worry unduly. They were content to follow the brand names in buying six billion cigarettes alone in 1906 from American Tobacco. For example, few knew then that the Wells-Whitehead Tobacco Company making 92 million cigarettes a year from Virginian Bright had been under the Duke thumb for several years.

Brand names known to smokers and under the Trust's tentacles included Richmond Straight Cuts, Sweet Caporal, Piedmont, Picayune, Coupon, King Bee, Home Run, American Beauty Cycle, Egyptian Deities, Mogul, and Trophies. Chewers of plug bought Thoroughbred, Schnapps, Browns Mule, Sweepstakes, Sun-Cured, Early Bird, Apple Jack, Wild Duck, and Red Meat.

Names were romantic, practical, misleading, and constantly changing. Cigarettes, twist, mixtures, cigars, and plug bore such other typical trade-marks as Battle Ax, Newsboy, Piper Heidsieck, Bradywine, Burr Oak, Crane, Standard Navy, Mechanic's Delight, Tennessee Cross, Bullion, Autumn, Black Bess, No Tax, Happy Thought, Black Diamond, Quality and Quantity, Climax, Keystone, Gold Rope, Nobby, Fancy Chew, Big Fig, Jack Spratt, Green Turtle, Forget-Me-Not, Rose Leaf, Honest Long Cut, Payroll, Hobby, Saw Log, Granger, Champion, Lucy Hinton, Double Five, Wheelman, Morning Glory, Five A, Good Luck, Oklahoma, Horse Shoe, Terrapin, and Burley Cable.

It was little wonder that consumers rarely knew the manufacturers' names, let alone whether or not they were independent of the combine. Critics of Duke were more persistent, and they painstakingly sought to unravel the tentacles to find what they were grasping. There was some astonishment when it was discovered that the Trust controlled Nall & Williams, which produced navy plug with a trade union approved label declaring that it was free of Duke's empire. Nall & Williams advertised itself as independent. Only the prickly Dick Reynolds enjoyed some considerable independence in running R. J. Reynolds, which had grown strongly since amalgamation, but largely because of Reynolds' refusal to tip his hat at Duke. The Reynolds business was among the biggest plug and twist suppliers in the East and South, remitting a rising two-thirds share of profits to American Tobacco.

Curiously, Reynolds was a friend of Josephus Daniels and kept the famous Methodist journalist well supplied with ideas for attacking Duke who was now divorced, abused in Washington, and ill-tempered. Daniels concentrated on the Trust's activities in tobacco auctions around North Carolina, claiming that as much as $5 million had been unfairly slashed off prices paid to farmers in 1904. By the summer of 1906 growers were militant, moving towards violent reprisals. About three thousand met at Rocky Mount in North Carolina and protested that leaf prices were being manipulated downwards by one-third, while taxation had been reduced and output prices raised. Protests spread to the Kentucky Burley belt where open hatred flowed from American Tobacco's decision to end open bidding on auction warehouse floors. Farmers who had carried their leaf many miles had to accept pitiful prices—under three cents a pound—or return to their land without money, dumping their crops to rot.

The leaf buyers of Imperial felt the mounting anger, too, for they were considered, rightly or wrongly, parties to Duke's activities. At Bristol, reports were received on what the directors called 'the Western situation'. Troubles spread into Tennessee as farmers gathered in their horse-drawn buggies to discuss the deteriorating system. It was difficult for the new peer Lord Winterstoke (formerly Sir William Wills) and his board to appreciate fully the dramatic events now taking place across the Atlantic, though in June 1906 a board report had given some warning about the new system of buying tobacco by personal transaction with American farmers to keep twenty-one processing plants well stocked. But, as if sensing a shift of history, African leaf-buying had begun in a small way, much to the delight of the pioneers in Rhodesia and South Africa.

Samples of Rhodesian tobacco had been examined by Imperial's executive committee in 1904. Now, two years later, the British Central Africa Company had approached the top men at Bristol with the claim that crops of smokable tobacco were being success-fully grown in Nyasaland but the planters needed guidance on better cultivation and curing. Imperial despatched a young expert, A. W. Boyd, from its Danville, Virginia, installations to study the potential. Boyd's report was to persuade Imperial to establish both an Africa Leaf-Buying Organisation and a processing factory at Limbe in Nyasaland (now Malawi).

Imperial directors were increasingly uneasy about Duke and his methods. The previous year there had been a row between Bristol and New York after a letter had been received claiming that an agreement on Imperial's buying and treatment of leaf for British purposes had been breached.

The letter stated: 'We have information that there have been violations of this contract in this respect frequently, almost from the date of the execution of the contract, by sale by you in the United States of leaf tobacco, scrap tobacco, and stem products of tobacco. We desire to call this to your attention and to ask that there be no further violation and that you kindly report to us past violations, with full details thereof, to the end that there may be settlement with respect to profits arising therefrom or such other adjustment, if possible, that may be agreed upon.'

This letter, and other complaints, hardly made for good relations between the truce-making British and American tobacco combines, but Imperial had to explain the need for some marginal operations within the United States market for factors not totally within its control. Now that there was unrest, Imperial was still sensitive enough not to challenge Duke and his American colleagues over the so-called Western situation. The board had resolved in June 1906 to send for Edgar Carlton, a top executive of Imperial's American Leaf Organisation, and he would spend three months working out branch requirements for Western tobaccos. Falling demand for chewing plug, and what Imperial increasingly acknowledged as 'the unsatisfactory nature' of the new buying system of personal offers, were about to produce violence, and arson.

The events overshadowed Imperial's other management decisions at this time, which included the formation of the British Nicotine Company, at Bootle in Liverpool, to make nicotine alkaloid and sulphate from tobacco waste for use in crop spraying, sheep dips and other farm purposes round the world. The growers of Tennessee and Kentucky decided to fight the Trust by the formation of cooperative marketing groups. Their agents would sell the pooled tobacco to manufacturers, tobacco brokers, and overseas agents, so stopping the practice of buyers quoting their own price. Tobacco manufacturers had to have leaf, the pool farmers reasoned, so strength lay in joint selling to avoid fragmentation of bargaining power. Unfortunately, not all farmers agreed to pool their crops—and so began violence. Under the cover of darkness, groups of masked horsemen, to be known to American history as the Night Riders, rode down on non-pool tobacco spreads, destroying the crops outright or by sowing mixtures of salt and grass seed.

Some farmers were to be tied to trees and flogged, some even lynched. Buyers attempting to buy crops outside the pool were stopped and beaten up. Barns and processing factories known to be handling non-pool leaf were dynamited, or razed to the ground with flaming torches. The resentment that forced farmers to such desperate and illegal actions was to be directed more noticeably at the monopolist manufacturers who were openly blamed for reducing the planter's income to as little as twenty cents a day for his hard labour.

On 30th November 1906, the mob violence erupted around the Imperial stemmery in Princeton, Kentucky, and it was burned to the ground. Bristol promptly approved the offer of a $5,000 reward for the arrest and conviction of the incendiaries, and the local authorities were warned that Imperial would withdraw operations from the region if law and order was not restored. Insurance companies were already threatening to cancel policies on tobacco premises. A few days later, at 1 am, three hundred armed men seized Princeton's fire-fighting equipment, and then burned two warehouses owned by the American Tobacco Company, warning off with their raised rifles those who tried to fight the fire. Some 300,000 lb of tobacco was lost, and the avenging farmers rode off into the night. Lawlessness continued for months with agitation against the combines growing to such a pitch that a year later, at 2 am on 8th December 1907, a band of around two hundred mounted Night Riders poured into Hopkinsville, Kentucky, along the railway track, cutting telegraph wires on the way. Police and firemen were detained. House lights were shot out. Two factories were then laced with paraffin and destroyed by fire, which began to threaten homes. Police and firemen were freed to let them save their homes. During the thirty minutes' raid, Imperial's local buyer, Lindsay Mitchell, was dragged from his home and hit over the head with a gun barrel.

Troops were sent in, and local communities organised law and order leagues. The Night Riders were never to be convicted, and for some time after 1907 factories kept racks of repeating rifles near to hand in case of new incidents. The violence subsided even if the militancy of many farmers remained obvious. At first Duke took the situation calmly and believed the authorities would quell the farmers who had been stirred up by those he branded as 'socialist agitators'. One thing that hit Buck Duke, however, was the newspaper reports in May 1907 that President Roosevelt was 'more than just unhappy' with the activities of the American Tobacco Company. And that summer the *Raleigh News and Observer* wrote:

'The Trust's desires are modest. All it wants is the earth with a barbed wire fence around it. The Tobacco Trust is a hog, and wants all the swill. The tobacco crop is short this year. It ought to have brought twelve cents a pound, but the Trust fixed it at seven cents or eight cents, and that is all that is being paid.'

That summer Duke married the beautiful widow of a Georgia cotton merchant, Mrs Nanaline Holt Inman, who would grace the $1.6 million mansion he was ostentatiously building on Fifth Avenue. During some other construction—at his Somerville estate—he intervened in a union dispute involving Italian brick-layers by calling the police and having the men taken to the County Jail. Duke's temper had not been improved by his still painful erysipelas foot, or by his wedding present from the United States Government—the filing of a suit to dissolve the tobacco combination on the grounds that it was a monopoly acting in restraint of trade.

Official investigations of trusts were nothing new, and Duke ought to have been prepared for tobacco to join the list of industries for Government scrutiny. The size of his group made it a prime target.

The new industries of America encouraged large-scale manu-facturing and processing. Inventions and mass production went hand in hand with discoveries of raw materials. In 1910 there were six million immigrants to swell the United States population, which had risen to sixty-three million between 1860 and 1880, and now reached ninety-two million. The United States Steel Corpora-tion and John D. Rockefeller's Standard Oil were symbols of industrial power—the latter resisting an attempt in 1890 by the Ohio Supreme Court to break it up by reincorporating as a New Jersey holding company. In 1911, the United States Supreme Court would again order its dissolution. Theodore Roosevelt caught the public mood. There was alarm at the power of the trusts and the men of great wealth. People looked to their politicians to counter their influence and financial power.

The United States Anti-Trust Act of 1890, steered through by Republican Senator and financial administrator John Sherman, was not seen by Roosevelt as totally ineffective, given a determined administration. He thundered against the 'malefactors of great wealth', and went after Buck Duke, a decidedly popular target, when thrust at forty-two from the office of Vice President to the Presidency on the assassination of William McKinley, Duke's hero. Unfortunately there were divided views within the Republican Party, which would stop the Nobel Peace Prize winner 'Teddy' Roosevelt from seeing his campaign against Duke speedily resolved. Roosevelt sponsored William Taft in 1908 as his successor, but became so dissatisfied he formed the Progressive Party to fight for the presidency in 1912, only to be defeated by Woodrow Wilson.

It would take four years of legal struggle, charges, counter-allegations, and weary sessions of taking evidence to back Duke into a corner. The testimony alone would fill several bulky volumes. Essentially, the suit saw the Trust as masterminded by American Tobacco with its three main operating subsidiaries, American Cigar, American Snuff and the newly established British-American Tobacco, in turn controlling eighty-two other substantial subsidiaries in the United States, Puerto Rico and Cuba, undertaking everything from billposting to making four-fifths of manufactured tobacco except cigars. The net capital, after excluding inter-combination holdings, was estimated at a colossal $316 million. And it was held that Duke and other stockholders (Thomas Fortune Ryan, Colonel Oliver Payne, Ben Duke, Anthony N. Brade, Pierre Lorillard, George Arents, Grant B. Schkey, and Williamson Fuller) commanded about 60 per cent of the voting stock of American Tobacco.

Named as defendants were twenty-eight individuals besides Buck Duke, and sixty-five American corporations, including United Cigar Stores, and the two English corporations, BAT and Imperial (in which American Tobacco now held a large minority shareholding).

As the United States authorities prepared their case against the Trust, the tobacco-growing areas had been facing other difficulties, flowing from the financial crisis of 1907 and 1908. Some banks experienced heavy runs on their deposits and hoarding of cash became a serious problem. Scarce money meant that farmers were being offered paper scrip pledges in lieu of hard cash, and many readily took low prices for cash rather than risk holding dubious slips of paper. Even Imperial, then Britain's biggest company, found its banks in New York and Richmond declining to remit currency needed for tobacco purchases even though strong balances were held. On 30th October, Imperial's secretary in Bristol received a cable asking for £100,000 worth of gold which was sent by Atlantic steamer three days later. It was a good move, as Imperial raised dollars quickly, bought its supplies, and, just as important, won the badly needed support and goodwill of tobacco dealers and growers.

The man who sent for the gold, Wellford Reed, the supervisor of American leaf-buying, died shortly after this emergency transaction, and the Wilson, North Carolina, Tobacco Board of Trade suspended its sales as a mark of respect.

The plain-speaking Duke was taxed quite early on by the Government prosecutor, Jim McReynolds, with the allegation that American Tobacco had conspired to hold down leaf prices unfairly. His answer, given in February 1908, was that the law of supply and demand determined prices. Farmers did not have to plant leaf, and, if not enough was paid, then they would stop growing tobacco and have to be paid more to get them to plant again. It was a simple enough argument in the era of unbridled free enterprise. But the anti-trust investigators might have been impressed if there had been more competitive buying. A monopoly buyer had to provide better justification, and, as the story of American Tobacco's growth and practices was set down, the credibility of Duke's early testimony was soon lost.

Like so many founding fathers of big business before and after him, Duke relied largely on his memory and never seemed to lack for quick answers under detailed questioning. His command was impressive. He had never acquired any business to eliminate competition. It was an investment, or a take-over to 'round out our business'. Particular deals were made to get 'a fair share' of the trade. When faced with evidence of obvious secrecy in ownership, Duke simply replied that former owners insisted on this when they became managers, retaining their trade-marks and business names. He did not mislead or misrepresent share ownership, rather he just declined to talk about the question. The success of his company was due to its advertising skill and drive. The vast empire existed, he stressed, because it happened 'to have more of the brands that please the people and consequently we sell more tobacco'.

McReynolds, who hailed from one of the hostile tobacco states, Tennessee, asked about his interest in Imperial following the settlement of the warfare in the British market. Duke replied that, while he was an Imperial director, he never attended a board meeting and knew nothing of the Bristol-based combine's proceedings. He said: 'I was put on the board merely as a compliment to us because we held a large amount of stock.' The questioning of Duke and others went on, and one after another came damning facts, figures, letters or documents that would destroy American Tobacco.

Some examples will suffice for this narrative, deserving as the Trust action may be of detailed examination. Nall & Williams and Wells-Whitehead, of Kentucky and Carolina respectively, masqueraded as independents, used by the Trust to destroy really independent competitors by subsidised price cutting. Many others pretended to independence in order to make products under the anti-trust Blue Label issued by the Tobacco Workers' Union. A national tobacco espionage system had been developed to help stifle competition. Uncovered were numerous examples of phoney names and secret postal addresses. Sometimes strikes were arranged in competitors' factories, with the labour force attracted away by specially inflated pay rates. Letters were produced showing that the Trust deliberately sought to conceal its involvement in business transactions and marketing attacks. British-American sought to stop by unfair means the exporting of cigarettes to China by Ware-Kramer, a very honest rival.

There was more, much more. Percival Hill, deeply involved in all the plotting along with Duke and such faithful lieutenants as Caleb Dula, was confronted with a letter in which he denied Trust ownership of the retail chain United Cigar Stores, whereas he claimed firmly in evidence that control was never concealed. The president of United was given written instructions to discourage the sale of rival products after spies reported on rival tobacco brands recommended by the sales staff. Other retailers, such as Acker, Merrall & Condit, received similar reprimands. Other letters were produced by prosecutor McReynolds clearly indicating that the Trust conducted accurate industrial espionage among rivals, whose deliveries were even monitored from source to customers. Often, Trust-owned companies attempting to give independent manufacturers reasonable access to markets were stunned by the spying system that kept them in line with combine policies and limited their so-called freedom of management in return for American Tobacco's claim on a share of profits. Some companies were even advised when it was expedient for them to show losses, or to subsidise short-term price cutting to undermine a competitor. Preferential allowances were paid to wholesalers and general tobacco jobbers who shut out non-Trust goods from the warehouses. Even heads of some American Tobacco departments were kept in the dark on some special discounts, often only disclosed by Hill, Dula, or Duke to their auditors for appropriately discreet book-keeping entries. Correspondence flowed between parties to such practices by the use of aliases and third-party postal addresses. Often plain unheaded notepaper was used.

Evidence was produced to demonstrate that tenders for Navy tobacco supplies were being rigged according to Trust instructions, even when the anti-trust action had begun.

Slowly the suit wended its way through the lower courts and finally went on appeals from both the defendants and the Government to the United States Supreme Court.

Across the Atlantic, life and business progressed. Imperial, which continued to build up its American organisation (in 1908 it bought Fallon & Martin of Durham and then continued to buy new processing plants), had learnt a trick or two from Duke. In 1908 it arranged to pay an annual window-dressing grant to a retail chain, Bewlay, in return for 75 per cent of the display space given over to tobacco goods. There was a new honour for the Imperial board room when that year King Edward VII took time off from opening a new dock at Avonmouth to knight at the Council House Edward Burnet James, twice Lord Mayor of Bristol. His father had been knighted by Queen Victoria at the same place in 1887. James was among those who had just approved the building of a steam-drying leaf factory in Nyasaland and the purchase of extensive forestry estates.

Tom Gallaher, worried by events in 1907 in America, bought the entire Irish tobacco crop that same year. In Scotland, the ninety-nine-year-old Dobie Company of Paisley, manufacturer of Four Square pipe tobacco, merged with J. and T. Hodge, an even older house which was the first to bring cigarette-making machinery into Scotland. At the same time, the Godfrey Phillips concern, which would in 1956 wind up Dobie and buy its brands, was converting itself into a public company.

Carreras was expanding rapidly with new brands and by 1909 had introduced the Baron automatic pipe filler and cartridge which would change pipe-smoking habits and sell by the million. In 1910 it built a new works at City Road and launched full-scale gift coupon schemes to cultivate the loyalty of smokers. In this year Louis Rothman acquired another showroom in Regent Street and a Royal Warrant for the King of Spain.

Match-makers Bryant & May opened a factory in 1909 in New Zealand, and one in 1910 in Australia (another had been established in South Africa in 1905), but warily assessed the news that the first wheeled-action petrol lighter had been successfully invented by Findeisl in Austria (two years later another Austrian, Russbacher, made his semi-automatic springloaded lighter box).

As the United States action against Duke moved towards its inevitable climax, Imperial became beset with its own problems. An important era was passing, and along with it some vital men would go. In 1909, Lloyd George introduced his first Budget as Chancellor of the Exchequer, and he turned to tobacco to raise new tax revenues. The duty was lifted by 8d to 3s 8d per lb and drew fierce protests from the trade and Imperial in particular, as it now commanded no less than 57.5 per cent of total trade. Cigarettes went up ½d per packet, and an ounce of smoking tobacco by a similar sum. Spending power was curbed in other directions and the consequence was the first fall in tobacco consumption after eight years of sustained growth. It was little wonder that the following year Imperial bought itself a new subsidiary, Murad, which specialised in less price sensitive Oriental cigarettes. The year 1910 also saw the first public auction of Rhodesian leaf, an event whose significance was totally ignored in the United States.

Death, which had removed in 1905 from the board room Arthur Hamilton Wills, who had most to do with tobacco buying, now took his father, Sir Frederick Wills, on 18th February 1909; his other son (Sir Gilbert A. H. Wills) would become the first Lord Dulverton and a chairman of Imperial for twenty-three years from 1924. Sir Frederick, a proven manager of factories, had stood firm against a sell-out when the idea of a merger with Duke's American Tobacco had once been put forward in the board room. Governor of Guy's Hospital and the father of six (many Wills had large families: Henry Overton Wills II had eighteen children), the Oxford-educated Sir Frederick was a political animal, fighting

several elections in Cornwall before becoming Unionist M.P. for
Bristol North from 1900 to 1906. He owned 1,500 acres of land
with homes in the fashionable Kensington district of London and
Bournemouth, as well as his Dulverton estate.

Within a month of Sir Frederick's death, Sir Edward Payson
Wills, whose strong point had been finance, died aged seventy-five.
Henry Overton Wills III, the family's elder, rarely attended any
Imperial board meetings. His son George usually held his proxy.
However, notes would sometimes be sent to fellow directors and
his cousin, the chairman, Lord Winterstoke, son of W. D. Wills.
Sometimes the messages came from as far as an estate he kept at
Romsdalen in Norway, but more usually from his main home in
Bath. He died in 1911 and left over £5,200,000.

But the most serious loss in terms of Imperial was that of the
most famous of these four senior directors and once partners in
the original W. D. & H. O. Wills business. On 29th January 1911,
Lord Winterstoke of Blagdon, formerly Sir William Henry Wills,
founder chairman of Imperial when seventy-one, died aged eighty.
His wise and lively humour would no longer permeate the board
room, though his twinkly eyes would look down on his successors'
deliberations from a recently painted portrait.

In spite of large charitable donations, his fortune was estimated
at £2,548,209. (The four Wills who died between 1909 and 1911
left well over £12 million, after numerous large donations and
endowments upon which much of Bristol's health, cultural,
political and educational institutions are founded.)

The loss of the wise old Winterstoke was eased by the fact that
Imperial was in strong hands, especially those of Henry Overton
Wills III's three sons, the sober George, engineer Harry and
Melville. Their contributions to the formation and early strong
management of Imperial almost matched those of the first chairman. The tennis-playing and organ music fanatic, George Alfred
Wills, was elected chairman on 21st February 1911 after a little
over nine years as Lord Winterstoke's deputy. His fortune would
grow to £10 million by the time of his own death in 1928, six
years after Harry, whose estate was put at a more modest £2.7
million. The Cambridge-educated Melville would survive until
1941, leaving over £4 million.

The continued dominance of the shareholding Wills family—
control would not cease for another seven years—was now to be

eased slightly by the appointment of the Scot, William Nelson Mitchell, as deputy chairman, drawn from the Stephen Mitchell & Son branch and an original founding director of Imperial. The brothers John Dane and William Goodacre Player would survive everyone, dying in the 1950s, and providing a moderating influence from Nottingham on Imperial's actions, helping avoid the worst temptations of monopoly power that one day, nevertheless, would come under official scrutiny.

On 29th May 1911, four months to the day after Imperial lost Lord Winterstoke, Buck Duke learnt that the United States Supreme Court held his combine as acting in restraint of trade. For one and a half hours Chief Justice White read out his opinion that the Trust had violated anti-trust law and must be dissolved by methods to be determined by the Circuit Court of Appeal of New York. American senators, members of the House of Representatives, teams of lawyers, Government observers and tobacco executives packed the Court chamber and milled around outside fighting for admission. Duke sat alone in his office, awaiting the telephone call that would tell him the decision dishonouring his name and dismantling an empire the like of which American capitalism would never see again.

CHAPTER EIGHT

Unlawful Conspiracy and Realignment

When a full transcript of the Supreme Court finding reached Duke, he read it with care. Search as he did, there were no mitigating sentences to flaw the damning indictment. The ultimate irony was that there could be only one man capable of unscrambling the complex enterprise—not the brilliant prosecutor, Jim McReynolds, who regarded the defendants as criminals and would soon become President Woodrow Wilson's Attorney-General, but none other than the 'Octopus' himself, James Buchanan Duke. This fact became painfully and embarrassingly clear as an army of stockholders, appeal judges, corporate and Government lawyers, public servants, auditors and others sought to dismember the creature reared by modern mass production, stock market manipulation, and good old native Carolinian cunning.

The judgement found that the combination, and all its elements, whether considered separately or collectively, was in restraint of trade, and represented an attempt to monopolise within the meanings of the first and second sections of the Anti-Trust Act. It went on:

'Undisputed facts overwhelmingly demonstrate that the acts, contracts, agreement, combinations, etc., which were assailed were of such an unusual and wrongful character as to bring them within the prohibitions of the law.'

The history of the combination, it continued, was replete with the doings of acts which it was the obvious purpose of the statute to forbid. From the beginning a purpose was demonstrative to acquire dominion and control of the tobacco trade, not by the mere exercise of the ordinary right to contract and trade, but 'by methods devised in order to monopolise the trade by driving their competitors out of business, which was ruthlessly carried out upon the assumption that to work upon the fears or play upon the cupidity of competitors would make success possible.'

Duke's worst enemies could not have drafted a more condemnatory conclusion. It rested on six main actions, held to be of a sufficiently unusual and wrongful character to breach the antitrust legislation. Briefly, these were:

1. Formation of the very first combination came from one or more parties to a previously existing fierce trade war.

2. Acts which ensued from the combination and its increase in capital justified the inference that intent existed to use its power 'as vantage ground to further monopolise the trade in tobacco by means of trade contracts designed to injure others either by driving competitors out of business or compelling them to become partners to a combination'. This purpose was illustrated by the plug and snuff wars, the conflict that followed the combination's entry into England, and the division of world-wide business in two foreign contracts that ensued.

3. By the ever-present manifestation which was exhibited by a conscious wrong-doing in various transactions to restrain others to monopolise and retain power in the hands of a few who from the beginning 'contemplated the mastery of the trade which practically followed'.

4. By the gradual absorption of control of all the elements essential to successful manufacture of tobacco products and placing control in the hands of seemingly independent corporations serving as perpetual barriers to the entry of others into the trade.

5. By persistent expenditure of millions upon millions of dollars in buying out plants not for the purpose of utilising them, but in order to close them up and render them useless for trade.

6. By the constantly recurring stipulations, by which manufacturers, stockholders or employees were required to bind themselves generally for long periods not to compete in the future.

The court, while not suggesting a plan for dissolving the combination, ordered that the plan or methods to be worked out by the parties in the suit in the Circuit Court of Appeals did define the objective. This was to recreate out of the combination's elements 'a new condition which shall be honestly in harmony with, and not repugnant to, the law, but without unnecessary injury to the public or the rights of property'.

That it was Duke who came up with the solution would, when it became known, raise new storms. His scheme had simplicity, for it was that American Tobacco should shed two-thirds of its plants and brands, to be handed over to two new corporations carrying the famous existing names of the P. Lorillard Company and the Liggett & Myers Company. At the same time, controlling share-holdings would be divested from a group of other well-known concerns, including United Cigar and R. J. Reynolds. This, he argued, would ensure competition, and this view was strongly reinforced when Richard Joshua Reynolds, Duke's old adversary, declared: 'Now watch me give Buck Duke hell.' When it came to his first ideas on the financial changes, there was trouble. He proposed that Lorillard and Liggett & Myers should issue and pay over to American Tobacco vast sums in preferential bonds matching the value of property transferred. While this was designed to safeguard the interests of American Tobacco's existing long-term public bond holders, there were immediate and obvious objections that this gave American a continued financial hold. Eventually, Duke came out with the alternative idea that the two new companies could create their own bonds, of higher interest, and exchange them for American Tobacco's bonds plus some Preferred shares, called in at high prices to ensure enough for the switch-round.

A howl of protest greeted the final scheme. Jim McReynolds, the prosecutor, even declined to sign the decree of consent until he was overruled by President Taft's Attorney-General. McReynolds wanted to institute criminal proceedings against Duke, Thomas Fortune Ryan, and the other share croppers. The Woodrow Wilson Democratic platform poured scorn on the Taft compromise, but when swept into power in 1912-13 on the New Freedom ticket it was too late. President Wilson recruited McReynolds as Attorney-General and as Duke's oldest enemy, Carolinian journalist Josephus Daniels, was also recruited to the Cabinet as Navy Secretary, the dishonoured tobacco tycoon knew he must retire as soon as possible from management, even if clinging on to his large shareholdings in the successor companies.

Selected to run the dismembered American Tobacco were

Percival S. Hill and his son, George Washington Hill. His old crony, Caleb Dula, was placed in charge of Liggett & Myers. Pierre Lorillard took over P. Lorillard, and Dick Reynolds continued with R. J. Reynolds, both men sure to give American Tobacco some tough competition. Plans soon emerged whereby the new top managements would have the incentive of receiving 10 per cent of profits while distributing the rest to stockholders, which ensured Duke and his fellow defendants would still receive handsome incomes. They would all 'battle like hell', keeping the Government happy, and Duke could not lose, whoever nosed to the front in the years ahead.

In Britain, of course, the decree had profound effects. American Tobacco's shareholding in BAT (two-thirds of the equity to Imperial's one-third share) was sold or distributed among the shareholders. At the same time, American Tobacco's large shareholding in Imperial, just under 14 per cent, was diluted and Buck Duke quit his ten-year-old directorship on 30th April 1912, and accepted under the revision of arrangements the chairmanship of BAT, promising to develop further its world-wide trading. Duke, whose new wife shortly bore him a daughter, was by now very disillusioned with the United States and felt he would enjoy more status and admiration for his business achievements in English society. Working more closely with BAT, registered in Britain, would take him regularly to London, and thoughts of settling in England began to dog him. He had also become interested in the money-making potential of white hydro-electric power, forming the Southern Power Company (later renamed the Duke Power Company).

A list was compiled of all Imperial brands which American Tobacco had sold in the United States prior to the anti-trust decree so that it would retain the rights.* But Imperial was now free to sell in the United States any of its brands not on the schedule. A similar list was prepared of American Tobacco brands in respect of which Imperial now retained trading rights in Britain. These included Old Gold and Richmond Gems.

The existing agreement between BAT and Imperial that the former did not market in Britain and engaged solely in overseas

---

* Player's Navy Cut (some years later American Tobacco transferred this brand's rights to Philip Morris), Wills' Capstan, Gold Flake, Three Castles, Wild Woodbines, Three Nuns and St Bruno.

marketing, handling Imperial's export business, was retained.
Imperial had little enthusiasm for destroying BAT as its agreement worked well, with several Imperial directors put on the BAT
board to ensure coordination and no overlapping. In any case, it
was not too happy at the prospect of trying to expand in the
United States market with its name somewhat tarnished in that
country as a result of the past connections with Duke.

The domestic market needed close attention because of the
check to consumption caused by the Lloyd George budget of
1909. Competition was growing much stronger, led by such as
Carreras, Godfrey Phillips, and Gallaher (which had greatly
increased its national advertising). New companies were even being
formed in 1912, notably the Ardath Tobacco Company, and
Julius Wix & Son, which would one day, by a turn of the wheel of
history, attract American Tobacco back into Britain and raise new
fears. Even Imperial's long-standing mastery of machinery was
vulnerable, for in 1912 one of the earliest competitors to the
Bonsack organisation, the United Cigarette Machinery Company,
formed with the packaging machinery pioneers W. E. & H. B.
Molins a new joint British company with working links with
United's machinery plant in Dresden.

An emerging monopoly, the match manufacturers Bryant &
May, decided that year to buy the fireworks firm Octavius Hunt,
an intriguing, if obvious, diversification.

That Imperial's board had a certain nervousness about its
involvement in the United States is an understatement. The
decree that allowed Duke to escape criminal prosecution and
retain his financial involvement had not gone down too well in the
tobacco-growing areas, particularly in the militant region of
Kentucky. Rightly or wrongly, Imperial was tarred with the same
brush in some Kentucky eyes, and the company and its buying
affiliate were charged under state anti-trust legislation 'with
conspiring unlawfully to lower prices of tobacco below its actual
worth and then to acquire it at the depressed rate'.

The indictment, recorded by a Grand Jury at Henderson,
Kentucky, brought Imperial's top leaf manager, C. S. Clarke,
hurrying to the United States as a witness for the court proceedings, transferred from the hostile Henderson County to Morgan-
field, in Union County, after Imperial's protests that the action
might otherwise be prejudiced.

It was to no avail, for Imperial and its local affiliate were convicted and fined $7,000, plus forfeiture of the Imperial Tobacco Company of Kentucky's corporate charter. A motion for retrial was overruled, and the case then moved to the Kentucky Court of Appeal. The conviction, however, would not be quashed until several years later (in November 1914) when International Harvester won a Supreme Court ruling that Kentucky anti-trust law was unconstitutional.

This residual antagonism was not the only factor in confining Imperial's expansion in the United States to its established leaf-buying. There were more solid reasons, too. BAT had long-term ideas for entering that market and Imperial could draw any benefits their way. At the same time, the successor companies to Duke's Trust were out to do each other down in a bout of intensive and costly promotions. There were already over fifty brands of cigarettes alone on the United States market, bringing a total consumption in 1910 of about 8.6 billion cigarettes.

Collaboration between BAT and Imperial took a new turn in 1913 when, to reduce their dependence on foreign supplies of carton board for packing cigarettes and tobacco, they set up a joint concern called the St Anne's Board Mill Company, bringing in an expert Buckinghamshire board maker, who ran one of the earliest domestic board plants under his own name, G. H. Hedley. While these groups got together, another very much smaller enterprise was splitting up. For undisclosed reasons, Louis Rothman broke his partnership with his brother Marx, who was given control of the Regent Street, London, business, while Louis remained at 5 and 5a Pall Mall, but bought himself a factory to make cigarettes at Underwood Street, close to the newly opened City Road factory of Carreras. The following year, 1914, Louis Rothman founded a new, but doomed, partnership with a life-long friend, Marcus Weinberg, forming the Yenidje Tobacco Company.

The society clients of Rothman were just the people that Buck Duke, the often rough-tongued former country boy, now felt he needed around him. In England, businessmen were the new aristocracy, respected for their contribution to the nation's industrial power. He began to buy in London art markets, and English society friends introduced him into their circles. The habit of smoking had Royal favour and cigarettes were increasingly acceptable in most drawing rooms and many public places. To be an American tobacco tycoon in the England of 1914 invited no sniggers, as it had in the past, and to be an apparently successful one even drew admiration. Prejudice against Yankees as figures of fun was fast vanishing with the rise of the American industrial machine and her emerging culture, often free of the worst features of European snobbery, and which reflected a freshness of thought and knowledge that was long overdue. Just how out of date and uncivilised the Europeans had become was to be demonstrated when they went to war in August 1914.

As if to demonstrate his desire to be adopted into English high society early in that tragic year, Buck Duke decided to find a London home. On 9th January 1914, *The Times* carried the following item:

THE TENANT OF CREWE HOUSE

Lord Crewe has let Crewe House, Curzon Street, to Mr J. B. Duke, the American tobacco merchant, for some months.

There is, we are informed, no question of purchasing.

The last paragraph of the short news item was not quite true. Duke's lease of one of Mayfair's most distinguished houses included an option after six months to buy the property on appropriate terms. Before he had settled in properly, Britain's attempts at mediation in Central Europe failed and 'the lights went out'. As a generation of young men enlisted for the slaughter in foreign fields, Americans in London found themselves suddenly isolated, bewildered by events. They instinctively sought to get back home across a sea that would prove a life-line to England in two World Wars. Buck Duke had no wish to be trapped within an economy placed on a war footing, and first reports were that the New York stock and money markets, inextricably intertwined with the great City of London financial machine, had fallen into immediate disarray. Worried investors were going liquid, and Duke desperately wanted to get back to protect his fortune by large purchases of gold and conversions of holdings into currency. Atlantic steamship offices were besieged by anxious Americans and not even Duke's wealth could help obtain a ticket. It was only with the intervention of the United States Ambassador, Walter H. Page, the man with whom Duke had once had a childhood fight, that he gained one of the few remaining places on an outgoing liner. His behaviour at this time caused so much comment—in America his every action was still big news, especially in the newspapers of the Bright tobacco belt—that there was speculation that Duke might even be thinking of taking British citizenship.

An associate issued a statement on his behalf stressing that as Duke 'found nothing attractive' in managing any of the smaller companies after the dissolution of the Trust, he had received a satisfactory proposition from BAT to serve as chairman, requiring him to spend six months a year overseas. Duke himself wrote a letter in September 1914 saying he had 'too much at stake' and 'too much hope in the future of American business and commerce to ever cease to be a citizen of the United States'. He went on: 'The result is that as soon as I could, after war was declared, I hurried home, because my first interest was here, and have since been giving my whole time to the situation, which demands the best of all of us.'

From this moment on, the ambitions of James Buchanan Duke seemed to shrivel as far as the tobacco industry was concerned. Share interests, of course, were to keep him well rewarded, and he kept an investor's eye on things. But new ambitions were to blossom during the years of war economies and tight central government controls on tobacco supply. He would plunge ever deeper into the power industry, textiles, and finally aluminium. Like a homing-pigeon, he would find himself drawn back towards the Piedmont region that knew him as a child and then embryo tycoon, devoting vast sums to higher education which one day would result in his statue scanning the campus of Duke University. In England, Duke's name would begin to fade from memory through the weary years of 1914–18.

The British tobacco industry had enough problems without worrying about Duke.

The outbreak of war in Europe had halved the price of tobacco in the markets of South Carolina, for Imperial had to withdraw purchasing as the buying season began until head office clarified its future requirements and assessed the implications. Buying soon resumed, for tobacco was to prove an indispensable commodity in wartime, and Imperial began to stockpile, financing the holdings locally to ease Britain's precious dollar reserves. Prices rose steadily. Whereas at one time in 1914 a price of $8\frac{1}{2}$ cents per lb was recorded, the basic cost would touch as high as $1 per lb. Farmers raised their crops as part of the war effort, stimulated further by the United States' declaration of war on Germany on 6th April 1917.

America was supplying up to 90 per cent or more of Britain's imports of unmanufactured tobacco during these years and continued to do so even as German warships and new submarines attacked the merchant ships that kept the 'hogsheads' flowing. Soldiers were heavy consumers* and the cigarette habit was to be cultivated beyond the wildest estimations of the manufacturers. In only one of the war years did supplies fall below 139,000 million lb—1917, when only 40,789 million lb arrived across the dangerous Atlantic waters. That stocks were built up cannot be doubted, for in 1918, the year of the Armistice, imports from the United States totalled an impressive 162,928 million lb (some 95 per cent of all imports of tobacco) whereas in 1919 the total rose mightily to 315,933 million lb—a figure not to be surpassed until 1946, when another war had just ended.

Some 8,000 million cigarettes were being smoked in Britain. Some 334 tobacco manufacturers' licences were held and some 401,872 dealers' licences issued by Customs and Excise. The war necessitated higher taxation and a 1s 10d per lb rise in September 1915 caused no surprise. But a further advance by Bonar Law of 1s 10d per lb in May 1917 met such a storm of protest that the Exchequer halved the rise, bringing the standard rate of duty to 6s 5d. April 1918 brought another advance, to 8s 2d (where it stayed for the next nine years).

The war brought its changes. There were few controls until 1917, when a Tobacco Control Board was set up after the Board of Trade made an Order under the Defence of the Realm Act. The Board set maximum prices for tobacco goods and restricted withdrawals of leaf from bond until the beginning of 1919. An advisory committee drawn from the trade assisted the Board in rationing supplies at levels not exceeding 1916 deliveries. During the war, manufacturers formed themselves into the Council of Tobacco Manufacturers of Great Britain and Ireland, and the National

* General Pershing once cabled the United States Government: 'Tobacco is as indispensable as the daily ration—we must have thousands of tons of it without delay.'

Union of Retail Tobacconists was born. Stocks fell badly in 1917, even rationing was contemplated. However, production controls were introduced.

The name of Wills was rarely off the lips of servicemen. Woodbines* were the most popular brand, and became part of military language. A five-funnelled cruiser at Gallipoli was dubbed the 'Packet of Woodbines'. In the trenches, a certain Army padre, the Rev. G. A. Studdert-Kennedy, earned his place in history with the affectionate nickname 'Woodbine Willie', distributing cigarettes with his prayers and comfort. The War Office saw to it that soldiers rarely went without the crumpled packs carried close to thousands of brave breasts in battledress pockets. The Wills branch of Imperial sold over 3.6 million lb of cigarettes in the Great War on War Office contracts, with tenders first invited in 1916. Even Harry Wills dutifully came out of retirement to re-enter management, heavily depleted as were all tobacco manufacturers' staff by service recruiting. Factories were so busy that there was some talk of profiteering. Player's found the war demand such that its cigarette manufacture rose sharply and, by the conclusion, was making over 20 per cent of Imperial's total cigarette supplies.

Militaristic themes had always been a feature of cigarette cards prior to 1914, but the Great War saw the cards being used deliberately for information and propaganda purposes. Recruiting slogans and a series of Punch cartoons attacking the Kaiser and his bloody deeds helped the war effort. There were patriotic scenes, such as the 'Old Contemptible' taking his farewell in his humble home, with the words:

> 'The bugle calls—"To arms" the cry
> 'A farewell kiss—A fond good-bye,
> 'No tears—brave soul, tho' rent her heart,
> 'Duty and honour bid them part.'

German nationals featuring on a series of Musical Celebrities were removed.

The conflict inevitably brought its shortages of raw materials, and by 1918 tobacco producers had to cease issuing cigarette cards for four years. But much earlier there were other difficulties. A

---

* The famous 'penny for five' price, set when Woodbines first appeared in 1888, vanished in September 1915 when it was raised to 1¼d and then 1¾d by the end of the war.

major part of Imperial's requirements of cigarette tissues and waxed papers came from French mills, so alternative arrangements for total needs were made with the Robert Fletcher paper processing company, in which the British tobacco combine took a majority shareholding in 1918, buying the rest of the shares seventeen years later. Fletcher worked happily alongside the newly established St Anne's Board Mill and Ashton Containers, another Imperial concern—making packing cases from timber supplied by a Bristol saw mill. Timber was a problem, and the war years saw match-makers moving into Brazil.

One company whose development was severely frustrated was the newly formed Molins Machine Company. The brothers Walter and Harold Molins, as well as their leading British-born employees, now had to withdraw from the United Cigarette Machines' German factory in Dresden, where they had been working on automatic packing machines, used by Wills for Gold Flake's paper packaging. In 1919 they would move into a small, derelict factory in Deptford, four years later buying out their American partners, United, and subsequently becoming the major force in British machinery manufacturing, firmly backed by both Imperial and BAT.

Patriotic advertising was not the prerogative of Imperial. Carreras, for example, engaged in widespread flag waving, and even sent pocket dictionaries and phrase books to the troops in France. Large quantities of cigarettes were given away to soldiers, helping to spread the habit as well as to bring comfort to those already familiar with cigarettes.

Just before the outbreak of war, Carreras sought to widen its base by emulating Rothman, buying itself a prestige firm of tobacco merchants, Alexander Boguslavsky & Company, and opening a showroom at 55 Piccadilly. There were, nevertheless, difficulties being experienced in this prestige sector by Louis Rothman, who found trade in special smoking tobacco blends and expensive handmade cigarettes somewhat confused. Wartime conditions increased the demand for low-cost cigarettes, especially low-cost Virginia brands, while supplies of Turkish tobacco, much used by Rothman's, were restricted. It did not take him long to decide where his trade had to be secured in the future.

Unfortunately, while Rothman advocated the mass production of Virginian cigarettes, his new partner, Marcus Weinberg, 'took the other viewpoint'. There were other differences of opinion, stemming from their conflicting personalities, which made it obvious the partnership could not continue. A court action followed in 1916, which created a precedent in English law whereby a thriving concern had to be compulsorily wound up by court order. The court decreed that the business should be offered for sale to each partner. The following year came the auction and, at the last minute, Rothman bid in guineas instead of pounds, securing control when his tender came out some £250 higher than Weinberg's offer. Louis took his son into apprenticeship determined to secure future family control with his policy of a switch to mass production to capitalise on his prestigious skills in tobacco blending.

The work of the Tobacco Control Board ushered in the era of Government intervention, which would, from then on, vary from swingeing changes in duty to health regulations. But no immediate need to impose restraints on the industry was foreseen in Whitehall in 1919. Indeed, a tobacco sub-committee of the Standing Committee on Trusts under the chairmanship of Mr Sidney Webb (later Lord Passfield) reported that year that the Imperial combination was not acting against the public interest. It commented that 'down to this date, the existence of the Imperial Tobacco Company, with its present policy, has not resulted in raising the price of tobacco or cigarettes to the consumer; but on the contrary has tended in the opposite direction'. It went on, 'Nor have we discovered that the Imperial Tobacco Company has so far exercised any injurious influence on the trade.'

These shining words contrasted sharply with American Tobacco's damning experience at the hands of the anti-trust authorities of the United States eight years before. The Control Board was abolished, and Imperial's chairman, George Wills, turned his directors' attention to the problems of peacetime competition and in particular soaring leaf prices.

The Exchequer was sensitive to the currency costs of United States leaf. The war had cost reserves dear, and the economy was moving into depression years, culminating in the General Strike of 1926. To ease the cost, the Government, which through 1919 saw United States leaf imports nearly double in weight on the previous twelve months as manufacturers restocked their bonded warehouses, decided in the September to discriminate against American supplies. A preferential rate of duty on unmanufactured

Empire tobacco imports was now introduced at five-sixths of the standard rate of 8s 2d per lb, lasting for six years when it was cut to three-quarters.

The move was to cause unexpected competitive forces to play upon Imperial which by 1920 controlled 91 per cent of the developing cigarette trade, then representing half of total consumption of tobacco. Overall, Imperial controlled 73 per cent of total trade in tobacco products.

The incentive to use leaf from Empire sources such as Nyasaland, Rhodesia, India, and Canada, was tempered by the smokers' existing preference for American Virginian leaf. Crops were often experimental and often of a poor quality, with aromas and flavour that could be readily detected. Growers, attempting to find markets for their plantings, were, however, making good progress with curing and supply systems. They knew, too, that only the year before, in 1918, the standard unmanufactured tobacco duty was raised very heavily, so raising substantially the costs of British manufacturers dependent on American leaf. Wills alone needed over 40 million lb a year and to offset higher production materials costs raised the price of cigarettes in 1920, with the brand leader Woodbine going up to 2d for five. Imperial, while cautiously encouraging Rhodesian and Canadian growers, did not rush to buy Empire leaf. There were not sufficient supplies of the right quality available, and the substantial investment in the American Leaf Organisation had to be protected. Another element in the situation was that Virginian prices were falling rapidly after the war demand and Georgian farmers were planting heavily to swell crops. American farmers were restless and setting up cooperatives. Their discontent helped prompt a Federal Trade Commission investigation into the tobacco industry to check up on whether monopoly abuses were reviving.

The preferentially priced Empire tobacco, therefore, tended to appeal more to the smaller manufacturers, now worrying how to survive in economic depression, without Imperial's resources of money and established range of popular brands. Both Godfrey Phillips and Carreras in 1919 introduced 'loyalty' bonus schemes for their retailers and wholesalers, and Rothman began advertising. The common marketing problem was the accelerating decline in sales of pipe tobacco, and it became clear, if by now there were any doubts left, that cigarettes, more profitable anyway with the right machinery, were the battle-ground for securing future growth.

The machinery industry was looking for new business. Molins had moved into its factory in Deptford in 1919, and in the same year the American Machine and Foundry Company set up a British subsidiary to expand sales of its increasingly successful Standard machine, which had been imported for some years. Imperial had been turning away from its famous Bonsacks to Standards and displaying customary shrewdness had, during the war years, taken a joint research interest with BAT in the Bristol engineers, Brecknell, Munro & Rogers, who started making the Standard under licence. The interest in Brecknell became a majority holding in 1920 and the new owners helped to improve the Standard specifications. There were other suppliers of rival machines. United Cigarette's established Triumph was a notable challenger to the Standards, Barons, and Bonsacks.

Imperial was expecting a new marketing attack. When it came, its executive committee was somewhat off balance, due partly to the determined competition developing between its Player's and Wills branches, placing the latter's four hundred expensive machines at some risk.

The thrust came from Carreras, who introduced Craven A, an immediately successful brand, and stepped up the Black Cat coupon promotion. Imperial were disturbed more by this thrust than by the casual action of Louis Rothman, whose son, Sydney, had entered the business, in marketing Mr Rothman's Own cigarettes, offered in discreet plain boxes and made from the finest golden bright Virginia. The discovery of a hogshead of leaf tobacco that had been overlooked in a dockside warehouse, during the war years—maturing to a rich colour and flavour—had given Rothman the idea of offering a very expensive brand. By adding other long-matured tobaccos to the original hogshead, he created 'the Napoleon brandy' of cigarette smoking. But it was a diversion, for the wily West End tobacco merchant was secretly planning something else—the Rothman Diary Service.

Pall Mall had become a familiar name through advertising after the Great War. In 1921, with twenty-five machines in his re-organised factory Rothman introduced Marksman Virginia and what he lacked were outlets; Imperial and others had a grip on the retail trade that would be expensive to ease. His Diary Service was a postal scheme that reached smokers direct and offered them low prices for bulk orders of one hundred cigarettes or more. In 1922, he gained 14,000 regular clients and changed the name to the Rothman Direct-to-Smoker Service. More brands were introduced, including, rather significantly, Rothman Rhodesian Virginia cigarettes.*

The direct selling contributed to a fresh outbreak of price cutting among retailers that increased to a pitch that not even the formation by some manufacturers, wholesalers and traders of the Tobacco Trade Advisory Committee could stop. Within Imperial, Player's seemed to gain so much ground on Wills, the dominant branch, that the co-ordinating committee began to think about revisions of organisation and structure. Wills faced some of its sales problems by seeking expansion in Ireland, starting manufacturing in Dublin in 1923, but were to be followed by Player's in this market the following year. Sir George Wills, honoured with a Baronetcy in 1923, began to think about retirement to make way for fresh leadership. An honour was a just reward for his charitable donations, and in the United States Duke, somewhat envious, had to content himself in 1924 with the creation of an £8 million ($40 million) trust fund to establish his University at Durham, North Carolina. Three-quarters of his holdings in the Southern Power Company made up a large part of the parcel of securities for the fund. He was not alone in his generosity for the day before George Eastman, founder of Eastman Kodak,† gave away $3 million to help American education.

The BAT exporting enterprise had progressed well on the lines laid down by Duke and with the mix of new and existing brand names built up in Britain and America. In March 1914, it had offered 1.4 million Cumulative 5 per cent Preference shares of £1 each at a premium of just 9d. It had factories in Britain and the United States and many depots round the world which bought up local firms or promoted many new companies. The share offer brought the capital up to its authorised Preference share ceiling of £4.5 million, but only £6,254,320 of £1 Ordinary shares were issued against the authorised capital of £10 million Ordinary.

* Imperial rigidly enforced until 1959 a rule that no tobacco packaging could carry the description Virginia unless the brand was made exclusively from leaf supplied from Virginia, the Carolinas, Georgia or Florida.

† Eastman Kodak was to be involved in cigarette filter development.

Though American Tobacco had to sell its interest in BAT after the 1911 Anti-Trust decree, Duke had a personal holding and Imperial had its original founder's half share in the shares, stemming from the peace settlement of 1902. The growth of BAT from its early years can be seen as follows:

Year ended 30th September	Audited profits	Dividend on Ordinary shares
1905	£ 711,483	12 per cent
1906	£ 751,780	14 per cent
1907	£1,031,325	23 per cent
1908	£1,062,729	23 per cent
1909	£ 930,647	19½ per cent
1910	£1,358,384	31 per cent
1911	£1,655,880	37½ per cent
1912	£1,981,159	26½ per cent
1913	£2,151,836	27½ per cent

Not even the big Buck Duke would dare imagine, after all that had happened, that BAT was destined to become a leviathan, the world's biggest tobacco firm with sales of 950 brands worth well over £1,800 million, yielding more than £156 million profits from 140 factories in 54 countries. Yet there were signs of the fantastic growth to come to be read in the figures after the difficult war years. The board in the summer of 1919 issued the rest of the Ordinary shares through a group of London and New York banks with Treasury approval, under the remaining Defence of the Realm regulations which licensed capital raising. Existing shareholders had preference, which increased Imperial's holding, but first a block of 141,000 shares (leaving 2,131,773) was neatly divided up among the directors and the head of the subsidiary Export Leaf Tobacco Company.

But within a matter of months the BAT board, claiming that the increasing cost of leaf, labour and general production was causing difficulties, were convening an extraordinary general meeting to raise the capital, now said to be insufficient, by an extra 5,500,000 Ordinary shares. Existing shareholders were to get one for every two already held. Imperial's stake grew fatter, even if it protested BAT's independence of action. In 1960 Imperial would hold £13,557,389 of the BAT Ordinary issued stock of £47,515,522, when its Ordinary dividend payments were heading towards the £12 million total mark.

The pointers to BAT's export-orientated growth were there at the end of 1924 as Sir George handed over his chairmanship of the Imperial combine to Sir Gilbert Alan Hamilton Wills, Bt, son of Sir Frederick, and who, like the founder chairman Lord Winterstoke, was to join the peerage as the first Lord Dulverton, holding the reins of Imperial until March 1947. BAT's cigarette sales by number had broken the magic 50,000 million by 1923. This compared with 10,000 million in 1910 and 25,000 million in 1915. The measure of the 1923 figure is that British consumption, the world's second largest national market and denied to BAT, was in that year 33,725 million cigarettes and not to pass the 50,000 million level for another ten years.

Statistics were becoming important to the tobacco manufacturers who wanted to measure their performance and develop better research into brands. What they told in 1924 was not encouraging, and explained the persistent price cutting among retailers, many of whom went out of business when their accounts went awry. In 1920, consumption of cigarettes (by weight) was 80.3 million lb and other smoking tobacco 70.3 million lb. Four years later the corresponding figures were 75.1 million lb and 58 million lb respectively, both down, but showing the proportionate swing to cigarettes within the total tobacco consumption.

What intrigued Imperial's early economists and market researchers was how Empire preference was working, for competitors were increasingly turning to Empire leaf, grown from acclimatised American seed and fast becoming more suitable for cigarette, as well as pipe tobacco, production. Whereas the Empire supplied in 1921 only $7\frac{1}{2}$ million lb out of the 228 million lb imported, it supplied around 18 million lb out of 182 million lb in 1924 (raising it to 41 million lb out of 222 million lb in 1927).

It seemed an ironic time for Imperial to open new headquarters for its American Leaf Organisation, described by one newspaper as 'one of the ornaments' of Richmond, Virginia. Of course, Imperial had given some help to Nyasaland growers and was contemplating trends. Its branches were too much preoccupied with the pressing domestic problem of proliferating brands from competitors, such as the new one introduced by Godfrey Phillips in 1924 called Army Club, to fortify its growing success in cigarette making. Phillips was also buying wholesale and retail interests. More than a few brands, including the newest, were utilising mixtures of American and Empire leaf, and costs were lowered when public acceptance was gained for pioneering all-Empire brands. Imperial had begun 1924 by giving its Ogden branch the British trade in the brands of the William Clarke & Son branch which was then transferred to Dublin. With the formation of the Irish Free State, it would work alongside Wills and Player's in undermining Gallaher's market hold.

Such reorganisation was perhaps necessary, but it served to divert central management attention away from the more important requirements at this time, such as that of protecting the mighty Wills branch which had just done a deal with the Molins Company for a score of fast packing machines for Woodbine. Wills and its brands were vulnerable because in times of depressed consumption trade had to be taken from the market leader if others were to grow. Craven A and Black Cat, for example, were gaining sales very rapidly and the Carreras directors were drafting plans for a big new factory eventually to emerge as the famous Arcadia Works at Mornington Crescent, London. It would make these and other brands, notably Piccadilly and Turf. Unfortunately the Wills management examined, but rejected, the idea of putting up a direct competitor to the Black Cat coupon brand, involving a brand called Autograph. Something had to be done. Player's was obtaining growth, helped by Weights and Player's Medium. There were four hundred machines at Wills capable of producing six hundred cigarettes a minute. This was a massive investment needing protection. Even Gallaher's Park Drive was creaming off valuable sales. There were rumours, well founded, that J. Wix, the Kensitas producer, was proposing to launch a coupon trading scheme, which it did in 1926.

But three months before that year arrived bringing as it did a worsening of economic depression, a General Strike, and the intensification of a tobacco price war, there came news from the United States of the death of a man with a manufacturing record the like of which the world tobacco trade could never see again—James Buchanan Duke.

The pigeon-toed Duke, aided by a heavy stick, had spent some of the last months of his life planning the unbuilt University that would bear his name and stand in a 5,000-acre pine forest a few miles from Durham, near the old Methodist institution, Trinity College, onto which his father had showered a fortune. Buck

Duke's endowment trust swelled on his death under clauses to his will and would pass the $120 million mark. At his New York home where he worked to the end, though stricken by pernicious anaemia, Duke finally died of bronco-pneumonia on 10th October 1925.

The boy pedlar, who flayed tobacco in a log cabin on his father's humble farm in North Carolina, was said by *The Times* to have left a fortune, besides his benefactions, worth £30 million. That newspaper's New York correspondent recalled Duke saying of himself: 'I have succeeded in business not because I have more natural ability than many people who have succeeded, but because I have applied myself harder and stuck at it longer.' There were plenty of grand eulogies as his body was carried by a special train to the tobacco region from which he sprang, finally resting in a family tomb alongside his father and other relatives at Maplewood Cemetery. Yet his last months had been far from happy. His plans for developing Duke University had their critics. His former wife, Lillian, had lost her £90,000 fortune at the hands of a society swindler and destitute she had sought to prove in court their divorce was illegal. Still no one could dispute his place in business history as the first Titan of Tobacco. His giant frame dominated those around him and that he should have resorted to the unlawful was a most unnecessary act for a man endowed with talents that his rivals should have tested fully in fair competitive struggle.

But the years when Duke strove to eliminate and to restrain competition were now passing into the shadows. The irony of 1925 was that price competition was flourishing once again on both sides of the Atlantic. And the combinations of Imperial and British American Tobacco, creatures born out of the strife he created, had at his death escaped unscathed from anti-monopoly forces. Indeed, just a few months after Duke's death, the Federal Trade Commission, reporting on Imperial Tobacco, checked up on relations with the dismembered American Tobacco and reassured the United States Senate that each was operating autonomously, and that there were only 1,245 American shareholders in the Imperial group, only five of whom held more than 100,000 shares.

That new and fiercely competitive forces had been unleashed in the United States market in the period between dissolution of Duke's Trust and his death was very evident to every American smoker. The Reynolds, Liggett & Myers, Lorillard, and American

Tobacco enterprises were locked in a marketing battle of national dimensions, a struggle which finally established cigarettes as the first choice of American smokers. Holding good his promise to 'give Buck Duke hell', Richard Joshua Reynolds had launched several cigarette brands, such as Reyno and Osman. They included one offered in 1913 in the Cleveland sales territory featuring the motif of Old Joe, a dromedary owned by the Barnum and Bailey circus. The brand, a blend of fine cured Bright, sweet Burley and some Turkish leaf, was called Camel, priced at 10 cents for twenty. Soon the nation's tobacco stores were queueing for stocks as smokers saw local advertisements heralding the new brand: *'Camels! Tomorrow there will be more Camels in this town than in all Asia and Africa combined.'*

Duke had outlived Reynolds by seven years. But that was time enough for him to see the dramatic change in cigarette marketing which flowed from Reynolds' Camel brand. It gave Reynolds no less than 40 per cent of the nation's cigarette consumption by the end of the Great War. Camels were firm, well-blended machine-made cigarettes. They were well named, for smokers seemed to prefer exotic names, even if some Turkish cigarettes were sham, oval-shaped blends selling alongside the genuine mixtures of Oriental and Turkish leaf. There was such a proliferation of names— at least fifty brands—that Camels, easy to say and remember, enjoyed an immediate acceptance. Reynolds had set out to establish Camels as a national favourite, taking on American Tobacco's Omar, Lorillard's Zubelda, and Liggett & Myers' pioneering paper cup-packeted Fatimas. Camels stood out amid the Deities, Moguls, Murads, Helmars, Meccas and Hassans. The Cairo, Zira, Oasis, Muriel and Condax brands were others to feel the competitive challenge. Turkish-type cigarettes had continued to sell well in spite of such bright Virginian brands as Sweet Caporals, Piedmont, Home Run and Picayune, among others.

Part of the reason for Camels' popularity was its bridging the gap between aromatic Turkish cigarettes and mild flue-cured bright American leaf products. Their markedly slow burning quality gave smokers a feeling of value for the price (twenty for 10 cents). Very heavy one-brand advertising by Reynolds stressed quality and emphasised that no gifts, coupons, or cards were offered because of the quality tobacco. Within two years of their introduction, some 2.4 billion Camels were bought in 1915, and a further 10 billion the following year, when American Tobacco, stunned by the challenge, hit back.

Percival Hill,* of American Tobacco, and his son George, had their chemists take the Camel's recipe apart and then decided to revive a brand name, used for chewing plug popularised during the Gold Rush, Lucky Strike. An attractive pack was designed, with a bull's eye target symbol, and the promotional campaign began with the slogan 'Lucky Strike—It's Toasted'. (Heat is commonly used in cigarette processing.)

Not to be outdone, Liggett & Myers improved its Chesterfield brand as a direct answer to both Camels and Lucky Strike, dropping slide box packaging for paper wrapping. 'They satisfy' was the simple claim. Battle was joined. Soon the nation was entreated to 'walk a mile for a Camel', or women to follow the example of a female opera star (who later recanted her testimonial) in the elegant choice of a Lucky Strike. Salesmen whispered nasty tales about rivals' products and advertising agencies waxed fat on the billings that were worth more than the value of the tobacco crops that made it all possible. With Reynolds dead and his well-rewarded executives rich beyond belief, young George Hill was to close rapidly on the lead of Camel. Domestic tobacco production boomed, helped by the wartime blockade on rival leaf from overseas. The age of standard machine brands began with advertising that grew ever more strident and would eventually dominate commercial radio.

The famed Duke was not the only giant to pass in a crescendo of competitive activity on each side of the Atlantic. In 1926, Louis Rothman died, and the following year Tom Gallaher went, too, aged eighty-seven. Sir George Wills went the next summer, leaving a £10 million fortune. The tobacco industry would never see such commanding figures again, even though George Washington Hill might lay good claim to the title of being among the last of the tobacco titans.

The establishment of the Anglo-American tobacco industry might be less than complete. Yet the statistical record indicates the dramatic growth which these and other pioneers of the machine era stimulated, helped by a world war that had made cigarette smoking not smart and fashionable, but commonplace and addictive.

* Percival Hill died in the same year as Buck Duke.

	United Kingdom		United States	
		Total tobacco		Total tobacco
	Cigarettes	products	Cigarettes	products
	(millions)	(million lb)	(millions)	(million lb)
1920	36,240	153.2	44,656	658.4
1925	36,030	140.8	79,976	715.8

The lack of dramatic growth over this period in the British market—it dipped to 33,725 million cigarettes in 1923—was due to the economic depression that contained consumer spending power. However, the fact that the market was held had been due to the emergence of new competitive forces in struggles that were not far removed from survival instincts. That Imperial found it necessary in July 1925 to sign an agreement with the Savoy Hotel Ltd to pay the hoteliers £2,000 a year not to sell any other Virginian brands except its own products was of little consequence to those unemployed men who had begun a not uncommon practice of buying their cigarettes 'on the slate', or singly, from an understanding corner shop.

Industrialisation had, of course, spread trade unionism in the struggle to improve conditions. The British tobacco industry had witnessed its growth at first hand. In 1925, the United Kingdom Operative Tobacconists Society was to change its name to the Tobacco Workers' Union, appointing the first full-time salaried general secretary, Andrew Boyd—such was the growth in membership. One reason for the high level of recruitment at this time had been a decision at the end of the 1914–18 war to extend representation from the skilled crafts of spinners, cutters and stovers to the hundreds of women operatives brought into factories as machines replaced craftsmen. A separate Cigarette Machine Operators Society had already been created with the advent of machinery.

The origin of the union was from the pipe tobacco trade, where craftsmen had formed themselves in 1834 into the Friendly Society of Operative Tobacconists, two years after repeal of the Combination Acts that forced groups of workers to organise themselves in secret. The numbers of skilled members was then small, all having to serve rigid apprenticeships. Any trade vacancies were only granted to the sons of journeymen, the craftsmen who had completed apprenticeships. Their original skills were the blending of tobacco by spinning leaf for pipe smoking. The spinners employed their own boys to open casks of leaf and to turn the spinning wheels. Craftsmen did not work for one employer, but jobbed from one place to another, often travelling long distances. It was quite usual for an employer to contact the society if they required a particular journeyman. Membership spread from the London area to the provinces and to Scotland and Ireland. The name changed in 1836 to the United Tobacconists Society, becoming the United Kingdom Operative Tobacconists some forty-five years later to allow in the hand makers following the steady introduction of cigarettes. Following the creation of the industrial union, one of the first, bargaining power increased immensely and by 1920 the Tobacco Trade Board had been established; a year afterwards the Imperial Tobacco Company made an agreement for minimum wage rates for all tobacco workers in all unions serving the industry. It was the first national agreement of its kind in any industry, and even resulted in the union being called before the Trades Union Congress, which wanted to stop recruitment from craft unions—a move that resulted in disaffiliation by the Tobacco Workers' Union.

In due course, the National Cigar and Tobacco Workers' Union would amalgamate with the Tobacco Workers' Union some ten years after re-affiliation to the Trades Union Congress in 1936, when the idea of industrial as opposed to craft unions was belatedly seen as the future by the movement's leaders. During the 1926 General Strike, the Tobacco Workers' Union was not directly involved, but the employers were forced to pay half of wages lost through the widespread short-time working which resulted from flagging demand for cigarettes. Members collected nearly £2,000 for strike relief funds.

CHAPTER NINE

Machinery with Strings

Hunger marches and the General Strike of 1926 were viewed with alarm by the men who marketed tobacco in Britain. They deplored the outbreaks of defiance as labour organised itself to win better times and a fairer distribution of wealth, though some tobacco workers had long organised themselves into societies and a union. Yet they knew from their travellers' sales returns that the new mass market for cigarettes was being placed in jeopardy. For this reason, price cutting and gift incentive schemes were seen as temporary measures to stimulate flagging demand. Efforts to impose resale price maintenance and guaranteed profit margins had been somewhat desultory but as earnings declined, so a few leading manufacturers would make fresh efforts to impose their past control.

Distribution systems were disrupted and, in many areas, retailers arranged to call at factories or wholesale depots to pick up stocks. Often their orders were small, a reflection of the lower rate of consumer spending.

Growth in sales had to be fought for, and, naturally, managements looked to their overseas markets for some compensatory expansion. For some time, BAT had been studying, with the care of the covetous, the affairs of the Ardath Tobacco Company, founded in 1895 but not incorporated until 1912. The reason for the interest was the fact that now, three years after attaining formal company status, Ardath was exporting 84 per cent of its production. The lusty, if small, rival to BAT had to be annexed, but how? The agreement with Imperial barred BAT from entering the home market, which would be involved in a take-over. Talks ensued between the two interlocking groups, which always denied collusion and declared themselves bound to the principle of independent management. Consequently, BAT asked Lord Dulverton and his board-room colleagues at Imperial to buy Ardath on a joint basis. The request was well received. Although Imperial can trace no other reason for the Ardath take-over, there is some evidence that the business was considered as helpful for future use in putting an end to coupon trading without directly involving the Wills or Player's branches, whose profitability was threatened by the erosion of loyalty to their brands.

The two groups linked up by forming a new holding company called the Universal Tobacco Company to buy Ardath, which was wound up in 1926. Universal retained the Ardath trading name and had a nominal capital of £6 million, with the holding company commanding all the important Ordinary shares of £3 million. Some £1.4 million of the £3 million Preference shares were held on the open market. The principal shareholding was halved and Imperial's share was put in the nominee name of Ardath's chairman.* A small advisory group was set up to exercise surveillance on general policy. It was a good deal, for Imperial was to receive half the profits, most of which were earned in overseas markets where BAT was allowed to influence policy without reference to Imperial, which had a similar freedom for the home market. A half-yearly bonus scheme was introduced for home trade customers, for Ardath's sales in Britain were a meagre 0.5 per cent of the total cigarette market.

Within a year Ardath would give Britain's smokers their fifth coupon-bearing cigarette brand, for in 1927 there were four well-established gift brands made by as many separate concerns and commanding around 4 per cent of all cigarette consumption. Among these was the family business of J. Wix & Sons, founded in 1901 and given limited company status a year later. There were persistent rumours, as the Ardath deal went through, that an American tobacco manufacturer was interested in Wix. They were dismissed as sensational and beyond credibility, for the British tobacco market was in a period of turbulence due to economic conditions, such as the serious unemployment that constrained the growth of consumption. Anyway, no American producer would

* Replaced six years later by BAT acting on Imperial's behalf.

surely dare return to Britain after the events at the turn of the century.

Price competition was becoming such a severe headache, even for some of the perpetrators, that in 1926 a group of British manufacturers (excluding the mighty Imperial) met with various retail and wholesale interests and formed the Tobacco Trade Advisory Committee which included Gallaher, Carreras, and Godfrey Phillips. They decided to introduce a 'stop list' which would cut off supplies from traders selling at below list prices. A rise in standard tobacco duty to 8s 10d per lb confused pricing policy. For its part, Imperial was busy on other significant matters, in addition to the Ardath negotiations, evaluating a new cigarette-making machine developed by Molins, the Mark I. Imperial's engineers were as excited as its salesmen were apprehensive. Molins had advanced greatly the technology of packing and general machinery, helped by Imperial's buying and patent controls. There was even a £10,000 mortgage advance from the tobacco giant and Molins put it to use in designing its first high-speed cigarette-making machine. The salesmen of Wills and Player's were apprehensive when they learned of the Mark I's capabilities. Its main feature was a running speed of 1,000 cigarettes per minute compared with 600–800 for the Standard Triumph and 800 for AMF's latest model.

Such a machine in the wrong hands would threaten the group very quickly. Wills alone had 400 expensive machines currently in action with average top speeds of 600 cigarettes a minute. Something had to be done, and quickly. Meanwhile, Imperial was securing and expanding its lines of tobacco leaf supply. Its sheer size, however, made the total operation vulnerable to competitors who had to grow in this period at each other's expense. Management nerves were becoming taut as 1927 brought a rush of important events.

Evidence of strains is provided by a dispute between Wills and Player's, with the former disputing the latter's decision to offer its growing Weights brand in packets of ten with cigarette cards when they had always been marketed in fives and had given little trouble to Woodbines, whose sales were more depressed by competition from outside the group. Wills' share of the national cigarette trade, while still very large, was nevertheless now the lowest for six or seven years. Imperial's management committee, with much else occupying its attention, simply told the quarrelling branches to get on with competing hard to protect the group.

That year, 1927, can be singled out for particular study, for development of the British industry then flowed to a new watershed. As if to reinforce the United States Senate report from the Federal Trade Commission, declaring that Imperial and American Tobacco were independent, the truncated successor to the Duke trust decided to re-enter the British market. George Washington Hill, who had demonstrated his ability by the launching of Lucky Strike to save American Tobacco from extinction by Reynolds, negotiated the acquisition of the coupon-giving J. Wix & Sons, then holding less than 2 per cent of the cigarette market. History seemed to be turning back the clock, at least to some, but Imperial was not immediately concerned since it was in a position to flex some muscle. What was obvious to all was that the original peace pact had been irrevocably torn up, and confirmed to be so by the Wix take-over. American Tobacco, it will be recalled, had agreed to stay out of the British market if Imperial stayed out of its backyard, a deal turning on the collaboration in forming the BAT export company.

There now came a tit-for-tat. For BAT had refrained from intervening too directly in the United States market, but now its board decided to try its hand against the Lucky Strikes, Camels, and Chesterfields. To do this, they bought Brown & Williamson, formed in Winston-Salem as a small snuff and plug firm ('Bloodhound, a dog-gone good chew') by merchants Robert Williamson and George Brown when holding a stock of 100,000 lb. BAT lost no time in introducing machine-made cigarettes to the firm's sales lists, notably a coupon brand called Sir Walter Raleigh and 10-cent packs named Wings and Avalon. Yet to come were the mentholated Kool brand and the filter-tipped Viceroy. The purchase of Brown & Williamson—the contract was signed on 1st March 1927—was to prove, many years later, a fortuitous one.

At first, BAT set out to carve its United States market niche by concentrating on speciality cigarettes and began experimenting with cork and other tips for filters to give a milder, tar-free cigarette smoke. This was novel, but not quite new. For some years processes for filters using crepe paper filler, sometimes with a cellulose wadding, had been available from a Hungarian inventor,

Boris Aivaz, and the marketing of the first Aivaz filter cigarettes was tested in Switzerland with some success. Gallaher showed interest in being licensed, but it was to be a fledgling company, Peter Jackson, that gave Britain its first filter brand, du Maurier, introduced in 1929, one year after the sons of Julius Wix quit American Tobacco's new subsidiary, J. Wix & Sons, to set up their own enterprise.

BAT had important negotiations under way back in Britain with Imperial and the Molins machinery company which had proved its technological brilliance with further improvements to the Mark I, but lacked the capital which could only be raised by the winning of orders from all comers. Imperial and BAT could not let that happen, and its directors went into a huddle with a Molins team 'to reach an understanding'. The absence of serious criticism of its dealings over Ardath* was encouraging when it came to tying up a potential Gulliver, like Molins, with restrictive conditions attached to a joint investment.

The Molins machinery agreements provided for a payment by BAT and Imperial of £450,000, and the raising of the authorised capital to £1 million. Directorships were specified. The brothers H. B. and W. E. Molins had the edge in voting control, but their new partners controlled 50.5 per cent of the total share capital. Brecknell's outstanding shares were bought up and the company handed over to Molins for just over £80,000. The services of the brothers were secured by contracts while the assignment of future patents and inventions was covered by a deal that was to last until 1957.

The talks with Molins resulted in two main agreements. First, Imperial and BAT took a major interest in the machinery company's share capital, including 49 per cent of the voting shares, to be raised to 50 per cent on the death of the survivors of W. E. and H. B. Molins. The other arrangement was that the new investors were to obtain various preferential rights on the use and prices of machines. Imperial gained exclusive home market rights for several pieces of equipment, including the cigarette-making machine. One consequence of the negotiations was that Brecknell, the machinery concern bought by Imperial and BAT seven years before, now became a wholly owned subsidiary of Molins and

* The parallel purchase in 1927 by Imperial of an interest in the Finlay chain of tobacconists raised few eyebrows.

changed its name to Thrissell Engineering Company. And a month after the deal was signed, Molins and United, the American producer of the Standard Triumph whose packing and other machines were made under licence by Brecknell, entered into a revision of an early arrangement that covered world sales rights on Molins equipment. Within three years the United Cigarette Machine Company, which had done so much to oust Bonsack from Britain, was in trouble and selling up its key Dresden subsidiary to the German engineers Muller.*

This agreement was to distinguish between 'marketed' and 'unmarketed' machines (including those yet to be developed) and between what was specified as Free Territory and Restricted Territory. The former covered all countries where the tobacco industry was then a state monopoly such as France, Italy and Spain. The restricted territories comprised the remainder of the world divided into eleven exclusive areas of which Britain and Ireland were one. Molins was free to sell in the free territory any machine, and 'marketed' machines in the restricted territories. But it undertook not to offer any 'unmarketed' machine for use in the restricted territory to any purchaser other than Imperial or BAT without first giving them the option to buy the exclusive rights. When a new machine was developed, one example had to go to Bristol for evaluation by Imperial and another to Liverpool for BAT to study. Time and payment arrangements were set out, too, for the evaluation period of sixty days, which could be extended in return for compensation monies. The complex arrangements also provided the terms on which options were to be exercised and minimum orders placed.

It is a tribute to the tight drafting that the pact lasted for thirty years, though BAT at no time exercised its option to exclusive rights. The main beneficiary was Imperial, who in this time secured exclusive rights for eleven out of fifty unmarketed machines.

What was important to Imperial was that it was able to secure the rights to the original first four Marks of the revolutionary Molins cigarette-making machine, developed up to 1933, and Marks V and VI. Records show that rights were also obtained for an automatic weighing attachment for the cigarette machinery, for packers and wrappers (including the hinged lid and wallet packet

---

* Muller, after a legal struggle with Molins, made patent arrangements with the British machinery maker, keeping it out of the British market.

machines), and the 'axial assembler' that was eventually to allow high-speed filter tipping. Later, Imperial was to justify its restrictive behaviour on three main grounds:

1. To secure an assured supply of the best machinery available.

2. To assist development particularly in cigarette-making and packing machinery, by bringing to bear Imperial's considerable practical experience.

3. To ensure that development was not hindered by lack of finance.

Imperial has always maintained that Molins showed great promise of inventive capacity which is why it was helping the company before the restrictive pact was signed. Molins was a willing partner for it 'had from the very beginning fought an uphill struggle against financial difficulties and it was obviously necessary for the company to have considerable capital if it were to expand and attempt to promote the development of new machines to an adequate extent'.

Monopolistic or not, the Molins investment was to be a highly profitable as well as defensive arrangement. The machine firm became the world's leading cigarette equipment supplier and even as early as 1948 was doing so well that it was able to lend Imperial £1.2 million. Its Deptford factory, extended many times, was insufficient and a new one was to be added near High Wycombe. That the deal was restrictive is obvious, and one of the first to get the cold shoulder was Gallaher when that company made applications in 1932, 1933, 1934 and 1936 to buy the Mark IV. In 1933, Imperial was supplied with a Mark V model, and Gallaher unsuccessfully tried to purchase the machine in 1935. Not until the summer of 1948 did Imperial allow Molins to supply the Marks I to V to other potential British customers.*

The embargo was not complete. For in 1939 Imperial did permit the sale of a Mark IV machine to Peter Jackson, the filter-tip pioneers which Gallaher had bought up five years before. But there were strange sidelights, particularly in the refusal to sell machines to Gallaher, as will be seen later. Imperial's executives felt that they took the risks in backing Molins and, after all, other machinery was available from other suppliers. Carreras had a link with Baron's inventions.

* In the machinery industry, the Molins Mark I–IV has been considered one machine due to the improvements on the basic first model.

Pipe smokers were proving the mainstay of the emerging Empire tobacco-growing industry. Over 250 brands of smoking mixtures—either solely from colonial sources or blended with American leaf—were available in 1927. The leaf came from British North Borneo, Canada, India, and Nyasaland, often dark in flavour and colour. But the development of cigarette leaf from acclimatised American seed and the price advantage of Imperial preference were gathering momentum. Indeed, there were some wild predictions, such as that of the Rt Hon. L. S. Amery, Secretary of State for Dominion Affairs, who in August 1927 suggested the British market could take six to ten times the crop of 18 million lb grown in Southern Rhodesia. It is little wonder that growers plunged into the growing of no less than 24 million lb in 1928, nearly five times the amount of flue-cured leaf produced just two years before when Imperial had made an unacceptable offer at the Salisbury Tobacco Warehouse for 60 per cent of the exportable crop. This was a disastrous course to take. Amery's prediction of what could be absorbed in Britain was irresponsible, for it ignored the British industry's investment in the United States, now reinforced by the creation of a Canadian leaf organisation for Imperial in that same year of the minister's statement.

Imperial wanted to help, but on a more planned basis. When the Salisbury Warehouse set up agents for growers in London with City merchant banking finance while crops waited to be sold, there was too much Rhodesian tobacco and too few buyers. Early in 1928 about seven years' reasonable requirements were clogging dockside bonds—and before that year's supplies were available. A loan from a merchant bank, Im Thurn, due for redemption, had to be borne on the growers' behalf by the already hard-pressed Rhodesian Government, and only a subsidy paid to growers who saw their leaf vanish into world markets, via speculators who were attracted by 'distress' pricing, kept the tobacco planters from abandoning the colony's main hope for future prosperity.

An anxious Mr Amery, regretting his own exaggeration, enlisted the help of Imperial in tackling what in 1928 he acknowledged was 'a grave and anxious problem' for planters. Imperial had recently established a small leaf handling and packing unit at Msasa, some four miles from Salisbury, and it now decided to see whether British cigarette smokers might accept an all-Rhodesian, Virginia-type brand. On 21st May 1928, at the Savoy Hotel,

Amery watched anxiously as guests of the Lambert & Butler branch (which had done so much for Kentucky leaf) smoked their inaugural samples of Rhodesian brand cigarettes. Samples were to be showered on MPs, peers, and others in the attempt to set a fashion and break the dominance of American leaf. One man even set up some shops to sell only Rhodesian cigarettes. A bankrupt tried to form a manufacturing company, but fortunately he was exposed in the nick of time by the Rhodesian High Commissioner, Sir Francis Newton, who himself had pestered the Royal Family for their endorsement.

The credulity of the Rhodesians at this time was only shattered when, after the initial polite and reserved comments of the English, a City man said their first cigarettes 'smoked and tasted like hay'. In 1929, production of Rhodesian leaf would plunge to 6 million lb when the officially supported Salisbury Warehouse fell into disrepute as a marketing organisation.

There were bitter remarks, aggravated when Imperial declared profits of nearly £10 million and paid a 23 per cent dividend to shareholders, plus a bonus issue of stock for 1929. Yet Imperial had tried it the Rhodesian way, and from now on its arguments that an all-Rhodesian brand would always be held to be an inferior substitute for American cigarettes would gain respect. Imperial knew that the best way was to introduce the leaf progressively as a blend, wooing smokers to new recipes.

Meanwhile, there were other pioneers struggling to raise their crops economically, not so far away. In England some several hundred acres were under cultivation again, evoking memories of three centuries before. Growers in Cornwall, Dorset, Hampshire and Cambridgeshire transplanted their seedlings, blissfully unaware that the Rhodesians and other sources of non-American leaf would eventually overcome their early difficulties and dash their hopes for indigenous growing. Manufacturers made little secret of the need to protect their American investments—Gallaher's operations in the United States were worth nearly £500,000, not a sum to be jeopardised by hasty switches in buying policy. Yet Gallaher was not uninterested in Empire leaf and had even introduced an appropriate brand of pipe tobacco called Foxhead Mixture.

The death at eighty-seven of Tom Gallaher in May 1927 brought its pressures on members of his family. On 18th January 1929, his successor as chairman and managing director, John Gallaher Michaels, posted a letter to the Constructive Finance and Investment Company, part of Edward de Stein & Company, of Pinners Hall, Austin Friars, London EC2. It set out the facts of Tom Gallaher's achievement in establishing a world-wide reputation for hard tobacco, including Irish Roll, 'War Horse' Bar, Uncle Jeff Twist, and Wrestler Plug, as well as quality pipe tobaccos such as Gallaher's Rich Dark Honeydew and Two Flakes. These were solid sellers, while sales of Gold Blend, Rotary, Golden Spangled and Park Drive cigarettes were no less profitable.

This letter, describing factories in Belfast and London, as well as warehouses round Britain, plus references to leaf-handling factories in Kentucky and Virginia, was needed to guide potential investors (customers and employees to receive 'special consideration') in the Stock Exchange's newest publicly quoted company, Gallaher Limited, which had been incorporated as a limited Irish company in 1896. Trustees acting for Gallaher family interests had sold out for £2 million to Constructive Finance, which arranged for Edward de Stein, of the same address, to sell 1 million Preference shares of £1 at 20s 6d. Average annual profits had been £195,373 over the five years ending December 1928 on assets worth around £1.8 million.

Gallaher was converted into a public company on 28th December 1928 with a new capital structure of £2 million. London and Belfast boards were set up with merchant banker Edward de Stein* (later knighted) as chairman and other directors who included Scottish shipowner Sir Charles Coupar Barrie and General Accident Insurance chief Robert Law. With its new status and access to share subscription to find future growth, Gallaher looked well set to push Imperial harder.

This move was to be quickly emulated by the smaller Rothman's of Pall Mall, who formed Rothman's (1929) Limited with a capital of £220,000 and in May 1929 offered a slab of Preference shares on the London Stock Exchange. The original Rothman share capital was only £60,000.

The direct-to-smokers mail order department of Rothman's was going well, as were export sales round the world, including China, South America and Empire territories. Working capital, however, was needed to develop the small chain of ten retail branches and

---

* The de Stein bank merged with Lazards in 1960.

open new distribution depots. Net annual profits were running around £40,000 a year and Sydney Rothman, son of the founder and chairman, was determined to leave his own mark by a more ambitious target. For this he had a great incentive, for besides a salary of £2,800 a year for acting as managing director, he also had a ten-year contract that would give him 1¼ per cent of profits over £75,000 a year. There were generous contracts for his two co-directors, too.

In selling Louis Rothman's original enterprise to the new public concern, the valuation gave the vendors £129,000 in cash and shares but left £80,000 for working capital. It was put quickly to use, buying new premises in Glasgow, Manchester and Bristol for the debut of White Horse and Dance Time cigarettes and Louis d'or and Tuya tobaccos. The most significant decision, however, was Rothman's entry into coupon trading with Navy Cut Virginia and Speedboat cigarettes offering the double incentive of gifts and wholesale prices if bought by the direct mail service. The less penny-conscious could buy instead packs of special order Virginia cigarettes with their initials imprinted in gold leaf.

The City ought to have been reeling with the activity in tobacco share dealings. In between the Gallaher and Rothman reconstruction, there had been the formation of the United Kingdom Tobacco Company (1929) with a £500,000 capital to buy for £333,331 an old-established East End business of the same ambitious name marketing cigarettes known as Greys, Sarony, Muratti, and Bandmaster as well as that of Marcovitch & Company, suppliers of Black and White and Con Amore cigarettes. Other tobacco manufacturers were very interested in the United Kingdom Tobacco Company of which little was really known beyond its public sales policies.

It had been incorporated as a private company twenty-two years before to buy the separate businesses of Major Drapkin & Company and Nicholas Sarony & Company, of Manchester. The company owned leasehold factories at Middlesex Street, London E1. Marcovitch was incorporated in 1909 to buy one of England's first Turkish cigarette-making houses, established a hundred years earlier for pipe tobacco mixtures. Marcovitch owned its own box-making subsidiary and leased a cigarette factory at Commerical Street, also in London E1 district. The combined profits, after tax, of the two main concerns averaged £62,273 over the five years to the end of June 1928, so Rothman was a smaller fish. Marcovitch and the original United Kingdom Tobacco Company were put into liquidation under arrangements preceding the change in ownership of the assets. Eventually the enterprise would pass to Godfrey Phillips.

As if this was not enough, before 1929 was out BAT (now under the chairmanship of Sir Hugo Cunliffe-Owen) offered another £6 million of its authorised shares to the public. This brought the issued capital to a mighty £34,074,036. Gilbert Wills, now Lord Dulverton, who sat in on the BAT board as one of Imperial's nominees, could not fail to be impressed by the sister organisation's spectacular progress, which now required twenty-one directors and five banks to monitor. For the previous three years BAT had net profits of over £6 million per annum. In 1928 it had also created the Tobacco Securities Trust to buy and hold shares in BAT's associated and subsidiary companies and act as an investment arm, operating from BAT's Westminster House offices on London's Millbank.

Just twenty-six days after BAT began taking in its £6 million of extra capital, the Wall Street stock market crashed.

CHAPTER TEN

The Martin Agreement

Buck Duke had been dead and entombed in his native tobacco country for five years, yet the British tobacco industry was again in more turmoil than even the mighty son of North Carolina could have precipitated. One of the Imperial branches, Wills, spent around £750,000 on advertising in 1930 using the emerging mass circulation newspapers that were not unhelpful to competitors wishing to bring their brands to wider attention. Machine concessions were acquired on railway stations—Imperial loaned the British Automatic Company fifty machines for the Great Western Railway stations on condition they sold only its brands.

Coupon trading was still proliferating. J. Wix, now an American Tobacco company, decided in 1930 to convert its Kensitas cigarettes into a gift brand—a move that raised the company's share of the cigarette market from 2.3 per cent to 6.3 per cent in 1931. That would have impressed Duke. Carreras, a pioneer of coupons, met the challenge by redeeming empty packets of some brands, such as Craven A, for gifts, and it bought its way into the distributive trades by the acquisition of John Sinclair Limited, a manufacturer with its own wholesale and retail branches.

Sinclair was a name also in the mind of Imperial. The Bristol combine bought the Robert Sinclair Tobacco Company which made some cigarettes and also wholesaled for other brands in the North of England and Scotland. The two Sinclair companies were big rivals in the Newcastle upon Tyne region and Imperial acted when news leaked that Gallaher was stalking the shares. It could not afford to let another leading wholesaler fall into competitors' hands, so it negotiated a deal under which Robert Sinclair became a public company with a large stake held in Bristol. (Imperial subsequently had to buy out the outside shareholders because of the company's poor performance, highlighted by its absence from ordinary dividend lists in 1934.)

Other structural changes in 1930 included the merger of the Hignett Brothers branch of Imperial with Ogden. Allowing for other transfers since 1918, this left twelve branches, cut to eleven when in 1932 Stephen Mitchell & Son and F. & J. Smith were put together. Since the end of the First World War, Imperial had left its traditional restriction on the transfer of Ordinary shares. From the original £15 million capital at incorporation in 1901, the group in 1930 had a £50 million capital and within two years some 40 million Ordinary shares would contribute to the even higher £55 million capital. In twenty years their sum would reach £85 million.

Yet the financial muscle that Imperial clearly could flex did not deter the opposition. Large enterprises are often vulnerable to smaller competitors, and gift-coupon trading, though it did not solely explain the disrupted sales returns sent in by branches to Bristol, was proving more than troublesome. It was hurting Imperial's share of the national cigarette trade which had fallen by 5 per cent to 75 per cent in 1929, and 70 of that 75 per cent was in the hands of the Player's and Wills branches (with 32 and 58 per cent respectively).

The depression—Britain went off the Gold standard in 1931—continued to slow the growth of sales, with many customers still buying cigarettes in small loose amounts, even one at a time. Shopkeepers had to survive and sought to supplement their income by showing preference to non-Imperial brands or ignoring the group's conditions of sale. In 1931 Imperial cancelled more than one thousand Bonus Agreements with distributors, many for the display of coupon gifts in shop windows. This did not improve trade relations at a time when Imperial was holding back on price rises for obvious reasons, though not appreciated by the then Chancellor who raised the tobacco duty and hence retail prices to 9s 6d per lb standard rate and so stiffened sales resistance at an awkward time. The trade was slipping rapidly into chaos, so now Imperial played a leading role in replacing the ineffective Tobacco Trade Advisory Committee by a new Tobacco Trade Association. This brought together a council of manufacturers and the two leading distributor organisations, the Wholesale Tobacco Trade Association and the National Union of Retail Tobacconists. The aim was to restore order by enforcing list prices and conditions of sale.

There were now twenty-two coupon brands on sale. Somewhat reluctantly, Imperial's top management decided it could not ignore the pleas of some marketing men to be allowed to hit back. Advertising was fierce, even omnibus tickets carried rival claims for brands. At Wills the ferocity of coupon competition had already led to secret plans for using the somewhat sluggish Autograph brand for entry into gift smoking. It was turned down for fear of the competition, though several new promotional schemes were introduced which included the offer of various smoking accessories such as ashtrays redeemable against empty packets. Commercials were filmed for the emerging cinema industry. In 1930, Lord Dulverton, chairman of Imperial, declared again that coupon schemes were 'inconsistent with the policy on which our business has been built up'. Two years later his staff at the Wills branch were working on a possible gift coupon brand, to be called Four Aces. The desire of smokers to receive gifts was established when Wills started a promotion for giving away playing cards and card tables. The Four Aces brand was launched, in the summer of 1932, selling at five for 2d, but also available in packs of ten or twenty. Wills' Four Aces would command over 20 per cent of the coupon cigarette market in twelve months. Part of this success was due to the offer of clothing and many items useful at a time of economic depression. Some 3 million Four Aces gifts would be given away in the next twelve months.

Such were the gifts showering down on smokers—for competitors stepped up their offers—that a Private Member's Bill was introduced in the House of Commons to ban voucher trading. Lord Dulverton made no secret of where his board's sympathies lay. He said coupon trading had reached 'distinctly unhealthy' proportions. There had been a general disturbance of ordinary channels of distribution, which was regrettable and ultimately against the best interests of the companies themselves. His one hope was that Wills would bring matters to a head—and he was right.

For too long one company in particular—Carreras, pioneer of coupons—had been allowed full rein in the market place. The Black Cat had been featured as a promotion as far back as 1905, when stamp albums and foreign stamps to stick in them were given away in return for vouchers placed in packs of cigarettes. There had been the Great Black Cat Football Competition, a forerunner of the modern system of football pools forecasting of results. A national Black Cat Day had been staged in 1913 when the whole front page of the *Daily Mail* was used to encourage the nation to walk the streets with their packs, hoping the Black Cat man would approach them with the rewarding question 'Are You a Black Cat Smoker?'; rewarding because thousands of gold sovereigns were to be handed out. The Black Cat had been sent into the First World War with advertisements showing him handing out cigarettes to the French soldiers at Verdun. There had been no let-up through the 1920s and now Carreras, with over 13 per cent, was a lusty challenger in the cigarette market. Conventional advertising was being increasingly supported by special promotions and Imperial was forced to introduce its own schemes. Football and cricket forecasting competitions were launched by Imperial.

The Governmental response to the 'give-away' era of tobacco marketing was to be a committee 'to consider the trading practices which the Gift Coupons Bill, introduced into the House of Commons on 28th November 1932, sought to make illegal, and to report whether, in their opinion, any of these practices are detrimental to the public interest'.

In the meantime Lord Dulverton was acting on another issue with a vital bearing on the level of future competition. Following American Tobacco's purchase of Wix, now in the thick of the coupon war, rumours were flying round the industry that it wanted to acquire Gallaher whose board felt increasingly frustrated by Imperial and BAT's grip on machinery patents. It was refused permission in 1933 to buy the Molins Mark I cigarette-making machine, and that same year Imperial snapped up exclusive rights in the newly introduced Mark V model. Gallaher needed more capital, too, to build on its steadily growing success in fighting the Imperial combine, for it was now the fourth largest manufacturer in Britain, whereas in 1928 the company's cigarette market share was less than 1 per cent. Carreras and Godfrey Phillips had bigger sales, though the latter was having an unhappy time against the coupon traders.

In November 1932, Lord Dulverton decided to inquire about the rumours by a direct approach to the chairman of Gallaher,

Sir Edward de Stein, and asked whether it was true that American Tobacco was contemplating a take-over. The reply was that no negotiations were taking place, but a representative of American Tobacco's subsidiary J. Wix had looked over Gallaher's factory in Northern Ireland, giving rise to the speculation. That was enough for Lord Dulverton, who promptly authorised negotiations with a view to a firm offer. Quickly, a highly secret letter was despatched to Gallaher's directors declaring that Imperial's executive committee was prepared to recommend to its board 'that this company should acquire an investment interest in Gallaher by taking, say, 51 per cent of the Gallaher Ordinary shares and leaving the management of the busines to go on undisturbed and unhampered, we using that interest in no way other than that appropriate to any other large shareholder with such an interest'.

Given Imperial's power and the knowledge that the combine was still pulling its punches in spite of the launch of Four Aces coupon cigarettes, Gallaher found itself with an offer it could not refuse. The investment cost Imperial £1,250,000 and would within thirty years attain a market value thirty-eight times greater, a capital appreciation that could not have been foreseen at the time. Gallaher would also grow into Imperial's greatest rival.

Dulverton and his colleagues were sufficiently sensitive to possible reaction about an extension of monopoly power to buy the shares in Gallaher secretly, through nominees, and not to place any representatives on the latter's board. BAT were informed in secret because of the 1902 agreement that acquisitions by Imperial gave the sister organisation the right to buy the export business of any new tobacco subsidiary. An agreement was made with Gallaher to take over its small and somewhat undeveloped export trade.

If news of the arrangements eventually came out, critics would be answered by the assurance that there would be no interference in Gallaher's management or marketing. To the charge that Imperial would gain a return from Gallaher's rising trade, Lord Dulverton could have said it was a much better prospect for Imperial to compete hard and make profits by its own direct marketing operations, which gave a far greater return. Meanwhile Imperial did its best to keep details of its investment secret. It argued to itself that 'it would be quite wrong for there to be an impression abroad that we in fact in any way control or influence

Gallaher's trading policy and that competition between us is in some way blurred and inhibited'. The investment was made on 'commercially protective grounds' because the group much preferred that the control of a business like Gallaher 'did not pass to the Americans'.

Many things at this time were hidden from public view. While smokers were collecting their razor blades, boots and ties for Four Aces vouchers, Imperial was tying up another important machinery deal with Molins for a new machine which formed a new type of wallet packet and filled it with cigarettes. Imperial gained an exclusive licence and introduced the packet for its Three Castles Medium, Churchman's No. 1, and Top Score brands. Yet as fast as it acted, new threats and opportunities would present themselves.

In 1932, the Austrian paper manufacturers Bunzl & Biach AG, who had been co-operating since the early 1920s in developing crepe papers and other materials for the Hungarian filter inventor Boris Aivaz, formed a company Bunzl & Biach (British) Limited. For a few years, Peter Jackson, now a member of the Wix group, had been selling a novel filter with its du Maurier brand. Gallaher had begun experiments, too. Imperial encouraged Molins to work on the development of filter rods, which were expensive and difficult to produce. (Crepe paper was proving difficult to compress evenly and assembling rods with cigarettes was far too slow for the new manufacturing speeds demanded by mass marketing.)

The success of Four Aces in quickly securing one-fifth of the coupon cigarette market (in 1933 one-third of all cigarettes were sold with gift schemes) placed Imperial in a strong tactical position. As sales soared, Dulverton let his competitors know that this was only a taste of Imperial's strength. It did not enter the coupon market directly until 'compelled to do so in self-protection'. Competitors took the point, though some muttered that Imperial's investment in Ardath was hard to reconcile with its policy, given Ardath's entry into coupon trading in 1927 when there were only four such brands about, not the twenty-two now on sale. Imperial was now about to use the muscles of all monopolies to bring about more controlled competition, for it now controlled Gallaher. But first Dulverton and his board had to await the Board of Trade committee report on gift coupons and the public interest.

The official report was published in July 1933. It was a disappointment. After reviewing the extent of incentive gift trading, costing one per cent of the total volume of retail sales and involving the annual handout of goods worth over £800,000, the committee declared that neither gift vouchers nor trading stamps were practices detrimental to the public interest 'and did not call for any special legislative action'. Clearly, the Government could not agree to outlaw coupons without backing from an impartial authoritative committee.

There was alarm at Imperial's headquarters in Bristol. This could be the signal for a costly coupon war of even greater dimensions which might bring Imperial and the whole industry into eventual disrepute. Unless there was some initiative to effect some sort of agreement, Imperial could see itself, if it won a power struggle, being attacked by the politicians for liquidating rivals to consolidate a monopoly position; or, if it lost, experiencing a slide in sales of such serious proportions that shareholders would seek to question their board's judgement. Already the sales record was looking unhealthy, despite Wills' Four Aces and Player's Weights. Between 1921 and 1933, Imperial's total share of cigarette trade had declined from 93 to 66 per cent. The share of total tobacco trade over the same period had dropped from 75 to 62 per cent. When sales returns were examined in that summer of 1933 it was obvious that Wills' Four Aces had bitten deeply into the sales of Wills' Woodbines. There was no sense in such a switch of productive and distributive effort, incurring the higher costs of coupon promotion.

Dulverton and his advisers correctly judged that competitors, also suffering an escalation of costs and the loss of standard price competition, might be willing to talk peace.

Their belief that others were suffering big cost increases, whatever the gains in sales, was increased when Carreras went to the Stock Exchange in March 1933 to raise new money in a Preference share issue, partly underwritten by the Prudential, worth £1 million. The chairman and managing director, Sir Louis Baron, claimed that in spite of trade depression and adverse world conditions 'the popularity of the company's leading brands remains unshaken'. But what struck Imperial was that profits for the immediate past financial year were only £744,379 compared with £1,280,630 in 1929. It meant Carreras' profits had been below £1 million for the third year running.

Costs had gone up with the introduction of a new brand, Clubs, to add to the list of Craven A, Black Cat, Clarence Tatler, Passing Show, Three A, Rubicon, Piccadilly, White Eagle, Empress, Beau Royal and Cerise cigarettes. It was a reflection of the pressures on profit margins that Craven pipe mixtures had not long been launched, based on cheaper Empire leaf. Other manufacturers were increasingly using Empire preference leaf, so much so that the amount in use was about 23 per cent of total leaf requirements.

The negotiations which ensued that summer and early autumn were handled with great care. They took place at the highest levels in board rooms of the leading manufacturers and were coordinated eventually through the new Tobacco Trade Association, created in 1931. Smokers, it was agreed, were to be deprived of their gifts from 31st December 1933. The terms of the armistice on coupon trading were enshrined in an agreement announced on 1st November. Martin's Bank was appointed to supervise the creation of a financial pool into which manufacturers, whose trade benefited from the end of coupon trading, would pay appropriate compensation for those which lost sales.

Parties to the Martin Agreement, as it became known, were Imperial, Ardath, Carreras, Gallaher, International Tobacco, Godfrey Phillips and J. Wix. Rothman's was not included, as it was not a member of the Tobacco Trade Association, whose rules were now to be changed to enable the organisation to impose strict resale price maintenance.

The age of restrictive practices was to be ushered in on New Year's Day, from which time the manufacturers would cease to supply 'coupons, certificates, vouchers, miniature cards, or similar things which have an exchangeable value'. The public was warned that the redemption of coupons would cease by 28th February 1934.

The pooling arrangements involved around £14 million, with Imperial bearing the brunt of the eventual cost until the scheme was terminated in 1945. Imperial paid out £13.5 million over this period. Gallaher received an excess of receipts over payments of £298,793 up to 1939, but had subsequently to pay in £461,435 from then to 1945. Imperial's associate Ardath took £3,611,752 in compensation payments of the period, while the totals for other beneficiaries were Godfrey Phillips £1,530,703, Carreras £3,954,318, and American Tobacco's J. Wix £4,563,905.

The Martin Agreement provided for the setting up of a manufacturers' committee, which was to consider 'various questions of general interest to the trade', reaching agreement on such matters as terms to the distributive trade and supplies to price cutters. To maintain prices and trade discipline, three specific agreements were framed, for retailers, for wholesalers, and for trade customers of wholesalers. Dealers who did not enter into the various agreements were termed 'non-signatory dealers' and could be denied supplies from all parties of the restrictive arrangements. A 'black list' would be operated, called the 'stop list', for disciplining black sheep. The maximum permitted trade discount on scheduled list prices was fixed at 5 per cent for cigarettes, cigars and whiffs and $1\frac{1}{2}$ per cent for all other goods irrespective of the size of order involved.

The embargo was not total. The English and Scottish Co-operative Wholesale Societies, supplying to dividend-paying retail co-operatives throughout Britain, were left outside the pact. J. A. Pattreiouex, the Manchester-based maker of Senior Service cigarettes, continued to offer large discounts to its distributors. More to the point, five manufacturers who had launched coupon brands before 1933 were not parties to the main manufacturers' agreement 'not to manufacture, offer for sale or otherwise handle coupon bearing goods and not to trade with anyone who did'. One of them was Rothman's which, though not a member of the Tobacco Trade Association, was a significant trade customer of a Godfrey Phillips' subsidiary. Some swift talking by Godfrey Phillips resulted in a separate deal whereby Rothman's dropped coupons in return for compensation.

These events were watched with great interest by members of the National Cigar and Tobacco Workers' Union, for they fell in the middle of the union's centenary celebrations. Members, many of them women, were assured that it all meant greater security of employment and more stable times, even though, before the agreement was signed, Carreras had recruited an extra one thousand workers to cope with demand, which would now revive through the rest of the thirties.

Whatever Imperial has said of these arrangements, their terms were clearly to reduce the level of competition and served to establish once again the combine as the undisputed price leader. A slipping monopoly position was stopped, and a number of subsequent actions by Imperial, Gallaher (its secret subsidiary), Ardath, the company jointly owned with BAT (whose cigarette sales had now reached the 100 million mark) and Molins, the machinery makers, undoubtedly promoted even greater concentration of power within the British tobacco industry. It is true that Imperial's competitors, drawing their Martin payments, placed some thirty-five new non-coupon brands in the next five years before smokers, bewildered by the sudden loss of their so-called free gifts. But the records clearly show an immediate transformation in Imperial's market position. The heavily reduced 66 per cent share of cigarette trade bounded to 79 per cent in 1934, while its slab of total tobacco trade jumped from 62 per cent to 72 per cent.

While manufacturers independently fixed their list prices to be charged by distributors—and enforced them at retail level under threat of cutting off supplies to anyone reducing prices—Imperial's price lists were generally followed. There were some variations, and price classes based on weight and size of cigarettes gave the illusion that price competition was not dead. On the latter, as it will shortly be seen in the Walters case, Imperial was not brooking anything other than an illusion. Meanwhile, 'all was not roses and joy'. Molins fell into a dispute with the Wix family, who had sold J. Wix to American Tobacco and who, because the Kensitas brand had lost its coupons, had received the biggest payout from the Martin pool. The row, not settled for three years, broke out over their patents for developments of axial assemblers for machine manufacture of filter cigarettes.

When the Wix family sold out, they had promptly formed Peter Jackson (Tobacco Manufacturer) and since 1929 pioneered filter-tipped smoking through the du Maurier brand. They had improved greatly the machine know-how with what they called the Edwards assembler. Unfortunately, Molins had developed its own equipment along similar lines. Imperial was to assert its right to exclusive use of Molins' axial assembler in 1935, but first Gallaher, its subsidiary, moved in 1934 to buy the Peter Jackson business along with two related companies, the International Tobacco Company and the National Tobacco Company. The deal involved the purchase of the home trade and the Aivaz patents, and export sales were held by the Wix family, who also at one time owned Benson & Hedges, but by now had formed Filter Tips so that their work on filter machinery could continue. The conflict over two patent specifications that were much the same was eventually resolved by a licensing deal under which Molins and Filter Tips agreed not to dispute further each other's patents. Imperial, in spite of Gallaher's intervention, next refused to allow the sale of Molins' Mark V cigarette-making machine to Gallaher. But as a consolation, Gallaher was given free access to the Molins axial assembler as it was now in the filter cigarette trade with du Maurier.

A complicated agreement was signed between Gallaher and Imperial on future rights and orders with the former buying eight axial assemblers at £1,500 per machine plus a royalty of 3d per 1,000 cigarettes. Imperial bought one (and ordered five more from 1935 to 1939) at £1,275 with no royalty. Imperial won every way. If sales of filter cigarettes proved popular, then the dividends from Gallaher would come in, plus the royalty profits earned on its investment in Molins. Imperial was in no hurry to offer filter cigarettes. Indeed, its first brand, from Lambert & Butler called Varsity, did not come on the market until 1935, with Matinee two years later. However, there was no great demand to justify an earlier marketing operation.

In 1934, as the Martin Agreement brought order out of competitive chaos, Imperial gave out a set of detailed rules for the dressing of display windows in tobacco shops to ensure its branches' brands were well represented. A department helped to supervise displays. Distributors had to comply under the terms of the bonus scheme, so they had little choice but to accept the regulations. Neon signs were to be banned two years later and after some Tobacco Trade Association arm-twisting Gallaher, Carreras and Godfrey Phillips also operated a similar ban. Essentially, Imperial obtained at least half the available High Street display space in shops selling all companies' brands. No one seemed to mind now that profit margins were being protected by the general resale price maintenance.

Next, Imperial consolidated its interest in Robert Fletcher & Son who made fine tissue paper for cigarettes by buying the business outright. Fletcher supplied other manufacturers and the only other major domestic supplier, Crompton (Stubbins), was to pass into BAT"s ownership. There was little concern over Fletcher becoming an Imperial subsidiary, for all eyes in the tobacco industry were now focusing on another problem that would test Lord Dulverton's resolve to preserve orderly trade.

Such were the improvements in the quality of cheap Empire leaf, especially that from Rhodesia, Canada and India, that a new company was set up in 1934, called the Walters Tobacco Company, with the main purpose of marketing an Empire cigarette called Walters' Medium Navy Cut. By 1935 it was evident that this company had a winner.

Walters did nothing to discourage rumours rife among smokers that its Medium Navy Cut was connected with Player's. The cigarettes were intermediate in size between the small and medium classes, but with the same retail selling price, at ten for 5d, as the then small class of cigarettes. It was obviously good value. The packing was not dissimilar to Player's Medium. This was a new and unexpected form of competition to arise so soon after the Martin settlement. Imperial was angry as Walters sped towards gaining about 4 per cent of total sales of small cigarettes by the end of 1936 (earning itself a 35 per cent return on its capital in 1935 and 75 per cent in 1936). Lord Dulverton and his management protested that the competition was unfair as the presentation and packing adopted resembled that used by their Player's brand. Other manufacturers complained it was disturbing their sales more than those of Wills or Player's. The 6d class brands from which Walters drew trade included Wills' Gold Flake and Capstan, Player's Medium (which had been doing very well indeed) and Carreras' Craven A. Some smokers were switching up market, too, from Wills' Woodbine, Player's Weights and Gallaher's Park Drive, at 4d for ten. Clearly, something had to be done—and it was, in 1936, in an episode that reflects little credit on Imperial.

The lapse in behaviour came when representatives of Carreras, Gallaher and Godfrey Phillips consulted with Imperial and agreed, in effect, that Walters was to be either acquired or brought quickly to heel, even liquidated by competition from a new rival brand also based on cheap Empire leaf. If the campaign worked, then Walters could be put on a 'reasonably profitable basis' by amalgamating the rival brand into Walters' operation, but not seeking to raise sales. It was agreed that Imperial would not introduce any other similar brand, nor would the other conspirators in dealing with Walters bring out a similar brand for six months (and would do so thereafter only on giving three months' notice). Commercial intelligence indicated conditions were right for the conquering of the tiny Walters, which was said to be running into difficulties in raising new working capital to cope with the growth of demand (sales were £1.8 million in 1937). Imperial agreed this was 'the most effective way of controlling this trade' and under instructions its Churchman branch duly announced the introduction in January 1937 of the Tenner Medium brand to halt 'the rising tendency of Walters' Medium'.

The owners of the infant Walters company did not stand a chance. Within twelve months exactly, Imperial had bought Walters, protesting its innocence and saying that the action did not result from any desire to obtain a monopoly of the new class of cigarette which the victim of the collusive action had tried to pioneer. Imperial was to declare that, while a willing party to the ganging up on Walters, the initiative had come from the other manufacturers anxious to preserve their existing trade in small cigarettes. It was to be many years before any official body commented on the Walters affair, when the Monopolies Commission in the small print of its post-war report on the supply of tobacco remarked: 'We do not think this explanation justifies the action taken.' Then it was far too late, indeed a long dead issue, to rectify any mischief in the public interest. Obviously, at the time of the attack on Walters, none of the parties saw that their victim was providing a cigarette for which there was proving to be a substantial public demand and that they ought to be trying to meet the competition by marketing similar cigarettes without concerted measures for their sale. Proof that Walters was right to spot a demand came as Imperial, now with both Walters' Medium and Tenner on open sale under its ownership, could not hold back a public demand as promised. Their combined share of the small cigarette market soared from 4.6 per cent in January 1937, at the time of the take-over, to 14.1 per cent within ten months. The following April the share was settled at 13.2 per cent, and continued to hold until 1941, during which time sales of Tenner advanced, while Walters' Medium fell, within the overall figure. Ironically, production of Tenner (which Imperial adamantly said it would have introduced with or without its joint pact with other producers) ceased in 1949 while Walters' Medium survived until 1953. The growth of a cheap intermediate cigarette class was stifled eventually by increases in the cost of Empire leaf, a reduced margin of preference in leaf duties, and weight adjustments. Eagle-eyed smokers had anyway spotted that Imperial had reduced slightly the weight of Walters' Medium and Tenner. This latter action had the effect of putting the gross margin on the same basis as the standard small brands. Nevertheless, at least one of the other big companies protested that Imperial had gained greatly from this period of sales growth, contrary to their understanding of the (conspiratorial) deal on Walters, and had been slow to cut trade back again.

While all this was going on, another challenger in the market place was falling under a take-over—J. Pattreiouex, owned by E. Robinson and founded in the North-West by Joseph Allan Pattreiouex, a Greek with a native attachment to the sea that was expressed in the main brand name devised in 1925, Senior Service, which featured white packs with the symbol of a galleon and gulls. Senior Service cigarettes were offered at a modest 6d for ten as 'a product of the master mind' and they did well against brands such as Wills' now ailing Gold Flake and Capstan,* Player's Medium, and Carreras' Craven A (now also tipped). Gallaher for some while had been regretting the fact that it did not own 'a cigarette brand of the standard type which appeared to have a favourable chance of being sold on a national scale to compete with the leading brands of the Senior Service price category'. So in 1937 Imperial's secret subsidiary bought E. Robinson & Sons, of Stockport, and its Manchester associate Pattreiouex, and proceeded quickly to market Senior Service throughout the country with great success.

Gallaher, which was not to have a general bonus scheme for distributors for another ten years yet, nevertheless continued Pattreiouex's previous practice of selling Senior Service at a trade price below its own and other companies' prices for comparable brands. This action was necessary for it to be competitive with Imperial's brands which benefited from that group's written bonus scheme.

A new-found confidence seemed to permeate Gallaher. It had a new managing director, T. Mason, and profits were at a record level of £500,000. At least Imperial could point at Gallaher to answer any criticism that competition had been stifled, an alterna-

* In 1937, Wills decided to introduce Embassy to restore its flagging fortunes in this section of the market.

tive to stressing the very heavy press advertising by all producers in the mass circulation newspapers. The competitive challenges, if limited, took many forms. In 1936, Carreras had bought the intriguingly named Rock City Tobacco Company. Rothman, noting the rise of smoking among women, brought out its Consulate menthol cigarette, and mentholised some other brands, then in 1937 bought Martins of Piccadilly which owned the North Borneo Cigar State Syndicate. Brands called West One, Kings Gate, Kanif Club and Cameron also came in the next two years from Rothman, who had also opened a factory in Ceylon and an office in Cuba.

A few concessions were made by Imperial. A six-year-old agreement with Metal Box on the exclusive supply of patented tinplate containers for tobacco goods was revised in 1937 and was worded to allow the sale of some existing types of boxes and cylinders to others, but a grip was kept on new designs. There was no relaxing of the strict control over machinery available to competitors. Molins, whose founder had died in 1935, had now developed a Mark VI cigarette-making machine which differed from previous models in its mechanism for feeding tobacco onto the paper. The product was much more uniform in its filling. Imperial in 1936 established exclusive rights and paid a voluntary premium on the prices. These rights were not to be fully relaxed for seventeen years,* and the Mark V machines of Molins were controlled strictly until 1948. A big programme of capital re-equipment was now instituted in Imperial branches who reported rising demand after the lean years of depression.

The steady roar of machines in Britain's tobacco factories, spewing out of their maws millions of uniform cigarettes or compressing pipe tobacco into tins, contrasted sharply with the trade's romantic past. Tobacco antiquarians had little with which to comfort themselves. The Westminster Tobacco Box, one of London's treasures, with its silver plate embellishments recording historical events and containing three pipes of tobacco, was still handed on by the custodians for safekeeping before members of the Parishes of St Margaret and St John. In Vienna, Professor Franz Löfler died, aged eighty, the last of the famous meerschaum

---

* The Mark VI, with a filter-tip attachment, was made available on certain conditions to other producers in 1949 to help conserve tobacco in a time of dollar leaf shortages.

pipe carvers, whose work is so prized today. Sensing the needs of future historians, the Tobacco Federation of the British Empire received for safekeeping from the Gluckstein family a collection of historical, general and technical books dating back to 1622. The tobacco companies were building up archives, even if the younger generation of managers, soon to help fight a second world war that destroyed some records, were more interested in the latest hinged lid carton packers of Molins or the cork tipping of a Player's cigarette that held great promise.

Mass markets demanded a relentless attention to standard buying, high-speed production, and bulk distribution. In 1939, some 185 licensed tobacco manufacturing units were supplying 530,400 tobacco dealers. Imports of unmanufactured tobacco retained for home consumption had passed the 190 million lb mark, yielding almost £85 million net for the Customs and Excise revenue collectors (that year standard duty was raised twice, from 9s 6d to 11s 6d per lb, and then to 13s 6d, while the Empire preferential rate was lifted to 11s 5½d per lb).

The age of high taxation of a popular product was firmly established, accelerated by the cost of waging a war with Germany that would see even the 13s 6d standard rate of duty changed four times to touch 35s 6d and 54s 10d per lb in the first two years of peacetime economic reconstruction. The cheap cigarette, the product of technical innovation and national marketing, would be no more. Wills' Wild Woodbines, introduced in 1888 at 1d for five, would cost 2½d for five by 1939 and Player's Medium Navy Cut, launched in 1900 with their bearded sailor symbol at 2½d for five, would rise to 7d. Five weary years, and longer, of restrictions and controlled competition lay ahead. Tobacco was too valuable a commodity and too much of a national comfort for War Cabinets to allow for anything else.

CHAPTER ELEVEN

The London Agreement

Early in December 1947, four sun-tanned men filed wearily out of a Central African Airways aircraft which for a little over four days had carried them from Rhodesia to London. Their arrival was anxiously awaited by Britain's cigarette manufacturers who had laid on a major programme of visits to theatres, factories, restaurants and offices. But it was round a table at Queen's House, St James's Street, that everyone got down to the real purpose of the visit—to secure for Britain the lion's share of Rhodesia's valuable tobacco crop at a time of desperate world shortages. Some thirty tobacco-importing nations had that spring been contending for leaf at the Salisbury auctions.

Five years of world war, the ensuing austerity, and shortages of dollars to buy United States leaf had not left the British industry unmindful that its very existence depended on an imported material. The United Kingdom went to war knowing well enough that her lifelines were the raw materials supplied from overseas. Tobacco had to be imported, not because it was essential for the production of weapons or munitions, or even survival, but because public morale might often hang on the momentary luxury of a puff on a Woodbine or a lingering pipe of some aromatic mixture in times of the direst distress.

Whatever the risks to health, or the waste of income, tobacco was the great national comforter. A new war leader would emerge, Winston Churchill, who defiantly smoked Corona Grande cigars and saw to it that his troops obtained a regular supply, however limited, of their Wills' Woodbines* or Player's Weights. Great

* From 1940 to 1945 the nation consumed 137,560 million Woodbines.

decisions were taken in many smoke-filled war committee rooms. Class barriers would tumble under the common stress. The offer of a cigarette from one to another was a great leveller, an expression of recognition of the unity of the civil population. A smoke was usually the initial, often the only reward after some act of bravery, and the passing on of a lighted cigarette became a film-maker's cliché that was guaranteed nevertheless to stir an emotive response from a cinema audience.

This time, patriotism was not to be vulgarly exploited by the tobacco companies who had established the cigarette in the First World War as a popular product, sometimes by the use of the most shameful stunts. The industry was older, wiser, and more concentrated in its structure. It was willing to surrender much to the national interest and Lord Dulverton, chairman of Imperial, even broadcast an appeal over the radio for moderate smoking to conserve leaf supplies. Even retailers, often short of supplies, raised no serious objection when Lord Beaverbrook, racing to raise aircraft production, obtained an order permitting factories to sell cigarettes direct to war workers to counter temporary absenteeism of people leaving their shop floors to buy their brands. Preference in supplies went to the NAAFI and War Office contracts, and the packs passing abroad to the troops were a familiar reminder of home.

Like all other industries, tobacco suffered its share of privations. But the fact that the Government established in 1940 a Tobacco Control, operated by the Board of Trade and an official tobacco controller, would ensure survival. Several committees—the Tobacco Manufacturers' Advisory Committee and the Tobacco Distributors' Advisory Committee—were created by inviting prominent individuals to serve as expert consultants on practical problems. Most of them were drawn from the ranks of the leading companies and Imperial, as the largest, was naturally and regularly the industry's principal spokesman.

The most immediate task was to frame regulations for the supply of leaf. In 1939, about 75 per cent of leaf requirements was imported from the United States, the other main sources being Rhodesia and Nyasaland (11 per cent), India (7 per cent) and Canada (5 per cent). Although leaf was not subject to official import licensing until 1st January 1940, the Treasury's exchange control regulations effectively took care of controlling supplies in the early months of the war.

Until 1946, all leaf from the United States was imported by the Government with the leaf-buying organisations of the leading manufacturers acting as agents. American tobacco markets were closed for a month after Britain's declaration of war. Market authorities were anxious that prices should not plunge, for British buyers had to suspend purchasing in order that dollars were deployed on vital war materials. Talks took place between the trade and the United States Government and these led to the Commodity Credit Corporation, acting under the umbrella of the United States Department of Agriculture, agreeing to finance purchases by Imperial and others until they were able to resume payments in dollars.

The bulk supplies were assigned to the big concerns, but a pooling system set up with Board of Trade agreement allocated a proportion according to grades to two main leaf banks from which other producers drew their requirements. Companies received allocations of dollars related to their pre-war clearances from bond to cover the cost.

At first, the buying of Canadian leaf was suspended but it was resumed on a limited scale under a licensing system in 1942. Licences were made generally available for Indian leaf and supplies from Rhodesia though for the latter source some restrictions had to be imposed from 1943. Special arrangements were made for Oriental tobacco. Annual purchases were made by the Government from Greece and Turkey from 1940, and manufacturers used a proportion of Oriental leaf in many of their products to conserve dollar tobacco.

These were not the only constraints. From 1940 the volume of output of tobacco products was to be regulated by controls on the amount of leaf cleared from bond. And in 1942 the amount of waste tobacco, such as stem, allowed for claiming repayments of duty under duty drawback arrangements with the Customs and Excise, was lowered from around 12 per cent to 6 per cent, thereby promoting greater economy in leaf usage.

By the end of 1941, as America directly entered the war, leaf stocks in Britain were down to six months' supply. Imperial's own docks at Norfolk, Virginia, were taken over by the United States Navy, and tobacco had to be shipped from ports all round the country, involving delays and disruption. Losses due to enemy action were comparatively small compared with other cargo carried across the Atlantic at great risk. Imperial, for example, only lost 32 million lb from bombing and fire incidents and 17 million lb from submarine ship sinkings. Labour became even shorter as the war progressed and in the tobacco-growing regions teams of casual employees were trucked from area to area—often two hundred miles a day—to cut the seasonal crop and handle the curing. The problem became so acute that eventually prisoners of war were hired under contract, with wages paid to the United States Government (part going to meet expenses of food and lodging for the men, but with a proportion accruing to their credit at the Post Exchange).

The privations of the British smoker were not to be so severe as those which beset Continental Europe. In 1941 Dutch smokers were puffing cigars made from beetroot pulp after the Germans impounded most stocks of cigarettes. A reader wrote to *The Times* urging the collection and sterilisation of 'dog ends' from buses and floors. His calculations were that £5 million worth of tobacco could be recovered. New pipes made from the best French and African woods were virtually impossible to buy, so many smokers resorted to improvisation and even wood carving.

Britain's Tobacco Controller, Mr (later Sir) Alexander H. Maxwell, a former leaf merchant, was asked by the Ministry of War Transport in October 1942 to propose a scheme to help effect economies in the use of the railways. Promptly the five largest manufacturers came to a voluntary agreement whereby proprietary brands of cigarettes bearing the name of one could now be made by any other producers. The zoning arrangement saved about 46 per cent of the then existing railway usage of the cigarette trade—an economy of 12 million ton miles a year. Machinery manufacture was curbed under various Government orders, releasing men and materials for other tasks.

The close relationship between the tobacco industry and Government showed itself in many ways. Lord Sinclair, a hero of the First World War, badly wounded at Gallipoli, became in 1939 deputy chairman of Imperial, after serving as secretary between 1927 and 1936. At the outbreak of war he was released by the board for full-time Government service, having impressed Whitehall as a member of the Prime Minister's Advisory Panel of Industrialists appointed to review the rearmament programme.

The wisdom of close collaboration between the industry and

Government was to be demonstrated by the fact that no official rationing of tobacco direct to smokers took place during the war, nor were there price restrictions. However, in late 1940 the manufacturers had to institute other arrangements on their own account for regulating supplies to ensure orderly trade. Leading brands were carefully allocated to distributors according to pre-war sizes of order and no new accounts were allowed by manufacturers other than with factories and general works canteens. From 1942, zoning arrangements came into force to cover both manufacture and distribution, including the interchange of production between competitors for some brands.

Everyone looked for economies to help the war effort. Shortages of package materials led quickly to the disappearance of hull and slide packets, prompting the reintroduction of paper cups for cigarettes. Cellulose film, foil, and tissues disappeared from packaging, and the supply of cigarette cards had to be stopped.

Consumption of tobacco, however, rose sharply during the war years in spite of manufacturers' economies. Sales of loose, roll, and dark tobaccos continued their pre-war decline as the popularity of cigarette smoking gained further ground. Smokers tended to accept what brands they could obtain and were not able to be discriminating. There was a uniformity, anyway, in many brands that made impossible the exercise of choice on grounds of different qualities.

In 1939, imports of unmanufactured tobacco retained for home consumption were 191,327,000 lb. The figure for 1945 was 218,369,000 lb. Over this period the Government drew huge revenues to fund war operations and justifying the allocation of scarce dollars to tobacco manufacturers. The £84 million of net customers' receipts from duties rose to £380,443,000 in 1945, boosted by the increases in duty in various budgets.

Towards the end of the war, the lack of tobacco supply was becoming very acute, even in the United States market. In January 1945 the National Association of Tobacco Distributors met in New York and set up a rationing system among its 2,800 members, who supplied 1,250,000 retail dealers. The plan was for traders to hand out cards to customers in the shops, which were to be punched for each sale, so ensuring fair buying. The tobacco distributors were the first industrial group in America to attempt wartime rationing of a scarce commodity. Fortunately, the end of the world conflict was close.

Members of the rod filter making Bunzl family fled to England following the 1938 Anschluss when their Austrian factories were expropriated. In 1940 they formed Tissue Papers Limited to carry on manufacturing, working through their Bunzl & Biach (British) Limited trading subsidiary, formed in 1932. It was a decision they would not regret. There were other structural developments, even in wartime. In 1944, Imperial bought the Anstie tobacco concern from the ageing family owners. Anstie, of Devizes (Wiltshire), was one of the oldest tobacco concerns in England, but curiously had failed to train a management to carry on the business beyond the 1940s. Early in 1941, Gallaher had to buy new premises at Lisnafillan for conversion into a tobacco factory following damage to the York Street installation. In 1944, it acquired Mono Pumps and its subsidiary J. E. Arnfield.

This was an intriguing deal for it gave Gallaher a machinery manufacturing capability. Gallaher, of course, had its troubles in getting equipment even in peacetime, due to Imperial's close control of Molins' sales. Its requirements were met largely by Amfoco's Standard machines and Muller's German-made Triumph by adapting their various bed and feed equipment. During the war it foresaw shortages of dollars to buy American machines and the destruction of Muller's Dresden facilities. The development of its own machinery with the help of Arnfield seemed logical and it could also engage in reconditioning as well as making equipment under licence for others.

That the wartime controls worked well enough does not mean there were no complaints. Some of the smallest manufacturers complained that leaf controls benefited the biggest concerns and preserved their positions. But Carreras felt they were 'fair and equitable', even though its growth and increasingly effective competition were telling on Imperial just before the war. Peace in any case brought its own problems.

The first full year of peace, 1946, saw a consumption in Britain of 222 million lb of cigarettes and 265 million lb of tobacco including pipe brands, cigars and other products. Imperial paid out £7.7 million, net of tax, in dividends—a sum not to be matched again until 1959. It was a temporary reward after the excess profits taxes and other controls of a war economy that were taking a long time to vanish in the early years of reconstruction and in the inevitable austerity of a post-war Britain which was surviving on lend-lease and the grit of a determined people who looked forward to an end to shortages. New regulations controlled the supply of dollars according to past clearances of tobacco for bond, so the fact that pooling of leaf supplies ended in 1946 seemed cold comfort for manufacturers contemplating the future of their enterprises. There was a record importation of 365,798,000 lb of United States tobacco in 1946, but in 1947 it would slump to 201,235,000 lb, and then to 172,383,000 lb in the following year.

It was not easy to maintain the optimism of the companies as their managements shed their uniforms and returned to their civilian jobs to wage the marketing war they once knew so well. Gallaher, faced with Imperial holding 78 per cent or so of total trade, was not to know the market would contract quite so sharply as it did in the first years of peace. Yet the company raised in June 1946 more money by a new issue of shares, hoping to finance expansion. This posed a problem for Imperial, not because of the threat of a better capitalised competitor, but because if it took up its proportion of shares' entitlement as the holder of a 51 per cent stake it would, before too long, have to consolidate Gallaher's results in its accounts. The Cohen Committee on Company Law Amendment had recommended in 1945 that holding companies must consolidate the accounts of all subsidiaries in which they held a majority interest. That recommendation was to be embodied in the 1948 Companies Act. Imperial refused its entitlement, preferring not to increase its monopoly position as it claimed to have invested defensively in Gallaher only to prevent a take-over by American Tobacco. The holding was now less than 50 per cent. Imperial contented itself with merging one of its oldest manufacturing branches, Adkin & Sons, with the W. F. Faulkner branch, to be followed by the merger of Walters with Edwards, Ringer & Bigg in the following year. It declined to join the Federation of Home and Export Tobacco Manufacturers, which in 1947 would replace the loosely organised Council of Tobacco Manufacturers formed in the First World War. The new Federation was created as a legal entity to undertake national tobacco wage negotiations with trade unions, but Imperial preferred to maintain more freedom of action, even if managements throughout the industry felt themselves affected by many factors not always within their control.

Supplies of tobacco leaf were becoming desperate as dollars became more precious to the Chancellor in the fight for Britain's survival. The year 1947 will be long remembered in the tobacco industry—it was one of devaluation and the greatest ever rise in tobacco duty, up from 35s 6d per lb to 54s 10d and a rate of 80 per cent against 45 per cent from 1900 to 1939. It was an ill-judged time for Imperial, now under a new chairman, Lord Sinclair, to resume mass advertising, especially in cinemas, and a policy decision would be taken in 1948 to cut the expenditure back again.

The scarcity of dollars forced the manufacturers to consider ways of encouraging greater leaf production within the Sterling Area. Naturally, everyone looked to Rhodesia where many ex-servicemen with their war-weary families had settled to cultivate the eternal weed for a tobacco-hungry world. The crop that they and the established colonial farmers raised was the valuable prize that their bronzed spokesmen carried when they flew into London at the tail end of 1947 for talks with the British manufacturers. A hectic and exciting year for those growers was about to close with the historic London Agreement.

The excitement began with drama, at the spring auctions, from which not even a coincidental Royal visit to Rhodesia by King George VI and Queen Elizabeth could distract attention. Growers, who in 1945 produced a record Sterling Area crop of almost 47 million lb selling at an average 1s 8d per lb, had, with a liberated Europe shopping for supplies, obtained 2s 8d per lb—a profit of more than 100 per cent*—in 1946. Now, a year later, a huge crop of 57 million lb was being put on the Salisbury auction floors, opening at an astounding 4s 11d per lb.

An emergency meeting of Britain's Tobacco Advisory Committee was convened to consider urgently the prospect of a crippling pricing battle against all comers for that crop. To make things worse, the Labour Chancellor, Dr Hugh Dalton, had of course raised the duty on tobacco not long before, both to conserve dollars and to discourage the growth of smoking (consumption was now 120 per cent more than pre-war levels) until better economic conditions prevailed. Manufacturers viewed the prospect of leaf

* The cost of growing tobacco in Rhodesia was then estimated at 1s 3d per lb.

prices soaring at the Salisbury auctions with great alarm. Something had to be done quickly. A cable was sent off to C. A. Barron, Imperial's general manager in Rhodesia, instructing him as a member of the Tobacco Marketing Board in Salisbury to put before that Board a joint request from the British manufacturers and the Board of Trade that the auction floors be shut down forthwith and kept closed until their special emissary, a director of Gallaher, A. V. Maunder, arrived from London to discuss prices. Auction bids of 4s 11d per lb were the equivalent of a landed import price in Britain of 6s 3d per lb, which compared with 2s 9d for Canadian leaf and 3s 9d for better quality American tobacco.

The Rhodesian Tobacco Marketing Board met hurriedly on 5th May 1947 to consider the unprecedented British request. Representatives of the growers had divided loyalties. Instinctively, they were sympathetic to their mother country, which had done much to help encourage the colonial planters in the early days of development, even if occasionally the amount of help had drawn criticisms from time to time from their predecessors. At the same time, the growers' representatives were acutely conscious that many of the new tobacco planters were working on borrowed money looking for big profits to cover their debts and justify the risks of settling down in Rhodesia. More than a few felt that auction prices could in a few years touch 10s per lb, providing nest eggs of new capital to cover the inevitably leaner years, or crop failures. The Marketing Board could not expect farmers to agree to suspending the auctions, depriving them of their expected high prices and disrupting the integrated system of moving tobacco from farms to warehouses and on to Beira for shipment. No, the auctions must go on.

From London came an unexpected and swift reaction—Imperial, Carreras, Gallaher, and Godfrey Phillips promptly instructed their Salisbury-based buyers to withdraw from all bidding. Many other countries might be in the market through leaf merchants, but the sudden withdrawal of British buyers, with their bulk orders and established procedures for acceptance, was enough to lower prices sharply. Average bids fell to 3s 3d, still a good price but not the lucrative level everyone was expecting.

On 13th May, Maunder of Gallaher had arrived and started talks with the worried Marketing Board. He told its members of Britain's plight over supplies but said manufacturers could not pay extortionate prices and expected some special understanding in the difficult times of post-war reconstruction. After all, Canada had made a magnificent gesture in 1946 in apportioning 20 million lb to the British market, diverting the supply from others. That action had helped the manufacturers get by. Maunder also let it be known that the British Government was supporting the industry's request for preferential treatment, though this could not be reflected in official negotiations at government level with Rhodesia because of an Article of the Anglo-American Loan Agreement relating to non-discrimination.

Maunder was well briefed by the Tobacco Advisory Committee, whose chairman, Sir Alexander Maxwell, had been Britain's Tobacco Controller at the Board of Trade and now enjoyed the status of chief tobacco adviser. Maxwell knew Rhodesia well— his former firm, leaf merchants Siemssen & Maxwell, had before the war bought up surpluses of local tobacco following the Ottawa Conference of 1932 which led in 1933 to guarantees of Empire preference to keep fluctuating tobacco supply on a more even keel. He had encouraged Winston Field in 1934 to go to the United States to see the auction system. The findings saw the opening of the Salisbury auction floors in April 1936 to replace the antiquated methods of farmers hawking their crop to the cooperative warehouse organisation. Growers got immediate cash at the auctions and were free of past losses and any missing consignments sent to agents from warehouses. Indeed, Maxwell's help had led to the formation of the Tobacco Marketing Board, and as the British Tobacco Controller he had a decisive voice in the allocation of wartime crops among the Allies.

Well, asked the Marketing Board of Maunder, the emissary, what did Maxwell and his Tobacco Advisory Committee of manufacturers want now of Rhodesia? The forcing down of prices clearly had, as Edward Harben, not long elected vice-president of the Rhodesian Tobacco Association had commented, 'somewhat chastened the growers'. Maunder put forward the idea that Rhodesia should introduce export controls which would ensure Britain bought two-thirds of the crop. In return, the Board of Trade would bring back wartime import restrictions to ensure fair distribution between manufacturers who would avoid open price warfare at the auctions. Board members now had to think deeply.

Other buyers might be jostling and clamouring for the valuable crops, but there was a strong chance that their custom would vanish overnight once the dollar scarcity was over. Rhodesians were still conscious they had quality problems and American leaf was still regarded as superior and consistent. Britain could be offered a guaranteed long-term market, if this could be negotiated, and the manufacturers with their great experience in the United States could be helpful in raising quality control standards. Many farmers were less sure about Britain. The withdrawal from auctions was an action that showed the teeth of a tiger. There was the monopoly trend of manufacturing. And, anyway, would not the British manufacturers turn to the United States for all purchases when it became possible?

The most immediate problem was to reach an uneasy peace on the auction floors and to resume talks later in the year, after all interests in Rhodesia had been more fully consulted. To find out what guarantees would be needed to bind the growers to the British market had to take time. Meanwhile, the British took 31 million lb off the auction floors, some 6 million lb less than they had originally intended to buy.

Import controls were ordered in London and, by July 1947, the largest manufacturers were making a voluntary 20 per cent reduction in their supplies of cigarettes to the public, reinforced a year later with a statutory 16⅔ per cent reduction in withdrawals from bond with the aim of holding supplies at the 1939 levels. To cover more serious temporary shortages, created by the loss of the 6 million lb of Rhodesian leaf, manufacturers turned to Greece and Turkey* for 12 million lb of aromatic tobacco to mix in with the milder cures from the Empire and the United States. Smokers viewed the curbs with painful resignation, for they were only too aware of the privations in post-war Britain, with politicians exhorting everyone to economy in everything. Old age pensioners were to be given tokens to buy their tobacco at reduced prices from 13th October 1947.

When Maunder returned to London in June to report on his mission, the Rhodesian Tobacco Marketing Board had agreed to send a team to London to develop the negotiations from the position of an unsatisfactory and temporary truce into a more lasting

---

* The United States Government could not object as these countries were excluded from the non-discriminatory provisions of lend-lease aid.

understanding. And so a small team, led by Ralph Palmer, newly elected president of the Rhodesian Tobacco Association of growers, came to be gathered round the table at Queen's House, St James's Street, in London. Sir Alexander Maxwell acted as chairman and besides Maunder of Gallaher the home team drew on representatives of BAT, Carreras, and Godfrey Phillips. Imperial sent three men, including a handsome young man called John Partridge, who was destined to become the combination's chairman and one of the big names of the Confederation of British Industry in the early 1970s.

Palmer chose a direct line of negotiation. He outlined, quite bluntly, a proposal for the British manufacturers to buy two-thirds of the Rhodesian crop over a ten-year period. That would mean the uptake from the projected 1948 supply of 46 million lb out of 70 million lb. Growers would expect an average auction price of 2s 5d or 2s 6d in return for the necessary export controls. It was quite a request, given the knowledge that the British manufacturers were hit by artificial restraints on earnings from the Government's attack on consumption.

However, dividend restrictions, imposed by law, required even the present returns to be re-invested, so Rhodesia was as good a place as any into which to divert a bigger proportion. The price asked was not a stumbling block. The arguments at first centred on the ten-year guarantee, resolved by an agreement to review the position annually for five years ahead. But a tough struggle soon developed over the issue of quantities—the growers' side held out stubbornly for 46 million lb from 1948, and the manufacturers refused to go beyond 40 million lb a year. It was deadlock. Ralph Palmer apparently dared not go back with a lesser commitment. He withdrew his team from the discussions and, with the nerve of a top-class poker player, sat it out in another room as the manufacturers rushed to the telephones to consult their board-room colleagues.

One of Palmer's team, Edward Harben, the Rhodesian Tobacco Association's vice-president, recalled: 'The farmers could hear the comings and goings of the manufacturers and the ringing of telephones while the big British firms consulted with one another. The tension and excitement grew until, at the manufacturers' request, the conference reassembled, when there came what was to the Rhodesians both a triumph and an anti-climax. Palmer was quietly told that his request for the manufacturers to agree to purchases of 46 million lb a year had been accepted.'

The London Agreement was to be provisionally signed in Sir Alexander Maxwell's flat. Much was being taken on trust, for it was not a watertight legal document and the British Government was not a signatory, even if it was pleased. Not so pleased were the leaf merchants, whose sales to other countries would now be severely limited by Rhodesian export controls that lasted until 1953. The agreement was finally accepted in Rhodesia after many passionate meetings around the growing areas. 'Give it a trial', was the plea of their leaders. One old grower, remembered Edward Harben, summed up the eventual majority acceptance with the remark at a meeting in Bromley, near Salisbury: 'All right; but I feel like the girl in a taxi who knows she is going to be kissed. I had better sit back and enjoy it.'*

In the event, the 1948 auctions would see 76 million lb on the auction floors, selling at 2s 8½d per lb, above the minimum asked at the London negotiations. The manufacturers in Britain took 42,500,000 lb, less than they promised. The agreement was thus off to a shaky but not totally unsatisfactory start. Things would get much better with Britain buying much greater quantities (helped by the 1949 devaluation of sterling) and even pressing planters to expand their crops. By 1951, Britain would have a revised London Agreement and be guaranteeing the purchase of 485 million lb spread over the following six years.

Clearly, 1947 was an historic year and a significant one for the long-standing Anglo-American alliance on tobacco supplies. The Rhodesian pact was the dominant event, but not the only one. There was plenty of domestic activity at corporate organisational level. For some time Gallaher, whose Senior Service cigarettes now enjoyed a big reputation which could not be fully exploited, had been studying the market for small machine-formed cigars. Profit margins looked attractive and some growth was seen for the future. This led to the take-over of Associated Tobacco Manufacturers, whose interest included J. R. Freeman & Sons, of Cardiff, makers of Manikin. Other moves included the purchase of new machinery patents by Imperial—this time from Tingey & Company, the engineering group that owned Oscar Legg. More

* *Leaf of Gold: The Story of Rhodesian Tobacco* by F. Clements and E. Harben. Methuen & Company, 1962.

important was an amendment by BAT and Imperial of their joint agreement for the ownership of Ardath whereby they would now share Ardath's Ordinary dividends in proportions reflecting the home and export trade contributions to profits.

The frustration of managements at not being able to engage in full-blooded marketing was felt in all board rooms. Young men emerging from war service foresaw great potential since it was obvious that cigarette consumption, given freedom of leaf supplies, had nowhere near reached saturation point. Their superiors tried hard to keep them from becoming bored by having tests run on mixtures to try and improve the quality of some cigarettes. Studies were put in hand of the growth of 'roll your own' cigarettes which enabled smokers to effect their own economies. Gallaher took its quality control drive a stage further by buying up the Rhodesian Leaf Tobacco Company and Tobacco Development Nyasaland, owning processing plants at Salisbury, Limbe, and Sedi (Malawi). The maintenance of morale was a constant worry against the background of tobacco shortages.

Another increase in duty in April 1948—to 58s 2d standard rate—was designed to hold down consumption. But the effect of another price rise on smokers seemed minimal when their preoccupation was with obtaining sufficient quantities of cigarettes. Packs were not often on general display in shops whose owners kept them under counters and discriminated among their customers. Some people tried pipes as mixtures were easier to obtain, but cigarettes were what they really wanted. Few wanted to take up pipe smoking, as did Sir Alexander Maxwell, the Government's increasingly hard-pressed tobacco adviser, and as did Harold Wilson, the young President of the Board of Trade, who answered a continuous barrage of Commons questions on the unpopular policy of trying to restrict smoking by measures just short of official consumer rationing on points. The National Union of Retail Tobacconists reported the steady emergence of a 'black market' and examined ways to ensure supplies were equitably sold and thefts reduced. Wilson warned in June 1948 that queues and complaints of shortages would grow as supplies were falling well behind demand. He said: 'The shortage is general, and there is every prospect that it will continue for a long time ahead. The fact is that as a nation we are trying to smoke more than we can afford.'

Shortly after that statement, the Board of Trade cut the level of tobacco that manufacturers could draw from bond for making cigarettes by 16⅔ per cent. The total was now down to 100 per cent of their basic figure for the year ended 31st March 1940. The Tobacco Workers' Union promptly went to Whitehall to plead for higher imports from the United States, for they were worried, with good reason, about employment—Gallaher had sacked workers after the Budget increase in tobacco duty. Statutory controls on bond clearances produced an inevitable result. On 12th August the manufacturers reduced their deliveries to retailers by an average of 4 per cent. Sir Alexander Maxwell, several weeks later, estimated that 1,600 million cigarettes were reaching the shops against about 1,450 million before the war. More women were smoking and some customers tended to hoard, exacerbating shortages. If all smokers were to consume one cigarette in ten fewer each day, he said, and refrain from hoarding, there would soon be an end to queueing in shops. Present supplies to meet demand depended on drawing from stocks as well as the purchasing of non-dollar leaf from Rhodesia, Greece and Turkey. There had to be priorities for using limited dollars on raw materials and food.

The National Union of Retail Tobacconists wrote a letter, received by Wilson on his return to the Board of Trade from a Cornish holiday, complaining about the latest cuts. An official statement from the NURT said: 'The consuming public are far less tolerant than during the war, and are very disgruntled and extremely dissatisfied. Reports are coming in from various parts of the country of rather ugly scenes.' Letters appeared in *The Times* calling for rationing on personal points, but few civil servants or ministers wanted to take such a drastic step. Ted Hill, the heavy-smoking general secretary of the Boilermakers' Union, warned: 'It should be clearly understood that the workers in heavy industries do not intend to give up beer drinking or smoking and the sooner the tax on them is reduced the better, otherwise they will revolt and their profound loyalty to the Labour Government will turn to hostility.' What no one was to know was that Sir Alexander Maxwell and Wilson were re-examining American leaf supplies and arranging for a United States deputation to be received in Whitehall. Fortunately, the Olympic Games, held in Britain, served to distract attention from one of the public's prime grumbles amid the many momentous events of Labour's first post-war administration.

In January 1949, Government representatives met a team from the United States Department of Agriculture for talks at the Board of Trade on securing a longer term programme for buying comparatively cheap tobacco during the Marshall Aid years. The outcome was the importation from the United States of 154,117,000 lb in 1949, and 143,699,000 lb the following year. This was a disappointing level, for in 1948 the supply was 172,383,000 lb. It was also well below the 201,235,000 lb of 1947 and the record 365,798,000 lb supplied in 1946. At least there was a clearer picture of the leaf outlook, justifying the rapid development of Rhodesian, Indian, Greek, Turkish and even Cypriot leaf purchasing. Manufacturers had now to take economies as a longer term affair than they had originally hoped. Something had to be done to improve the quality of blends, to make smokers less resentful, and to reintroduce a more competitive environment even within the climate of shortages. One potential development was under everyone's nose—the little used axial assembler, the equipment that made possible rapid production of filter-tipped cigarettes.

Crepe paper filter-tipped cigarettes had sold well in Switzerland and South Africa, but British manufacturers were not impressed with the papery taste or 'look' of the products. Cigarette holders were felt to be the answer for smokers who wanted a filter. Gallaher, with du Maurier, was gaining experience. The developing expertise in making rods and rod materials was, of course, centred on the Bunzl family, whose expropriated factories in Austria were returned after the war and so were able to supply special papers to Cigarette Components, a company set up in 1945 by the Bunzl family to work under their Tissue Papers subsidiary. By 1946, Cigarette Components had forty workers* engaged on filter production in two tiny factories, turning out rods for export only. The original patents of Boris Aivaz, the Hungarian inventor of crepe filters, had expired during the war. He had cooperated pre-war with Hugo Bunzl who supplied him with filler materials, including some cellulose wadding to combine with crepe paper for variations of the original filters. In March 1948, Cigarette Components registered UK Patent No. 639,919 for a process of applying fibrous fleece to crepe paper. This was a great step forward in improving the quality of filter-tipped smoking.

* Ten years later there would be 3,100 people employed in twenty factories in Britain and overseas.

The more the manufacturers studied their difficulties over leaf supplies the more it became obvious that filter-tipped cigarettes might offer economies. The tip would enable a manufacturer to make a cigarette with a smaller tobacco content while retaining the overall dimensions, avoiding the waste of leaf in the unsmoked butt. Discarded butts represented duty paid. Besides conserving leaf, reasoned the advocates of tips, an appreciable saving could be offered to the smoker, confronted with higher prices after the big rises in taxation. With poor quality leaf and unsatisfactory mixtures, filter tips might improve the flavour and pleasure of smoking with a greater degree of 'coolness' and an end to loose bits of tobacco sticking to the tongue. Curiously, few at this time realised that smokers would come to believe that filters might reduce health hazards, a claim that manufacturers have never made even if they were to respond eventually to a big demand based on that belief.

Discussions between the main cigarette manufacturers were arranged. There was a basic problem, machinery. There were four potential machines—the Molins axial assembler already in use by Gallaher and Imperial on a small scale (subject to Imperial's control), the Wix family's Edwards machine with the patents held by Filter Tips but used for export trade, an attachment developed jointly by Imperial's Player branch and Molins, and a machine independently developed by an inventor, Hyman Policansky. Everyone was agreed that part of the demand for cigarettes should be met with the economies of filter-tipped production, but first there had to be a general availability of machinery. Effectively, this meant that Imperial had to ease its monopoly constraints on Molins.

In February 1949, Imperial released the axial assembler for use by all manufacturers with the proviso that no one, other than Gallaher, should start selling filter brands assembled on Molins machinery before the group marketed its own products. The Player attachment was also released for open market sale and all the manufacturers together secured rights to the Edwards and Policansky patented machinery. As a further gesture, Imperial released the main Molins Mark VI high-speed cigarette maker to other manufacturers on condition it was used with filter attachments. That autumn a number of filter-tipped brands were made widely available to customers, including tipped Capstan, Woodbines, and Gold Flake.

The move involved some self-sacrifice by Imperial, for, as many in management observed, leading manufacturers were being placed on equal terms for filter-tipped competition whereas given the patent rights Imperial could easily have stolen a march on its competitors. However, there was one advantage. It enabled Imperial to assume outright price leadership, for prices and margins had been discussed for filter brands and in these inter-company consultations—such collective discussion would be made illegal in the fifties—Imperial seized the opportunity to state what it intended. Part of the filter-tipped deal was that marketing would start when everyone had acquired enough specialised equipment to supply 5 per cent of their total cigarette production with tips.

So began the progressive weaning of smokers on to tipped cigarettes. Advertising was stepped up again with an appropriate emphasis on the new style of cool smoking. But demand would not boom until public consciousness of health hazards was stimulated some years later. Nevertheless, the response was encouraging and had its effect on leaf stocks.

For its part, the Government responded by lifting official controls on the level of withdrawals of tobacco from bonded warehouses, even though dollar controls would continue to complicate buying operations. Talks between the Board of Trade and the Tobacco Advisory Committee yielded the Substitution Plan, a five-year scheme for the progressive substitution of Empire leaf for United States tobacco,* reducing the American content in cigarettes to half from about 70 per cent. The ability to step up the supply of cigarettes had been improved by the creation of a market in filter-tipped brands, but import quotas and dollar shortages effectively acted as a restraint on the rate of growth for the next four years. There would also be plenty of grumbles about the poor quality of tobacco received; even United States leaf had suffered a sharp fall in standards and Imperial had to double its efforts to maintain quality control by taking details of its requirements right to the growers, whether in Rhodesia or the United States, crop by crop, year by year. This was a lengthy process, but meanwhile smokers were offered varying recipes in an attempt to

* In each of the years 1950–54, the sterling values of tobacco imports from the dollar area were £36m, £56m, £24m and £50m. Of the total £166m, some £46m ranked for American aid.

hit upon a consistent brand content that would cultivate loyalty through a reasonable quality rather than illusion.

An oddity at this time was a half-hearted decision by Imperial's executive committee to meet the promotion of Cope's Old Holborn for hand rolling of cigarettes. In 1950, it was ruled that some branches—but not Wills, Player or Churchman—could use the words 'For Pipe and Cigarette' on packets of tobacco or in shop promotion, but not in newspaper or poster advertising. Pictorial representation of hand rolling was banned outright, as were any references to economy. However, a small, if growing, army of hand rollers had already hit upon the merits of Imperial's Ringer A1 Light mixture as an alternative to Old Holborn.

That April a Fleet message was despatched by the Admiralty that there would be a 20 per cent cut in the issue of duty-free tobacco on ships and at home naval establishments. This ended a long dispute going back to 1931 when Customs and Excise first challenged the sailors' concession (their first was granted in 1793) on the grounds of excessive consumption and evidence of their smuggling the cheap tobacco to people outside the 'Senior Service'. The British Navy was not the only source of smuggling onto a black market. Tobacconists in East Anglia complained that cigarettes were changing hands illegally from the United States. Service bases and the American authorities ordered that all their men sign undertakings that the issue of tobacco was for personal use only.

The steady return over the next four years to free marketing ought to have enabled Wills, the pioneer of machine-made cigarettes, to develop a new sales strategy. The Player's branch (John Dane died in April 1950) was proving a lively rival eroding Wills' Woodbine in Class A cigarettes with Weights and Wills' Capstan and Gold Flake in Class B with Player's Medium. Contrary to expectations, it was in the Class B market that growth was to come for the manufacturers and Wills' dominance in the economy range with Woodbines was not enough to underpin Imperial's total position. Sales of Capstan and Gold Flake were being lost to either Player's Medium or, more seriously for Imperial, to Gallaher's Senior Service. The Gallaher brand was made with what was called a 'dense ender' which packed the tobacco firmly at each end of the Senior Service cigarette. This gave a better smoke and customers believed it to be a larger cigarette.

But new brands could not yet be contemplated so competition was still very restricted, enabling Imperial to engineer a manufacturers' price rise in 1951, the first non-duty increase since the war.

Aware that a price advance might have a short-term demand effect, so disrupting the Exchequer's revenue forecasts, the manufacturers under Imperial's lead gave the Board of Trade advance notice of their rise of ½d on ten small cigarettes and 1d for ten of the bigger classes. There would be a weight adjustment for tobacco content to keep the variation in cost in line with coinage. Duty now accounted for 80 per cent of the retail price of cigarettes, with manufacturing costs plus profits at 11 per cent—the rest being the distributor's margin. The record was a good one. Retail prices generally had soared, indeed doubled since 1939. The Board of Trade was not happy and called for an accountant's report. This led to a request to Imperial, as price leader, to limit the 1d for ten rise for medium and some higher grade brands to ½d, plus some weight changes.

Another burst of corporate take-overs and general re-alignment followed the price adjustments. Each deal, however, had its separate motivation, even if controlled pricing restricted the urge to compete. Gallaher, not having Imperial's inhibitions about hand rolling, bought Cope Brothers & Company which also traded under the name of Richard Lloyd & Sons. This deal gave Gallaher the Old Holborn brand of smoking mixture, much favoured by hand rollers, and there were other advantages. The board 'felt frustrated' that the allocation of dollars for buying United States tobacco precluded Gallaher from fully meeting demand for its cigarettes, such as the increasingly popular Senior Service, as well as Park Drive. Cope Brothers' dollar quote was, therefore, an important factor in the take-over. Among other moves was Ardath's acquisition of three other manufacturers, John Wood & Son, Charlesworth & Austin, and the Express Tobacco Company. Imperial bought J. & H. Wilson and, not to be outdone, Carreras swallowed Murray Sons & Company, of Belfast, and R. & J. Hill, both old companies severely hit by the post-war tobacco controls. But the most important Carreras decision in marketing terms was a licensing arrangement under which the 'Black Cat' group obtained exclusive rights to sell cigarettes in the United Kingdom market under the trade-marks of Alfred Dunhill. Rapidly Dunhill White Spot cigarettes were introduced to the market. In 1952, Tissue Papers changed its name to Bunzl Pulp & Paper and, in the same year, Cigarette Components, its subsidiary, took over all filter manufacturing activities.

The pressures for reorganisation were reflected in an Imperial branch merger between W. T. Davies and Faulkner. Rothman's needed finance for expansion and became a subsidiary of the Rembrandt Tobacco Corporation of South Africa, a merger effected by 1954 as the industry's steady progress with the introduction of filter cigarettes added to the pressures. Molins was alarmed to learn that the Wix family were being wooed in mid 1953 by the German machinery makers Hauni Werke Körber & Company KG, as well as the American Machine & Foundry Company—the former with a view to using the Wix family's know-how, and the latter with a view to buying up Filter Tips, where the know-how was applied. Rather than let in foreign competition, Molins bought up Filter Tips, so avoiding the possible payment of royalties to a competitor for the existing patent relationship between Molins and Filter Tips. Later, Bunzl's Cigarette Components turned the screw tighter on filter-tipped supplies by obtaining a non-exclusive licence to Eastman Kodak patents to make rods of acetate tow in all countries except the United States.

If there was any common theme to all the 'wheeling and dealing' within the industry it was the need to anticipate the future. Small companies had to take refuge in better capitalised groups. Big manufacturers had to consolidate their manufacturing capability. It was becoming obvious, as wartime controls were progressively dismantled in other industries and trades, that a return to abundant leaf supplies could not be long delayed, even if quality or dollar problems might persist for a while longer.

CHAPTER TWELVE

A Question of Monopoly

When Gilbert Alan Hamilton Wills, the first Lord Dulverton, and chairman of Imperial Tobacco for twenty-three years, died, aged seventy-six, on 1st December 1956, it took some time for the family lawyers to work out his surviving personal fortune. Disregarding provisions made in his life-time for his heirs, there was still a gross estate of over £4 million of which the Exchequer promptly demanded more than £3 million in death duties. Like other members of the Wills family, his munificence to the City of Bristol was beyond doubt. Not long before his death, Lord Dulverton had footed the bill for restoring the war-blitzed Great Hall of the local University, founded in 1908 by a donation from Henry Overton Wills, who became the first Chancellor.

That the Exchequer wanted a £3 million plus cut of Lord Dulverton's personal fortune, much reduced by good works, was too much for his son,* who declared: 'It may seem regrettable that the capital fund of my late father's estate, which he had used wisely and for the benefit of so many others besides himself, is to be lost as a small drop in the ocean of State income.'

The disgruntled heir spoke bitterly of the revenue authorities' windfall in an interview with a local correspondent of *The Times*. He stopped himself on the brink of alleging the money would be squandered by the State, instead of being preserved for some worthy task. That £3 million should be regarded as 'a drop in the ocean' raised many eyebrows in less affluent circles, yet tobacco

* The second Lord Dulverton became a Council member of Oxfam in 1962.

manufacturers are always conscious of the huge sums that their products have raised in State taxation and levies. Since 1900, net receipts of tobacco duty in Britain had yielded well over £9,700 million.

Whatever the merits of the second Baron Dulverton's remarks on the heavy taxation of private wealth, the complaint served largely to focus attention on one individual's reward from Imperial Tobacco. The company had total sales of £640 million and profits of around £23 million. In 1955, it accounted for 79 per cent of the total United Kingdom tobacco market. Public sympathy for anyone with an income partly deriving from such an enterprise was bound to be muted. Indeed, it gave a further point, however distantly relevant, to an inquiry authorised by the Government, only forty-eight hours before Lord Dulverton's death.

On 29th November 1956, G. H. Andrew, a Secretary of the Board of Trade, signed two papers called 'references' which were immediately despatched to the Monopolies Commission. They required the Commission, which had already prepared twenty-one reports since its creation under the Monopolies and Restrictive Practices (Inquiry and Control) Act 1948, to investigate and report on the supply of cigarettes and manufactured tobacco as well as the supply of tobacco machinery. The terms of reference were to establish the existence of monopoly, scrutinise corporate behaviour for anti-competitive actions, and to indicate what practices operated against the public interest.

Public knowledge of the tobacco companies' history and development was very restricted. Brand names were familiar enough. The heavy and successive rises in taxation were understood, if not always popular. Large-scale manufacture and supply, however, was impersonal and the tobacconists' old-time personal service of individual smokers' requirements had become a mechanical affair, interrupted, anyway, by wartime shortages and the economic controls. Price levels had become a talking point among smokers becoming increasingly suspicious that they were being exploited not just by Chancellors but perhaps by the companies. There were few business writers to dispel the romantic notions about tobacco or to examine what common beliefs there were about the industry. Even tobacco traders and many senior executives in non-Imperial companies did not understand the sheer scale of the monopoly. Imperial had never felt much cause to outline its activities to anyone other than shareholders, who seemed content with the minimum of information. The secrecy was not calculated, just appropriate to managements used to public ignorance.

Consequently, Imperial felt aggrieved that the Board of Trade, with which it had so fully co-operated in war, and in austerity, should now embroil the tobacco industry in a costly and revealing inquiry. Yet no Government, especially one as sensitive to the public mood as the Conservative administration which had wrested power from Labour's central planners of the 1945–51 ilk, could ignore a developing public thirst for more facts about those who made and sold consumer products.

Whereas the pressures for the anti-trust investigation of Buck Duke's American Tobacco had sprung from farmers, the long-overdue inquiry in Britain into Imperial had its roots in the consumer revolution.

Mr Peter Thorneycroft (later Lord Thorneycroft), as President of the Board of Trade, was anxious to stimulate competition, and it was necessary to fire a warning shot or two across the bows of established industry in general now that the era of protection and cosy regulation of markets was over. No longer was the consumer to be the manufacturers' pawn. In future, the shopper must have freedom of choice in the High Street, where new self-service shops were beginning to proliferate as rationing began to disappear. Thorneycroft had appointed R. F. Levy Q.C. as chairman to give the Monopolies Commission a more active role than before in promoting vigorous competition* by the systematic examination of any industry where at least one-third of goods was supplied by one or two companies. Levy understood his task well and agreed that tobacco was eminently suitable territory for a purposeful study.

If Imperial's board, other directors, and their predecessors had really acted with rectitude and consideration to the requirements of the public interest, now was the time for them to prove these claims with hard facts and figures about themselves. However it did not stop the industry responding to the references with a chorus of 'surprise and puzzlement'. The reaction showed in itself a curious insensitivity to the public mood, which earlier in

---

* A Commons Select Committee had already prompted some amendments to the monopolies legislation to improve the speed and quality of the Commission's work.

1956 had persuaded the Government to pass the Restrictive Trade Practices Bill, outlawing groups of manufacturers' collective enforcement of fixed and common retail prices (but permitting individual suppliers to maintain with the full force of law their separate standard list resale prices in shops they did not own).

Yet the tobacco industry had some grounds for wondering why it should be selected for specific investigation so soon after the introduction of greater freedom from the Whitehall controls they had borne for so long after the war. Competition was developing. G. C. Larkin, of J. Wix & Sons, whose company had that very month embarked on the first major cigarette gift coupon scheme since the war (Kensitas), called the proposed inquiry 'rather ironic just at the time when competition is making itself felt'. He saw Imperial being able to claim: 'Look at the competition we are getting.'

One of the answers, of course, was that Thorneycroft had access to the Board of Trade's accumulated confidential information on Imperial and the industry. He knew well enough there were plenty of reasons for assuaging the public's emerging thirst for information. Disclosure of some of the industry's many secrets would surely do no harm, and probably help to avoid possible abuses by Imperial in the future of its obvious market power.

In the three years before the Monopolies Commission inquiry was ordered, there had undoubtedly been a transformation of the industry from one of restricted and collaborative control to one of free marketing. Thorneycroft was aware of this transitional character of supply arrangements and wanted to ensure that Imperial would resist any temptation to stifle fair competition. After all, in 1954, Imperial held 75.4 per cent of the tobacco sales, and it had risen higher in both 1955 and 1956. In contrast, Gallaher held 11.2 per cent in 1954 against 11.9 per cent for Ardath, Carreras, Godfrey Phillips, Rothman's and J. Wix combined, and 1.5 per cent for the Co-operative Wholesale Societies and all others. What no one knew, outside a small circle, was that Imperial had a large shareholding in Gallaher and Ardath as well as their shares in fifteen other manufacturers outside its own combination of branches such as Wills and Player's.

Imperial's restrictive practices such as controls on retailers' displays, loyalty bonuses, machinery rights, refusal of supplies to price cutters, market sharing with BAT were all matters requiring an independent assessment of whether they conflicted with the public interest. Was the competition now developing an illusion, or even constrained? Were remedies to actual or possible abuses of market power needed? Thorneycroft looked to the Commission to provide the details, and some appropriate recommendations.

Although special committees officially probed Resale Price Maintenance in 1920 and 1930, the drive to bring about its end had not gained much impetus until the early fifties. In 1949, there was the Lloyd Jacob Committee which reported to the then President of the Board of Trade, Harold Wilson. That committee gave qualified approval for price fixing, providing enforcement was not undertaken collectively by groups of suppliers or trade associations. But Wilson was not convinced by the arguments that severe price cutting would be against the public interest and subsequently a White Paper was issued stating that all forms of RPM must, with a few special exemptions, end. Unfortunately, the Attlee administration passed out of office and both Wilson and his successor as President of the Board of Trade, Sir Hartley Shawcross, lost the chance to implement their ideas.

During the next four years, the Monopolies Commission, established in 1948, drew public attention to the restrictive nature of resale price fixing and there were frequent startling reports about private trade courts 'trying' enterprising traders for price cutting. By 1956, the Conservatives were securely established in office. Taking account of public disquiet, the Government turned its attention confidently to problems of monopoly and restrictive practices. The result was the Restrictive Trade Practices Act 1956, which banned the collective enforcement of resale prices, but permitted the individual supplier to determine retail prices for his goods with the full authority of the law.

Yet doubts lingered on and many members of all the main political parties felt RPM must eventually go. With the grocery trade switching to self-service techniques and undermining fixed prices as competition grew fiercer, most politicians opposed to RPM felt the practice would wither away by voluntary abandonment and there need not be fresh legislation.

Not until the Great Trading Stamp War of the 1960s did the Government of the day feel obliged to face the issue squarely.

By the middle of 1954 the supply of leaf had improved sufficiently for the tobacco industry to adopt what became known as the

Freedom Scheme. Manufacturers were allowed to import all the North American leaf they thought they needed to meet full demand for their brands, on giving an undertaking to the Board of Trade that the dollar proportion of the light and Oriental tobacco used in manufacture for the home trade would not exceed 61 per cent. This was effectively a limitation on the dollar content of cigarettes. With Imperial and Gallaher agreeing to an initial reduction in their dollar allocations, all manufacturers now received licences to import tobacco according to their estimates of requirements. The broad intention was for manufacturers to meet all their available trade and to maintain reasonable stocks as free marketing accelerated.

To avoid initial strain, Imperial gave the Board of Trade an undertaking that, during the first twelve months of the Freedom Scheme, it would not raise output by more than 5 per cent, nor run down stocks of dollar tobacco below eleven months' needs. This proved to be a sacrifice as there were plenty of smokers anxious to buy more Player's Medium and Weights or Wills' Capstan and Woodbines. Gallaher gave no such assurance, and, as Senior Service sales immediately boomed, Imperial obtained a release from its undertaking within three months. So, in January 1955, manufacturers voluntarily ended the rationing of cigarette supplies.

The dam of demand broke and, by 1955, both Gallaher and Imperial were having difficulties in supplying the market. Both had to put some brands back on 'quota', rationing supplies to the trade on a temporary basis. Gallaher took over Benson & Hedges to raise output of Senior Service as well as to acquire a distinguished new trade-mark for its stable. Competition was more evident, in spite of the individual supply problems. Imperial transmitted its first commercial television advertisement, for Woodbines and Capstan, and actively began recruiting new trade accounts. Demands from retailers for better margins were met with price rises that summer, the result of joint meetings and Imperial supplying advance copies of its price list to other producers. Meanwhile, Imperial ordered the building up of a £1 million stock of cigarette cards as contingency planning for any outbreak of pre-war style promotion.

All this, however, risked the very severe loss of market position by the smaller manufacturers. Only Gallaher seemed able to expand against Imperial's onslaught. It was no consolation to see Wills and Player's battling for supremacy (in 1955, Player's overtook Wills as the biggest manufacturing unit within Imperial and the total market). Player's had introduced Bachelor tipped and proved the acceptability of a low-priced filter cigarette with a consistent quality. To this challenge, Wills responded with Bristol, a brand based exclusively on Commonwealth leaf to guarantee supplies. The trend was towards milder-tasting cigarettes and more variety in price ranges. Tipped cigarettes still only accounted for 2 per cent of total sales, but the future seemed to augur well for new brands.

It quickly became obvious to the Board of Trade that freedom was producing a worrying rise in Imperial's total position. The combine's share, by virtue of an expanding market, rose from 76 per cent to 79 per cent for all tobacco products between 1954 and 1955. Gallaher, in which Imperial had its secret shareholding, had lifted its share of cigarettes from 6 per cent in 1953 to 10 per cent in 1954, and then in 1955 went over 14 per cent, with a 15 per cent holding on all tobacco products. In contrast, the market shares of Carreras, Godfrey Phillips, Ardath and J. Wix fell back. Carreras, once the chief rival to Imperial, saw its slice of the cigarette market cut from 8½ per cent in 1953 to 3 per cent two years later.

Two very small manufacturers, Amalgamated Tobacco and B. Morris & Sons, found themselves falling foul of the Tobacco Trade Association's restrictive pacts when they tried to launch coupon brands. Imperial withheld supplies of its brands from retailers who handled the first coupon cigarettes to appear since the Martin Agreement (though executives knew that a recent Monopolies Commission report on Collective Discrimination in trade was making Whitehall think about banning collective resale price maintenance practices).

That the tobacco industry engaged in widespread resale price maintenance was beyond any doubt. Price fixing was made possible by the existence of the Tobacco Trade Association and the power of Imperial in the market place. No trader dare risk cutting prices when supplies could be quickly cut off. Manufacturers might be competing more than at any time since the Second World War, but Imperial was certainly not anxious to encourage a return to the free-for-all conditions that had produced the Martin Agreement.

Most distributors were also keen on standard pricing as it guaranteed them margins and limited the nature of competition between shops. They were always grumbling about cooperative societies being permitted to give dividends on tobacco sales, but then the cooperative movement kept its own cigarette factories in reserve in case Imperial should dare to amend conditions of sale to ban deferred customer discounts on non-cooperatively made brands in its shops.

There was a long history of collaboration between manufacturers. Between 1945 and 1956 there were fifty-four meetings, and many other discussions took place involving the Wholesale Tobacco Trade Association and the National Union of Retail Tobacconists. Within these consultations, it was comparatively easy for price maintenance to be enforced and margins carefully controlled.

The enactment of a new law banning collective enforcement of fixed prices to the consumer led to changes in the tobacco industry's arrangements. The Tobacco Trade Association had to be wound up in September 1956, and so the twenty-year-old coupon trading pact signed under the Martin Agreement came to a sudden end. Imperial let everyone know of its intention to continue to enforce resale price maintenance on an individual basis—a clear hint to other producers that its standard conditions of sale ought to be followed without breaking any law. There were other actions by the group to hold the threat of full-blooded competition at bay. Cash bonuses to traders were raised, plus extras for customers who paid accounts promptly. Weights of some brands were amended to improve profitability. An arrangement was made with an old-established independent manufacturer to undertake production of Imperial cigarettes (not implemented, for Molins now came up with the Mark VIII machine capable of producing 2,000 cigarettes a minute).

Attitudes towards Imperial were changing. Carreras became disgruntled when Molins refused applications for hinged lid carton packets because Imperial insisted on the licensing agreement for machinery being kept. Molins was not happy, either, aware that a competitor, Hauni, was offering a rival product. In 1956 and early 1957, Imperial relented and allowed the sale of three- and two-row packets alongside hull and slide packets. This, and other actions, prompted some disquiet within the tobacco industry which the sensitive ears in Whitehall quickly picked up.

There were rumours that Imperial wanted to wind up Ardath, which had moved into a loss position, and was only subsidising the joint subsidiary as some form of insurance against a new outbreak of coupon competition. An internal Imperial committee had, indeed, been considering a strategy for fighting anyone who re-introduced coupons, even if Wills and Player's branches did not want to use coupons.

Imperial's view via its executive committee, after the winding up of the Tobacco Trade Association, was that it should be prepared, and in October—one month before the Government ordered the Monopolies Commission investigation—Ardath was permitted to inquire among manufacturers of consumer goods about the possible supply of their products for gift coupon smoking. The chairman of Imperial thought any attack ought to be met by resorting to consumer competition rather than gift voucher collections for he was 'by no means yet convinced we would want the Ardath Company with a paltry £1.5 million sales to bell the cat'. So much for the independence of Ardath's management. It was obviously a creature of Imperial, subject to the combine's sanction.

For Imperial's part, the executive committee regarded the group, with 76 per cent of the tobacco market, as more vulnerable with the ban on collective resale price maintenance. Profits of over £26 million a year were at risk if competitors became more daring and flexible in exploiting the advantages of smaller size. Imperial might enjoy the economies of large-scale production, but size had disadvantages when it came to responding quickly to market challenges. The costs of launching new brands or switching mass production routines were huge. A sign of nervousness was Imperial's representation at shareholders' meetings of competitors in 1956, with observers keeping ears keen for words about possible coupon trading.

But Imperial's board knew there was the large financial interest in Gallaher on disclosure of which the public might draw the wrong conclusions about the group's methods for maintaining market leadership. Gallaher's Senior Service and Park Drive cigarettes were already making inroads into Imperial's sales without coupon trading.

Corporate antennae had already picked up Government moves towards ordering a monopolies inquiry. On the face of it, there seemed to be more vigorous competition to assuage any Whitehall disquiet.

It was an ironic twist to the situation that, when the reference of tobacco supply to the Monopolies Commission was ordered, J. Wix & Sons should promptly introduce, as the fifth largest cigarette maker, a coupon trading scheme for Kensitas Extra Size—a scheme subsequently enlarged to the company's filter brands (by 1960 Kensitas tipped with coupons was Britain's second best-selling filter cigarette). The response from smokers was beyond even Wix's wildest expectations. The company had been in some financial trouble, for, in 1954, sales had been £17.3 million, but by 1956 had plummeted to under £3 million. Coupons helped tobacco sales to rise spectacularly in 1957 to £12.7 million and touch £23.8 million by 1959. During this time, 1956-9, Imperial's sales fell from £641.2 million to £592 million. Only Gallaher would perform better in these three years, raising sales from £156.3 million (they had been just over £87 million in 1954) to £273.6 million.

Another company in trouble had been coupon pioneers Carreras whose sales in 1956 at £22 million compared with a 1954 level of almost £60 million. Carreras was strangely reluctant to follow Wix's method of hitting out at Imperial in the 'good old-fashioned way of the thirties'. The board even had talks with Imperial to see whether some means might be devised to protect the trade from gifts and competitions on the lines of the Martin Agreement. Discussions were abortive, for lawyers constantly declared that any agreement would take the industry before the Restrictive Practices Court. So, in May 1957, Carreras re-introduced coupons for Black Cat cigarettes and a limited gifts scheme for the Turf brand. Unfortunately the enthusiasm of the marketing men was blunted by the board's half-hearted support for the step. Not even Imperial's subsequent permission to Ardath to introduce two coupon brands could stimulate a more vigorous and positive selling campaign.

During the next few years, as the Monopolies Commission slowly and patiently gathered its information, seeking evidence of behaviour against the public interest under the post-war competition legislation, Imperial would market eleven new brands (up to 1960) in its efforts to maintain market strength but one-third of all brands sold by Imperial made losses. Profitability was sustained, however, by the still considerable sale of old favourites and, more particularly, by two general price rises—in September 1957 and August 1959—not resulting from duty charges. It pushed the price rises through by informing other manufacturers of its proposals, while avoiding joint meetings with them, which would have been illegal. As it was, the practice of advance notification of changes to margins would be considered questionable when a Monopolies Commission inquiry (the preliminary conclusions of the Commission were not put to Imperial until October 1959) was investigating how Britain was supplied with 260 million lb or so of tobacco via 430,000 licensed retailers.

Price cutting was feared within Imperial. It had asked wholesalers to stop supplies to any retailer who dared break conditions of sale and, on at least one occasion, employed private detectives to investigate one troublesome price cutter's activities. In the four months after the Tobacco Trade Association arrangements for collective enforcement of standard list prices were banned, Imperial's conditions of sale department handled thirty-five cases of price cutting compared with only eight in the first eight months of 1956. Imperial made no secret of its intention to take any trader to court, if necessary, to obtain injunctions under the new Restrictive Trade Practices Act, which banned collective action on price maintenance but allowed manufacturers to set retail prices as an individual company.

More tactfully, and perhaps wisely, Imperial and BAT were quick to modify their arrangements over the jointly owned Molins machinery monopoly. A few months after the Commission was asked to undertake its task, the two giants signed separate agreements with Molins which effectively cancelled the 1927 restrictive pact. Royalty payments between Molins and Imperial stopped. All machines subject to restrictions were released on to the market, but certain preferential rights were preserved on prices for the two big shareholding tobacco groups. For several years, Molins had pressed for less constrained conditions, worried not only by the trend of British legislation on restrictive practices, but also by the United States anti-trust legislation that the rival Amfoco might have invoked, perhaps banning Molins machinery in the American market because of the preferential arrangements made for Imperial and BAT. Molins had always stopped Imperial from trying to go too far by any 'undue degree of interference' and at one stage, Imperial even thought of selling its shareholding because of Molins' sensitivity.

The size of Imperial and all its ramifications sometimes made for insensitivity. After all, it was now selling cigarettes through 100,000 trade customers (some of the largest in group ownership). However, there had been times when other qualities of the management were to the fore. For some time, the Anstie business had been kept alive 'on sentimental grounds' and it would survive until 1958, when it ceased to manufacture and Imperial gave the brands and goodwill to the Ringer branch, continuing the structural concentration that in 1957 also saw the Stephen Mitchell branch merging with Wills, and Davey with Edwards, Ringer & Bigg. There was an external structural change, too, effected about this time when the Robert Sinclair Tobacco Company, an Imperial member, bought the goodwill and certain assets of Carreras' Newcastle subsidiary, John Sinclair. This brought Imperial's acquisition of wholesale tobacconists since 1930 to thirteen.

This sale by Carreras alerted the rest of the industry to that company's difficulties. Coupons were proving a costly venture, and big money was needed to revive Carreras' fortunes in the years of freedom of leaf supply. The Baron family, who had held a controlling interest since the early 1900s, realised that a recent commitment to build a big new factory, sited at Basildon New Town in Essex, might be too ambitious. Coupon cigarettes were not providing the growth that the productive capacity demanded, nor could the introduction of a new filter brand called Guards, a popular enough cigarette, restore the company to its former glory. More overseas marketing was needed as well as capital to deploy in national promotion at home. In November 1958 the Baron family sold their shares to the Rembrandt Tobacco Company, run by the South African Dr Anton Rupert, a one-time university lecturer, who four years before had taken control of Rothman's.

Rupert was a dynamic new figure on the world tobacco scene. His Rembrandt group, founded only a decade before, was already a major corporation, selling its brands in one hundred and twenty different countries. His first act was to begin integration of Carreras and Rothman's, eventually transferring all British manufacturing to Basildon and setting up export arrangements under various associate managements. His aim was to keep Carreras identifiable as a British company, operating in its own right—an objective that pleased the British managers, who often bristled when newspapers occasionally referred to the concern as a subsidiary of a South African parent. The Carreras Rothman's marketing division was formed within a year, and Carreras brands were cut down to six for cigarettes and twenty-three for tobacco. New men were brought in to refresh top management.

The new team, including Ronald Plumley, managing director, had ideas for solving the sales problems. Rothman's was set to work marketing king-sized filter cigarettes, offering a longer smoke. This was to be a winner, especially in the duty-free travellers' market as well as the general trade. Black Cat coupon cigarettes were scrapped.

Carreras and Rothman's were to go after the 'classy' trade to raise profitability. A breed of king-sized cigarettes such as Dunhill International, Craven A and Peter Stuyvesant was reared alongside Rothman's. Menthol Consulate 'as cool as a mountain stream' appeared. The quality range was enhanced by more active promotion of Murray's Erinmore pipe tobacco. Later there would come Piccadilly Filter-De-Luxe and the world's first multi-filter cigarette, Ransom.

Perhaps the realigned Carreras group's most successful move was the general policy switch to go for filter-tipped smoking which was where its new experts believed the future rested. Even by 1960, filter cigarettes represented only 15 per cent of the market, so it was a bold decision not just to push Guards in the lower price ranges of smokers' choices but to stake so much on king-sized categories. Market research was yielding some interesting findings. Player's Bachelor, an early filter brand, had done much to give that brand ascendancy over Wills by the time of W. G. Player's death in June 1959, when Player's held 49 per cent of Imperial's cigarette production. Large spending by Wills on the rival but less successful Bristol helped to spread the practice of filter smoking, as did even newer brands such as Gallaher's Nelson, sold with all the Navy traditions that had long characterised much of the industry's advertising, and the less successful Olivier.

Marketing men were divided over the trends of consumer preference in the late fifties. The general trend appeared to be away from A class cigarettes such as Woodbines and Park Drive to the more expensive B class cigarettes like Player's Medium and

Senior Service plain. Smokers seemed to want higher quality and presentation while looking for economy. It was a conflicting requirement they placed on manufacturers, now thrashing around with menthol, king-sized, economy filters or whatever. Before the final decontrol of tobacco supplies, five to eight brands had been the stock-in-trade of an average retailer. Now the shopkeeper had to carry around fifteen or so, and there was always a rush to try the newest brand, fair or foul. Carreras' policy was to break the gap between the A and B classes with its Guards filters, which were attractively packed and well advertised on television, while meeting demand elsewhere with king-sized filters which contained layered cigarettes with the price economy of 'non-taxed dog-ends'. Wix's Kensitas coupons were regarded as an isolated success, not to be emulated on a large scale until the market gave a more settled indication of trends. If anyone seemed to point the way, it was Gallaher, whose Senior Service was a source of constant worry to Imperial, in spite of the latter's huge sales still resting on traditional brands, whatever the claims for tipped Bristol, Bachelor and the more recent Kingsway and the disastrous Strand ('You are Never Alone with a Strand' ran the haunting theme of a television commercial much exploited by comedians that became notorious in the trade).

The simple fact was that, at 30 per cent, Gallaher's share of the cigarette trade was larger than that of any individual competitor of Imperial throughout its history. It was proof that a small manufacturer could build up trade against the monopoly supplier, which in 1960 offered the public 57 brands of cigarettes and 183 brands of tobacco. But there was a reminder of the difficulties, too, as the chairmanships of both Gallaher and Imperial changed for a new decade.* This was the decision by Godfrey Phillips in September 1960 to hand over five-sixths of most of its tobacco brands' home trade to the ailing Ardath, which became sole concessionaire in the home market on a royalty basis. A once great manufacturer—at one time the third largest cigarette maker— had to face the choice of ceasing home market manufacture or closing down its main factory altogether. De Reszke filter cigarettes had suffered badly in the market place against newer filter brands.

* In March 1959, Lord Sinclair of Cleeve's twelve-year reign ended and R. S. W. Clarke succeeded as Imperial's chairman. Sir Edward de Stein handed on the Gallaher chair to C. W. S. Mason.

The Four Square–Marcovitch–Passing Clouds–De Reszke concern of Godfrey Phillips had previously hoped to do a deal outside the Imperial empire. It could not afford the sums needed to survive in an era of expensive national advertising. Ardath's business had not long been again reorganised—in June 1960 the High Court sanctioned the repayment of Preference shares and a new company called Ardath (UK) was created as a wholly owned subsidiary of Imperial to take over the former company's operations in the home market (while BAT took the overseas side and the original Ardath Tobacco Company Limited). Ardath (UK), the new company, now took over a trade of 30 million cigarettes and 50,000 lb of tobacco mostly from Godfrey Phillips and switched the production to Imperial factories. The Ardath (UK) company, confined to marketing and distribution, would only last until the end of July 1964 when the Churchman, Lambert & Butler brand took over selling operations as well as manufacturing.

It was a sad emasculation of Godfrey Phillips, a once great name of tobacco, which would nevertheless survive, if with less prominence, until a final surrender before a take-over by Philip Morris. Various decisions had been taken because of the concern to keep the company in a growth posture, such as the launching of Four Square Books in 1957 and general diversification into printing and greetings card manufacture. The retention of the Abdulla & Company and Pritchard & Burton brands ensured a useful presence in the market for speciality cigarettes, such as blended Muratti, or Turkish and Egyptian types such as Abdulla No. 11, or De Reszke Turks. In retrospect, Godfrey Phillips took the right course, as profits of the enterprise did revive quite markedly, free from the demanding task of fighting the Imperial combine directly in the British market-place. The kind of profit margins which might be acceptable to large producers of Imperial and Gallaher's ilk were insufficient for smaller manufacturers with some ambitions of growth.

Godfrey Phillips was better off on the sidelines when Imperial's Player and Wills branches decided the time was ripe to demonstrate its market muscle power to the increasingly ambitious Gallaher.

CHAPTER THIRTEEN

The Ugly Duckling Project

There was no greater testing time for Britain's tobacco managements than the advent of the sixties. In America king-sized brands helped by a favourable tax situation* were accounting for 95 per cent of sales of all filter brands, which accounted for over 40 per cent of total cigarette sales. Filters were selling very well in Germany, Switzerland, and South Africa. The increase in smoking by women was boosting demand for filter-tipped cigarettes everywhere. But the greatest growth was yet to come from a combination of factors, not least of which were more swingeing rises in duty and health scares.

It was necessary for marketing men in Britain not to underrate the importance of the fact that Excise duty accounted for about 75 per cent of the retail price of plain cigarettes, on shifts in demand. Successive rises in price intensified 'the smoker's search for better value for his smoking money', as one Imperial research document put it.

Brand strategies had increasingly to take account of price changes. The real dilemma in promotion was the option of quality versus price in marketing a cigarette.

An example of the dilemma was the conflicting position of two brands that were making ground—Gallaher's Senior Service, recognised as a quality product, and Wix's Kensitas coupon, appealing to the instincts for quality. Heads were scratched at John Player, anxious to maintain the momentum of their growth and displacement of Wills as the largest single cigarette-making

* King size were in the same tax class as regular filters.

unit in Britain. There they knew well enough the rising demand for filter cigarettes, helped by the large rise in women smokers who disliked plain brands and the stray tobacco bits that 'got on the tongue'. In the summer of 1961 came a development that disrupted one trend—that of many smokers moving from the A class of the Wills' Woodbine type cigarette to the more expensive B class such as Player's Medium. It arose because that summer the Chancellor used his tax regulator powers to raise the duty element by 4d on B class packs of twenty cigarettes, to which the manufacturers added 1d. Player's chose this moment to launch a new brand, Gold Leaf Virginia Tipped in a striking Sultan red pack, embossed with the traditional Player's 'lifebuoy' trade-mark so familiar on Medium plain. It was a breakthrough in marketing terms, for the B class filter cigarette drew an immediate response by offering the same overall sized cigarette but at 8d per twenty less because of the lower tobacco, and therefore lower duty content. It was also a high quality product with a consistent recipe.

A sizeable proportion of smokers promptly switched to Gold Leaf and sales of Kensitas coupon cigarettes were improved by the heavy tax on rival standard B class brands. At Wills there was consternation. The Wills brand had already suffered two costly setbacks with the failure of king-sized Kingsway and Strand, which was an intermediate sized cigarette, not as good as Carreras' Guards. Executives in 1960 had commissioned a market research study which demonstrated that there were no longer any important adverse associations for coupons in smokers' minds and, indeed, were likely to be regarded as a 'plus'. Coupons did not necessarily ensure the success of a brand, as Ardath and Carreras were finding out. Coupons could only be regarded as an integral part of a marketing concept. The time seemed ripe for a Wills quality tipped cigarette in the B class which included coupons, an enforced savings element that Kensitas smokers 'actively desired' and did not just accept. The Wills response to the rival Player's branch of Imperial was now to put in hand a confidential plan for a completely new brand involving coupons. In the summer of 1961, highly secret files were opened, marked with the code name Ugly Duckling. It would be another year before all was revealed and the cigarette market in Britain would undergo its most dramatic transformation since the end of wartime restrictions.

While the marketing men at Wills and elsewhere prepared to

fight off Player's Gold Leaf, the most senior directors of the leading parent groups were contemplating another pressing problem— the Monopolies Commission inquiry.

The inquiry hung like the sword of Damocles over the tobacco industry, and Imperial in particular. Never before had the industry's affairs been subject to intense investigation and the measure of disclosure that answering official questions had required. Imperial's board had been advised by the Commission in October 1959 that monopoly conditions prevailed and meetings had taken place in 1960 to discuss whether those conditions, or any of the 'things done', operated or might be expected to operate against the public interest. An equivalent procedure had been used for telling Molins that there was a similar provisional conclusion for the supply of machinery. What was more important was what the Commission would now recommend in its public report, first received in confidence in January 1961 by a new President of the Board of Trade, Reginald Maudling, and published a few months later for Parliamentary scrutiny.

It was a measure of Imperial's board-room sensitivity to the group's future that, even as secret talks were taking place with the Commission on various questions, the subsidiary Robert Sinclair acquired the Golden Wonder Crisp Company, a lusty new challenger to the monopoly of Smith's Potato Crisps. It was Imperial's first real diversification outside tobacco and the related paper and packaging industries. Not only was there a real worry about the group's future reliance on tobacco for growth, when branded a monopoly and so subject to constant Governmental scrutiny, but there was a growing public consciousness over the dangers of excessive smoking.

The board felt satisfied that Imperial's actions throughout its history would not attract undue criticism. Their combine was no Buck Duke operation and, indeed, the American Tobacco Corporation's worst mistakes had been studiously avoided. But one worrying item, among others, was the large shareholding held secretly through nominees in its principal rival in the market-place, Gallaher. The Commission were bound to disclose the size—and they did. It was a $42\frac{1}{2}$ per cent holding of Gallaher's Ordinary capital.

In a 245-page report the Commission conducted a masterly survey of Imperial's relentless development, attaining the lion's share of a retail trade in cigarettes and tobacco worth £1,050 million a year, of which duty averaged more than 70 per cent. What ought to have been the one consoling feature against critics of Imperial's position was the recent loss of ground. From a peak market share of 80 per cent, Imperial had slipped in its Jubilee year to 63.5 per cent, largely because Gallaher had been making more strenuous efforts and, with a market share of nearly 30 per cent, was in a better position than any competitors of Imperial throughout the monopoly's fifty-year history. Unfortunately, a big shareholding in Gallaher was not a fact to attract much public sympathy. Any success by Gallaher clearly meant profits on the shareholding, making any loss of market position to that company a less serious affair. The holding was becoming a kind of insurance policy rather than a defence against a new American invasion, which anyway had happened again when American Tobacco bought J. Wix, now marketing Kensitas coupon cigarettes with notable success.

The scale of competition to Imperial, discounting Gallaher, was puny, as seen in the table on the next page, even if it indicates the monopoly group's lack of new gains since the advent of freer marketing after the Second World War.

Why had Imperial kept exact details of its shareholding in its chief competitor from its own shareholders, the industry at large, and the public? It had even maintained a lofty silence whenever newspapers spoke of rumours of 'a large minority stake'. The Commission report revealed that the group had argued that public disclosure would 'inevitably lead the rest of the tobacco trade to assume a degree of control by Imperial over Gallaher which does not in fact exist'. It 'would be quite wrong for there to be an impression abroad that we in fact in any way control or influence Gallaher's trading policy and that competition between us is in some way blurred and inhibited'.

There was still a danger that American tobacco manufacturers would 'attempt to regain a footing in the United Kingdom' if the shares were to be sold, a repetition of the original motive for the investment. Observers of the industry were not impressed, however, by either the defensive nature of the original share investment, or the claim that it had not interfered with Gallaher's management. Circumstances had much changed and the board ought to take account of the contemporary view that foreign

Manufacturer	Sales of Cigarettes and Tobacco (a)						No. of Factories 1959
	1954	1955	1956	1957	1958	1959	
	£'ooo	£'ooo	£'ooo	£'ooo	£'ooo	£'ooo	
The Imperial Tobacco Co. (of Great Britain and Ireland) Limited (Imperial)	585,377	636,013	641,226	635,700	617,723	591,856	15
Gallaher Limited (Gallaher) ..	87,321	122,749	156,325	200,279	238,992	273,580	6(b)
J. Wix & Sons Limited (J. Wix)	17,313	1,919	2,975	12,725	15,461	23,799	1
Carreras Limited (Carreras) ..	59,395	26,199	22,036	21,813	20,106	20,339	3
Rothmans Limited (Rothmans)	56	195	694	1,924	4,767	8,562	1
Godfrey Phillips Limited (Godfrey (Phillips).. ..	7,005	7,537	8,829	8,458	7,977	6,855	2
Scottish Co-operative Wholesale Society Limited (S.C.W.S.) ..	3,898	3,231	3,380	3,371	3,285	2,910	1
Co-operative Wholesale Society Limited (C.W.S.).. ..	3,418	2,157	2,111	2,174	2,082	1,923	1
Ardath Tobacco Company Limited (Ardath) ..	8,118	2,585	1,492	1,696	1,632	1,525	1
Others	4,628	4,226	3,303	2,600 (c)	2,200 (c)	1,800 (c)	
Total	776,529	806,811	842,371	890,740	914,225	933,149	

(a) Not all manufacturers' sales figures are for calendar years (e.g. Imperial's figures are for years ended 31st October). In such cases the figures have been allocated to the nearest calendar year.

(b) Including one very small factory making limited quantities of special cigarettes.

(c) Estimated figures.

Source: Monopolies Commission Statistics.

investment in British industry was stimulating to competition and efficiency in serving the consumer. There was a history of restricting Gallaher's supply of the best cigarette-making machinery and display in shops.

Yet there was a good deal of truth in Imperial's assertion that it had allowed Gallaher a large degree of management freedom, markedly, at least, since the return of free marketing and political action on monopolies. The management of Gallaher itself attested to Imperial's general good behaviour, even if over the years it had had a number of scrapes over machinery supply and other matters.

The Commission firmly recommended to the Government, which held powers of enforcement, that Imperial should divest itself of any direct or indirect financial interest in Gallaher. The report stressed that before the recent determined competition from Gallaher, Imperial was not compelled to exert its maximum effort. And it went on: 'The company has lost trade to Gallaher in recent years and is now taking steps to recover its position. We consider that the stimulus to efficiency which Gallaher's competition provides might have been even greater if Imperial were not, through its investment in Gallaher, insured to some extent against the potential loss of profit. Imperial's interest in Gallaher renders less financially serious to Imperial the effect of any increase in Gallaher's share of the market at Imperial's expense, and this might tend to weaken Imperial's incentive to achieve the highest possible standard of competitive effort. In our opinion it is in the public interest that Imperial should be continuously exposed to the most strenuous competition and, although we see nothing improper in the company's attitude in this matter, we think for the reasons given above that the continuance of Imperial's investment in Gallaher operates and may be expected to operate against the public interest.'

Another recommendation was that Imperial should terminate its existing bonus agreements with distributors and remove any restrictive elements from future discount schemes. No tobacco manufacturer should in future enter into an arrangement with a distributor the effect of which was to force the distributor who advertised a competing product to advertise the manufacturer's product as well.

Apart from the recommendation on the Gallaher shareholding, Imperial was not displeased with the report, for its paramount conclusion was that Imperial's monopoly position, as such, did not operate against the public interest, nor might it be expected to do so. The Commission declared: 'Our review of the development of Imperial's monopoly position has led us to conclude that the absence of the stimulus of effective competition was reflected for many years in the company's organisation and commercial policy but that in spite of certain points of criticism Imperial has exercised responsibility and restraint in making use of its power as a monopolist. In examining certain features of the existing position we have also concluded that Imperial does not earn a rate of profit which is so high as to be contrary to the public interest and, in the conditions of present-day competition, is not likely to do so; that it is contrary to the public interest that Imperial retains its substantial investment in the equity of Gallaher but that its interests in Ardath, Sinclair, Bewlay and Finlay are of little significance; that its interest in Molins and in companies making packing materials and cigarette paper are unobjectionable; and that its distribution system is unobjectionable except for the bonus arrangements, which are contrary to the public interest.'

This general clearance allowed the Government to temper its handling of the Commision's report. Maudling, at the Board of Trade, was impressed by the evidence of considerable internal competition within Imperial because of the adoption of the branch system. There had, of course, been a drastic reduction in the number of branches to a point where there were just Wills, Player, Ogden, and the newly formed Churchman, Lambert & Ringer supplying 57 brands of cigarettes and 183 brands of tobacco.* The regulation of branch competition by central controls, handbooks of practice, and an executive committee was thought to be reasonable to ensure the implementation of corporate policies on those issues which could not be left entirely to branches. Talks promptly began between the Board of Trade and Imperial on the issue of the stake in Gallaher. Imperial argued persuasively that the shareholding was not against the public interest.

The upshot was that Imperial was not to be required to divest itself of the Gallaher holding, but the Government obtained an undertaking from Imperial not to intervene in that company's affairs over and above its private undertaking to Gallaher's management. The Government reserved its right to intervene in the future should circumstances change to justify such action.

No one took much notice at the time of a part of the Commission's report devoted to a minority note of dissent by one member, Professor G. C. Allen, a leading authority on monopolies law. He was concerned with the tobacco industry's pricing policy. He declared: 'I consider that the weight of evidence and argument shows that resale price maintenance in the tobacco industry is against the public interest and that this restrictive practice should be abolished.' Though this comment attracted little attention

* In 1938 Imperial supplied 191 brands of cigarettes and 596 brands of tobacco.

then, it was to prove a pertinent and troublesome one for Imperial and not before too long. Wills' still secret Ugly Duckling brand marketing plan was to prove a powerful influence in eroding the arguments for retaining manufacturers' rights to fix shop prices and, indeed, helped create conditions for a later President of the Board of Trade, Edward Heath, to ban the practice by law.

Nor would the Government's refusal to order Imperial to sell its shareholding in Gallaher necessarily indicate that the overall Commission report had been a damp squib at the industry's heels. Constant reference in newspapers and public discussion about the tobacco industry—it would swell up with the health issue— eventually required the board to act voluntarily on the recommendation.

At Gallaher's Granite House headquarters in the City there was discussion about the future. Imperial was bound to demonstrate its competitive claims more vigorously to reassure smokers, and Player's Gold Leaf in late 1961 was undoubtedly selling very well. Wills was rumoured to have a major new brand under review. Above all, if ever there was an opportune moment to take some bold new move, even of a structural nature, it was surely now. Imperial was hardly in a position to raise any objection even if it wanted to, and in any case the directors could not be sure that Imperial might not choose at some time to disturb morale, however accidentally or intentionally, by a reduction or even an outright sale of its shareholding.

The immediate issue was to hang on and improve on the 30 per cent market share that had impressed the Government.

With one bold step, Gallaher raised its market share to 37 per cent by persuading American Tobacco to sell the whole of the issued capital of J. Wix, the Kensitas firm, in return for £3.2 million Ordinary stock (with a market value of £14.4 million) in Gallaher. It was an ironic, if sound, acquisition, bound to leave new questions in the public mind. Now American Tobacco would hold a 13 per cent interest in Gallaher alongside Imperial's 42.5 per cent shareholding. This was an intriguing development so soon after a Monopolies Commission report which had revealed that Imperial's original purchase of a big interest in Gallaher had been intended to prevent any further American incursion into Britain. Once again Imperial, with its shares, could expect a share of a competitor's profits even if the deal, tacitly approved, was not of the making of the men in Bristol. And Wix was making good profits. Secret figures made available to Gallaher's board in deciding the take-over disclosed a startling change due to the Kensitas coupon brands. Wix had made a loss of £341,327 in 1955 but in 1960 had earned, after expenses and pre-tax, £1,368,358. It was little wonder Gallaher was willing to pay £14.4 million in the form of an issue of new Ordinary shares for a company that had net assets of only £4.4 million.

Treasury consent for the deal was given but some Government advisers were nonetheless intrigued at the new share structure. American Tobacco finally said it intended to retain the holding it now had in Gallaher, rather than sell the shares at market value, 'as it is their wish to keep an interest in the United Kingdom tobacco trade'. There was now a new option for the future in periodic reviews of Imperial's position for, allowing for the public holding, American Tobacco was in a tactical position to bid for regaining control according to market circumstances.

But there was a problem for Imperial in that a voluntary decision entirely to reduce or sell its share in Gallaher could easily let American Tobacco gain control. As if to reassure Imperial, American Tobacco declined to have any directors on Gallaher's board and said the shareholding was an investment. A 'sound British payment' was all that it wanted. With these words, the Americans withdrew, content to collect their dividends. No one envisaged that executives of the American giant would be rushing back seven and a half years later for a fierce take-over battle that would despoil the City's good name in some influential eyes.

The view was firmly being taken by Gallaher that future growth must rest with filter-tipped brands, and indeed the management had introduced Nelson and Olivier to test public reaction. There was also a rising demand for cigars and a new factory for Freeman's was opened. The Benson & Hedges acquisition was later to bring Hamlet small cigars to sell alongside Freeman's Manikin. In 1961, filter brands were holding around 23 per cent of total cigarette sales compared with 10 per cent in 1958. The lines of sales graphs for filters were getting steeper now Gold Leaf was moving into third place in the then 3s 10d for twenty market. To launch a new brand with coupons would be a costly operation, with all that was entailed in setting up buying operations and redemption facilities for gifts. There was one big advantage in buying Wix. For smokers who had begun collecting the coupons towards a gift there was a strong disincentive to change to a new cigarette. No one would want, surely, to stop hoarding their coupons when approaching the point of collecting their prize. And there was no reason to give coupons with established brands that sold well enough, such as Senior Service. The Kensitas brand offered coupons on both tipped and plain cigarettes and built new choices into Gallaher's brand range.

About to be dramatically tested was Gallaher's belief that smokers would be reluctant to switch to a new coupon brand when hoarding coupons for an existing and popular product such as Kensitas, whose packet had the famous motif of an old English butler carrying a tray on which rested a pack with a similar motif— and so on to infinity. But first came the publication by the Royal College of Physicians of a report* in March 1962 entitled 'Smoking and Health'. This was a document of major importance to the tobacco industry, which had given large sums to the Medical Research Council and conducted its own studies of potential risks.

The take-over of Wix by Gallaher was proof of Wills' wisdom in preparing for an even stronger challenge by the contingency planning of a coupon brand. The costly Ugly Duckling project, approved by Imperial's executive committee in August 1961, suffered an internal setback when the Royal College of Physicians health report appeared, producing as it did a sharp, if temporary, drop in the consumption of cigarettes. Imperial was sensible enough to realise that an announcement of a gift coupon brand by a company that had a history of opposition to usage of such a sales incentive would generate criticism. Here were distinguished physicians providing new evidence of the health risks. No responsible tobacco manufacturer could risk the public censure of immediately marketing a brand that cultivated the loyalty of smokers and might encourage excessive consumption in the pursuit of gifts. MPs were already calling on the Government to introduce new controls on the industry to reduce the health hazards. Wills was told by Imperial's executive committee that the coupon project must be postponed. However, by August 1962 permission was reluctantly given for Wills to go ahead. Before anyone changed their minds, the Wills management called sales briefing conferences

* See Chapter 14.

in London and provincial centres for retailers and wholesalers to outline incentive schemes for a new brand (containing gift vouchers)—Embassy.

The trade and the press, which was separately briefed, were staggered by the lavishness of the launch, which alone was to cost over £1 million in promotional support besides the investment in stocks of gifts for the Robert Sinclair subsidiary to handle and distribute. The price of Embassy was the same as for a standard B class cigarette and the vouchers given determined at the same rate as Kensitas, with the weight specification making allowance for the value of the gift vouchers (Imperial was not giving anything away, whatever smokers might believe). It was an enforced form of saving on price and not a reward for the loyalty of Embassy smokers, even if many thought otherwise. The name of Embassy, packed in hinged lid crush-proof cartons, was not the first choice. Wills executives had originally planned to base the brand on the historic Gold Flake to derive the prestige of a top-quality name. But Imperial's central co-ordinators put their foot down, arguing that it was too like the new Gold Leaf name, given to Player's new tipped brand. Embassy was a dominant name in the Wills stable of trade titles and it was chosen because it had a 'snobbish' ring to it which helped overcome any feeling among smokers that the coupon brand was a cheap product they might be ashamed to be seen pulling out from their pockets.

The brand was so sensational that it made front-page news in the national newspapers. Virtually overnight, smokers switched to Embassy, and retailers promptly ordered bigger stocks, drawing incentives in the rush. Wills factories went onto overtime, and new capacity had to be hurriedly installed. Dutch printers (chosen to preserve secrecy in the planning stages) airlifted in fresh supplies of gift catalogues and vouchers. Expensive television commercials and heavy press advertising kept up the excitement, which was to give Wills back its position as the biggest cigarette maker in Britain, deposing the sister Player brand. In 1965, Embassy Filter would lead all other brands, plain and filter, with an 18.4 per cent share of the cigarette market. Other coupon brands would hold 3.6 per cent.

The movement of the market both with coupons and in overall terms can be seen from the chart on the next page.

From the introduction of Embassy in 1962, the next seven years

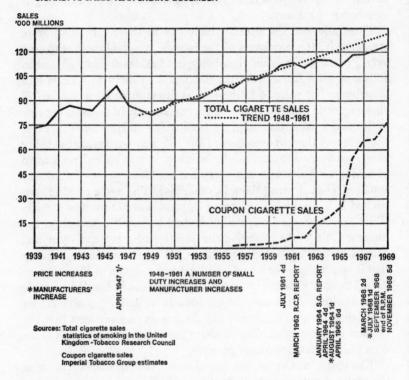

TOTAL CIGARETTE SALES AND COUPON
CIGARETTE SALES YEAR ENDING DECEMBER

SALES
'000 MILLIONS

TOTAL CIGARETTE SALES
••••••••• TREND 1948-1961

COUPON CIGARETTE SALES

PRICE INCREASES

∗MANUFACTURERS'
INCREASE

APRIL 1947 1/-

1948–1961 A NUMBER OF SMALL
DUTY INCREASES AND
MANUFACTURER INCREASES

JULY 1961 4d

MARCH 1962 R.C.P. REPORT

JANUARY 1964 S.G. REPORT
APRIL 1964 4d
∗AUGUST 1964 1d
APRIL 1965 6d

MARCH 1968 2d
∗JULY 1968 1d
SEPTEMBER 1968
end of R.P.M.
NOVEMBER 1968 5d

Sources: Total cigarette sales
statistics of smoking in the United
Kingdom - Tobacco Research Council

Coupon cigarette sales
Imperial Tobacco Group estimates

would see seventy new brands of cigarettes go on the market. Yet
the popularity of the coupon brands could not be shifted. Both
Gallaher and Carreras were forced to respond with coupons on
new and existing brands, with a varying degree of success. The
actions of both Player and Wills had the effect of improving
Imperial's monopoly position and cutting back Gallaher's market
share to 31 per cent in 1966 and then 27 per cent three years later.
Smokers relentlessly switched to smaller sized, lower weight
cigarettes and if they offered gift vouchers and filters, so much the
better, such were the pressures of prices due to successive duty
charges. Long established brands such as Player's Medium and
Wills' Woodbine went into rapid decline.

Smokers were more sensitive to price levels in their choice of
brands than to advertising, even if a powerful lobby had built up

to control advertising expenditure on the evidence of health risks. Before long the tobacco industry's critics, and the Government, would call for restrictions on coupons, but their appeals were lost in the public clamour for more price competition in the shops. If Imperial had unleashed new marketing forces in the tobacco trade after the Monopolies Commission report, not all competitive pressures were to its liking. A new breed of shopkeepers, the supermarketeers, were waiting on the sidelines, impatient to cut the cost of smoking but denied the opportunity by resale price maintenance.

Not even a Government ban on television advertising of cigarettes, introduced in July 1965, could counter the appeal of coupons. Overall consumption of tobacco was disrupted both by the health scare and Budget rises in duty (4d per packet of twenty standard cigarettes in 1964 and 6d in 1965), but coupon cigarettes were a growth sector in the market. This was to be recognised in December 1965 by Player's, who introduced their own coupon brand, Player's No. 6, at an economy A class price and size. No. 6 was another winner, securing an astonishing 13 per cent of the cigarette market within a year (and about 19 per cent by December 1969), eventually giving Player's back the leadership in the manufacturers' league table. In 1969, Player's obtained a 33 per cent cigarette market share,* compared with the 32 per cent of Wills, whereas in 1964 it had fallen to 20 per cent under the onslaught of Embassy, and Imperial's general mastery in marketing filter-tipped cigarettes with a mass appeal.

The success of Embassy cigarettes coincided with the adoption by several major supermarket chains, notably Tesco and Fine Fare, of trading stamps. Vociferous opponents of trading stamps called on manufacturers to invoke their powers of individual price enforcement, even cutting off supplies of new stocks to reduce the effectiveness of the stamps. Tobacco companies found themselves being pressed hard to take action against any shopkeeper who used them with tobacco goods. Retail tobacconists did not want their share of cigarette sales disturbed, and the manufacturers were not anxious to experience the kind of hard bargaining on bulk supply terms that had broken out between food manufacturers who had allowed RPM to erode in the grocery trade.

The Big Three tobacco groups—Imperial Tobacco, Gallaher

* In terms of numbers of cigarettes sold and not value.

and Carreras—had written reports in 1963 on Fine Fare's policy of openly giving away Sperry & Hutchinson pink stamps with tobacco goods. For some time the stamp companies, such as Green Shield, had urged retailers to be wary of offending the cigarette manufacturers who insisted on rigid fixed prices. Imperial decided to approach Fine Fare with a request that it cease to undermine resale price maintenance by the use of the stamps as a hidden price discount. A refusal might be followed by stronger action, such as stopping supplies, or legal action to test the validity of stamps on price-maintained goods. Fine Fare's management was told that Imperial Tobacco's conditions of sale were being contravened, and the supermarket chain agreed to exclude tobacco goods from stamp giving.

Imperial Tobacco's determination to deal with similar cases was clearly shown in a letter sent by the manager of the company's Conditions of Sale Department to William Judge, managing director of the Melias group of stores. 'This company regards the inclusion of its price-maintained goods in trading stamp schemes as a breach of its conditions of sale and its policy is to take up strongly any such breaches brought to our attention. We are glad to know that our attitude has your full support. We think it likely that your letter may have been prompted by the recent introduction of trading stamps by Fine Fare and we can advise you that as a result of prompt representations which we made, this firm has issued instructions to all branches to exclude tobacco goods from the scope of the scheme.' The letter promised similar action with other stamp traders.

Unfortunately, Embassy coupon cigarettes were to prove an embarrassment to the tobacco industry in the fight to retain resale price maintenance. Many opponents of price fixing were openly exploiting the national controversy over the use of trading stamps by shopkeepers—so out of control that supermarketeers were using the stamps to give a form of discount on RPM goods. How, they argued, could a manufacturer giving away coupons with cigarettes possibly object to a retailer, at his own cost, giving away trading stamps on tobacco products? Ronald Plumley, the managing director of Carreras, was quick to spot the way in which the tobacco industry's case for retaining price fixing was being weakened. Plumley said: 'If an industry generally supports retail price maintenance it seems hard, in my opinion, to defend that position if price maintenance should be used to any degree to assist in the support of the cost of the gifts provided by stamps or coupons.'

Newspaper reports of the way in which manufacturers were insisting on the observance of fixed retail prices, even to the exclusion of stamps, provided consumers with a timely reminder that their desire to see more cut-price competition in the High Street, expressed by their support for supermarkets, was not shared by suppliers to shopkeepers. The issue of price fixing attracted the Government, now led by Sir Alec Douglas-Home, and attempting to revive flagging support as the time for a general election drew near.

Sir Alec Douglas-Home needed to get across the idea of a modernising administration, orientated towards the consumer, before going to the country. Public opinion polls were very worrying, and the Labour opposition had been climbing whole-heartedly on the consumer protection band-wagon. Price maintenance had assumed the dimension of a major political problem following the outbreak of the stamp war, and Ministers were worried about a situation in which some manufacturers appeared to be indulging in restrictive but lawful practices. A Labour MP, John Stonehouse, led a Private Member's Bill before the House, and the Government was being forced to kill it by taking on the job of abolishing RPM itself. Such action might offend strong Conservative supporters, but they would hardly forsake the party for Labour, or the Liberals, both of whom opposed RPM.

Heath, as President of the Board of Trade, preferred to risk antagonising established shopkeepers and manufacturers rather than offend a large number of housewives now greatly aware of the issue as a result of recent events. In addition, he had the support of a departmental investigation into the merits and disadvantages of RPM, conducted a year earlier by Frederick (now Lord) Erroll. Behind the scenes, Stonehouse indicated that he would be happy to give his Bill to the Government.

The Cabinet met at Downing Street on 14th January 1964, and Heath impressed Sir Alec Douglas-Home with his argument that RPM should be tackled as part of a general plan to deal with restrictive practices, monopolies and mergers. It was agreed that any action should be postponed until after the election. Support was not unanimous and Heath had to deal with considerable opposition from some colleagues, promising safeguards for any manufacturers with a reasonable case for keeping RPM.

Within twenty-four hours, Edward Heath, whose brilliant negotiating skill had enhanced his reputation for courage during the great Common Market controversy, lit the fuse under resale price maintenance. He announced in the Commons after a morning of further Cabinet wrangling that RPM was to be made illegal. But manufacturers and traders would be given the right to seek exemption from the ban on the grounds that, in their particular case, RPM did not operate against the public interest.

Elmo Stores, operating twenty-one supermarkets in London and the Midlands, greeted the news of Government action by promptly selling cigarettes well below list price and defying the big manufacturers. One of the stores involved was at Bristol, then headquarters of Imperial Tobacco. This action took everyone by surprise and it came at a time when the tobacco companies were beginning to make headway in restraining other defiant and cheeky chains from price-cutting tobacco goods with stamps. Elmo gave stamps, too.

The Resale Prices Act of 1964 provided temporary exemption from the general ban on RPM for goods registered for subsequent Restrictive Practices Court investigation. The next few years were to see a stream of registered price fixers voluntarily abandoning resale price maintenance rather than fighting on through the Court. They included manufacturers of prams, garden chemicals, clocks, furniture, home appliances, musical instruments, slimming foods, sewing machines, glassware, stationery and shotguns. Supermarkets and others scrutinised the products to sift out suitable lines for price cutting, knowing that no manufacturer could now refuse to supply on grounds that prices would be slashed.

Many other manufacturers decided to let their cases stand choosing only to withdraw from the struggle at the last possible moment. But their defiance was being undermined, both by the advice of lawyers—aware of narrow gateways for winning the permanent right to enforce list prices—and the hostility of informed public opinion. Their confidence was badly shaken in January 1967, when the most notorious price maintainer of all, the Imperial Tobacco group (Wills and Player's) apparently decided to withdraw from the tobacco industry's joint defence of RPM well ahead of the full case coming before the Court.

News leaked out that Imperial's board was on the brink of a decision to end price fixing—and for one hectic, thunderous week the company maintained a stoic silence about its intentions as supermarketeers and leading grocers engaged in a premature price war that brought down the cost of a packet of twenty cigarettes by as much as 5d. The rival Gallaher and Carreras cigarette manufacturers were quick to protest and to demand an early statement of Imperial's position. Thousands of small tobacconists voiced alarm.

As prices tumbled there were at least two thousand retailers scrambling to make the headlines—Imperial finally called a major press conference to confess that it had considered ending fixed prices. But, explained the chairman, Sir John Partridge,* the group had decided to reverse its decision and would continue maintaining the wholesale and retail selling prices of its cigarettes and tobacco goods. He said the offer by supermarkets of unreasonable price cuts had caused the company, holding over 64 per cent of the cigarette market, to change its mind. Cigarettes had been used as 'loss leaders' a tired-looking Partridge declared: 'Second thoughts are everyone's prerogative. We are not fully persuaded that the decision is in all the circumstances of the tobacco industry the right one.'

Amid howls of protest from the cut-price grocers and supermarket chiefs, the price war was soon brought under control. Backed up by Carreras and Gallaher, Imperial warned that writs would be issued, or supplies cut off, unless normal conditions of sale were restored. One chain, Pricerite, had taken the opportunity to cut chocolate prices too. But Cadbury Brothers and Rowntree immediately obtained ex-parte injunctions to restrain the chain from reducing confectionery prices.

Yet the writing on the wall was clear. Imperial had hesitated. Before the month was out, many other consumer goods manufacturers were pulling out of the fight to retain price maintenance. The list of goods where price fixing was outlawed—formally authorised by a Court order as companies withdrew without a full hearing—swelled week by week.

The Registrar of Restrictive Trading Agreements was having a field day. It had taken just over two years to reach the stage of putting eight hundred different classes of goods formally before the

* Appointed Imperial chairman in March 1964.

Restrictive Practices Court for full-scale investigation. And by May 1967, about 250 registered products had already been voluntarily freed from price control.

Yet the Registrar's work was far from over. Later that month came the first full defence of RPM when the Big Five sweet and chocolate makers began presenting their case for obtaining general exemption from the general ban. For forty-three days witnesses streamed into the Court to argue for and against. They included supermarket executives, representatives of thousands of corner sweet shops worried about price competition, and health experts. It was the longest ever case to be heard before the Court, and the first of its kind under the Resale Prices Act.

So important was the decision—other manufacturers were likely to be guided by the Court's final attitude—that judgement was reserved. Meanwhile, more voluntary withdrawals were made. Nevertheless, more than two hundred manufacturers of branded goods, ranging from records and cameras to toys and cosmetics, waited nervously for the Court's ruling on chocolates before joining the rush, too.

The decision came on 25th July 1967, when Justice Megaw spent an hour delivering an adverse ruling and then made an order declaring that the Court refused to exempt chocolates and sugar confectionery from the general ban on RPM. Supermarket observers rushed from the Court to nearby telephones to give instructions that brought down prices within minutes of the judgement. More than ten thousand grocery stores made cuts, throwing the £350 million market into temporary confusion.

As expected, the decision appeared to influence the attitude of others seeking exemption. Infant milk food producers caved in, as did the photographic equipment manufacturers. Christmas 1967 saw the £67 million a year toys and games industry deciding to give up, too. The New Year was to bring news of another determined price maintainer sliding out of the struggle—the Prestige Group, the kitchen utensils firm with a long history of legal action against shopkeepers who attempted to reduce prices.

The list of withdrawals mounted. Hot water bottles, toilet paper, cement, electric tools, mirrors, pencil sharpeners, artists' requisites, eye baths, and weighing machinery were among the typical products next freed from price fixing. Ended too was RPM on branded stockings.

Anxious, but still determined to battle on, a group of branded footwear makers appeared for the second and full-scale Court case, at an estimated cost of about £70,000 in legal bills. Throughout the spring of 1968, the Court was to sit for forty-six days—the longest hitherto in the history of the Court since its inception (beating the chocolate hearing by three days). While the Court reserved its judgement, there came news of another major abandonment—this time by more than forty manufacturers of toiletries and cosmetics. No one really doubted the outcome of the footwear case—another order outlawing fixed prices. The remaining handful of diehard price maintainers were now isolated. Their cause had clearly been lost. Out of five hundred classes of goods grouped for official scrutiny since their registration between August and November 1964 (the original eight hundred registered manufacturers were cut down by regrouping with similar products) the Restrictive Practices Court, by May 1968, had made declarations of non-exemption from the ban on RPM for four hundred and fifty classes and parts of over twenty others. These were heavy casualties.

Imperial could not maintain its position of enforcing standard minimum shop prices for much longer. But before the position could be reviewed again—and the lawyers were pointing out that a defence of tobacco RPM before the Court would be a costly and fruitless affair—the group set in train a course of events that would see Gallaher caught up in a fierce take-over struggle, reviving memories of the swashbuckling Buck Duke.

CHAPTER FOURTEEN

Smoking can Damage your Health

With Lady Barrett in the chair, the Society for the Study of Inebriety met in London on the night of 12th April 1932, to hear discussion by distinguished doctors and surgeons on such matters as 'smoker's throat'. The part played by tobacco indulgence on heart and circulatory systems was described. A Dr J. D. Rolleston said the group considered it a definite precursor of cancer. Unfortunately, his otherwise careful analysis was to be partly ruined by his enlisting President Hoover's name to support the view that cigarettes were a source of crime.

In spite of the Society's valiant and seemingly 'cranky' efforts at public education on the dangers of smoking, in the following year no less than 163,896 million cigarettes were consumed by British and United States smokers. Some thirty years on, the rate would be 624,788 million. Then some more influential words would be uttered on the question of health risks—influential enough for some 12,941 million fewer cigarettes to be smoked in 1964 than in 1963, when speculation on the gravity of those hazards ended once and for all.

The words were: 'Cigarette smoking is a health hazard of sufficient importance to warrant appropriate remedial action.' They were to be broadcast, cabled, and telephoned around the world by the rows of journalists who rushed out of the United States State Department's auditorium (familiar to television viewers for President Kennedy's open press conferences) clutching copies of a 387-page document entitled 'Smoking and Health'. The journalists had been behind the auditorium's locked doors for one and a half hours—and 'no smoking' signs seemed to emphasise the explosive quality of the report, which the Federal Printing Office had produced under top secret conditions. It was a Saturday, 11th January 1964, so Wall Street was closed and tobacco shares were safe for forty-eight hours from panic selling.

With great skill and attention to the close questioning, the Surgeon-General of the United States, Luther L. Terry, and an eleven-strong advisory committee took the newsmen through the document. For fourteen months the committee had studied thousands of scientific papers and questioned hundreds of witnesses with the purpose of assessing 'available knowledge' on smoking and health to make appropriate recommendations.

Three years before, President Kennedy had been asked by many of America's voluntary health organisations to establish a commission on the medico-tobacco issue. Subsequently, Kennedy asked the Public Health Service about its policy, partly to arm himself to answer questions which were coming his way now that Senator Maurice Neuberger was actively campaigning for some action and even badgering the Federal Trade Commission for some stronger action. In spite of some compelling evidence presented in the fifties on the statistical relationship between cigarettes and lung cancer, both President Kennedy and the Federal Trade Commission knew they needed some further authoritative research before they could take on the tobacco companies in seeking to defend the nation's health.

Surgeon Terry seized the chance to give President Kennedy a review of the evidence with a gusto that alarmed the tobacco industry, already embattled by critics of its advertising policies and past rejection of medical criticisms. Terry was even shrewd enough to give the industry a chance to help choose the advisory committee's members, drawn from a list of one hundred and fifty experts with no significant record of public criticism. Five of the chosen team smoked. All their medical and other specialities, and skills, were beyond reproach.

It was Terry's determination that the tobacco manufacturers would be given little chance to discredit their work. The drama of a security-shrouded press conference at the State Department ensured that press interest was doubly heightened. For months, journalists had tried to break the secrecy of the committee's deliberations.

American smokers were to be deeply shocked. There was no disputing either the eminence or the independence of Terry's team. Ignorance and suppressed discussion about the fearsome disease had been sufficiently dispelled for smokers to know quite clearly the risks they might be taking, yet they were baffled enough by the conflicting arguments heard in past health scares to give the benefit of their doubts to the reassuring statements issued from Richmond, Winston-Salem, Madison Avenue and wherever manufacturers gathered. Smokers wanted the evidence to be evaluated with the utmost authority. Meanwhile, they had switched to filter tips and hoped their admittedly desultory efforts to cut down or 'kick the habit' would one day be justified. They were not to be.

The advisory committee report associated smoking causally with lung cancer. It stated: 'Cigarette smoking is causally related to lung cancer in men; the magnitude of the effect of cigarette smoking far outweighs all other factors. The data for women, though less extensive, points in the same direction.' The report declared smoking was a contributory factor in emphysema, chronic bronchitis and contributed to cancers of the throat, mouth, and respiratory tract. The habitual use of tobacco was related mainly to psychological and social drives, reinforced and perpetuated by the pharmacological action of nicotine on the central nervous system.

The question 'Why do people smoke?' had been asked for many years. A longer term response to the Terry report's findings, by way of Governmental action, would require much deeper consideration of this basic question, from which sprang the health problem now so clearly stated.

The question was simple enough, but when the National Society of Non-Smokers was formed in Britain in 1927 (absorbing the British Anti-Tobacco and Anti-Narcotic League) the answers were no less varied than they are today. They included the belief that people smoked tobacco to soothe the nervous system, boredom, irritation; from a desire to feel grown up, the reluctance to be unsociable, from inability to break a habit, and the pressures of advertising. Those British doctors who had rejected a then current *Lancet* statement that habitual cigarette smoking in any quantity 'was only slightly less harmful than drinking spirits between meals' were more preoccupied with their early researches into consequences than cures for a habit as old as the weed's misty past.

Not until they and their successors amassed enough evidence could they turn their attention to the most fundamental question. Tobacco companies had spent enormous sums on research into the motivations of smokers, not to stop the practice but to encourage people to buy their brands by appropriate advertising or other forms of promotion. Their skill in understanding the latent desires of consumers made them more than a fair match for medical authorities who could only patiently wait for their theories to be confirmed, or to be passed onto a new generation of scientists. Medical knowledge and expertise in statistical recording lagged well behind the explosive growth of tobacco consumption. Whole generations were weaned on to the habit, which transmitted itself to the young in a never-ending chain of innocent indulgence.

Naturally, those anxious to reduce smoking turned their attentions to the advertising policies of the manufacturers. Within a week of the Surgeon-General's report being released to the press, the United States Federal Trade Commission had stated it would introduce new regulations for tobacco labelling and rules for advertising cigarettes.

Ever since Buck Duke ran foul of the United States anti-trust authorities, the ceaseless and strident struggle between United States cigarette manufacturers for market dominance had continued to pour millions of dollars into the coffers of the advertising industry. Madison Avenue was to be paved with golden Burley as domestic leaf increasingly replaced Turkish to give a milder, cooler smoke. 'Blow some my way' cooed voluptuous women from the street hoardings. Young male models invited the adolescent to buy their manhood by smoking Camels, Lucky Strike, and Chesterfields. Stars of the cinema and radio personalities endorsed products. Slogans were repeated with a frequency that reshaped the senses. The allegiance of smokers had to be bought and fought for with an aggression that caused frequent lapses in both taste and behaviour.

R. J. Reynolds and American Tobacco engaged in a titanic fight for supremacy. American Tobacco's George Washington Hill, who would wear his hat at his desk and act on impulse, proved a worthy successor to his father, Percival, and the legendary Duke. His advertising was frequently based on dubious or misleading claims. When his father's famous sales message 'Lucky Strike, It's Toasted' eventually drew from Reynolds, the Camels maker, the response that 'It's Fun To Be Fooled' (the American Tobacco 'toasting' process was no more than the common curing process of tobacco production), George Washington Hill came back with 'No Throat Irritation—No Cough' (Hill had unfairly suggested for some time that competitors had sheep dip in their products).

Later, Hill came up with 'Reach for a Lucky instead of a Sweet'. This slogan did much to encourage figure-conscious women to take up smoking. Slim actresses and models dominated the advertising, which was so successful that the confectionery manufacturers protested and formed a protective committee that sponsored rival propaganda on the virtues of candy. Since Hill made extensive use of radio commercials, there were appeals to American Tobacco's conversion of sweet-eaters into cigarette smokers. The tobacco–candy struggle proved a lengthy and costly affair before the Federal Trade Commission finally stopped the sale of Lucky Strike as a shining health aid.

By 1930, Lucky Strike had achieved a leading position in the league table of brands. It would alternate for the next two decades for the prime sales position with Camels which had once given Reynolds, in 1918, some 40 per cent of the United States cigarette market. Liggett & Myers with Chesterfields ('They Satisfy') and Lorillard's Old Gold ('Not a Cough in a Carload') struggled valiantly for their positions below the leaders. In 1933 came a strong and new challenge from Philip Morris with a brand of the same name. Over the nation's wireless sets came the repetitive cry 'Call for Philip Morris' (a New York page boy had been hired for his shrill voice). Within seven years, the brand held about 7 per cent of the United States market for cigarettes, proof of the power of radio commercials.

Up to this time the big manufacturers were concentrating their promotional efforts on just one or two brands. Yet one producer which resisted the concept was British-American Tobacco, which had owned the modest Brown & Williamson subsidiary since 1927 and progressively introduced various speciality brands and pioneered both filter and menthol cigarettes. Sir Walter Raleigh was to be compromised, and joined by such stable brands as the low-priced 10-cent cigarettes Avalon and Wings. Filter-tipped Viceroys and mentholated Kools—introduced in the mid 1930s—had 'unisex' appeal, helping to give Brown & Williamson about 3 per cent of the national market.

Before World War II disrupted the developing marketing war, Hill and his American Tobacco made another and highly significant move, in 1939 (seven years before Hill's death), by relaunching Pall Mall, once a Turkish blend sold in a striking scarlet pack, as a king-sized brand. Pall Mall cigarettes were now sold at an individual length of 85 millimetres, whereas the standard had been 70 millimetres. In response came similar sized Chesterfields and new king-sized brands such as Herbert Tareyton (also from American Tobacco). It was an ironic time to introduce longer cigarettes as the years of tobacco shortage loomed ahead. No one among the majors believed in filters, with their little-understood sales potential. There was scorn in 1932, for example, when Benson & Hedges had brought out Parliament, featuring a tube mouthpiece filled with cotton.

In spite of leaf shortages and queues outside tobacco shops, the war years encouraged consumption. Tobacco was classified as an essential material by President Roosevelt and some farmers were to win deferment of military service. Between 1939 and 1945, cigarette sales rose by 50 per cent and manufacturers faced peacetime with a known, if still restricted, demand for nearly 270 billion cigarettes in the home market, that would soon be swelled by returning servicemen who had taken around 18 per cent of total output for overseas supply during the war years.

The attempts to re-establish abundant supplies of cigarettes were to be bedevilled both by Governmental commitments to supply leaf to Europe and recovery from war disaster, and then, when freer competition became possible, by the despairing controversy over the health risks of smoking. A swing to filter brands in the fifties had more to do with the reassurance of troubled consumers than the grounds of price economy experienced in Britain. The cigarette market fell into a frenzy of filtration and mentholisation of brands. New packs, new names and new sales slogans burst on American smokers, bewildered by the medical evidence collated by researchers into the health hazards. The message seemed to be that filters offered safer smoking, a claim that British manufacturers studiously avoided making, even if this did not actively discourage the popular belief that harmful elements were removed.

Not all the filter brands were, of course, new. Brown & Williamson's Viceroy experienced a marked surge in demand and by 1954 was the leading filter brand, improved by the adoption of cellulose acetate tow filler in the top after Liggett & Myers came up with what it called a 'pure white miracle tip of alpha cellulose'. A filter was added by Brown & Williamson to Kools and Raleighs.

Smokers were faced with a variety of choices, from the Herbert Tareyton Kings from America—who introduced the concept of a cellulose filter containing 'activated charcoal' as a smoke purifying agent—to Reynolds' Winston. Philip Morris astutely acquired the Benson & Hedges filter brand Parliament but then developed Marlboro, with a 'selectrate' filter, a brand which sold well under the endorsement of a virile and craggy tattooed male model, whose obvious choice of tipped cigarettes was no indication of femininity. All this activity had the effect of reducing the popularity of the first filter cigarette to be promoted on a national scale with a full advertising budget—Kent, put on sale in 1952 at a high price by Lorillard with the reassurance that its 'protection' was priceless.

The Kent brand offered smokers a 'micronite' filter said to hold back half the normal tar and nicotine drawn from standard plain cigarettes. Lorillard's marketing team for Kent received an unexpected boost to their sales campaign when the *Reader's Digest*, long a troublesome publisher of anti-smoking articles, helped circulate in 1954 the idea that filters could reduce risks of lung cancer and bronchial disorders. Unfortunately, sales graphs looked much sorrier a few years later, after smokers found it hard to taste Kent. The filter specification was then demanded and the nicotine content revised upwards.

Although the growth in United States cigarette consumption did pause in 1954 and 1955 as a consequence of rising public awareness of the relationship between lung cancer and smoking, the number of cigarettes supplied continued to climb through the fifties—reaching 470,136 million in 1960 compared with 360,199 million at the beginning of the decade. During this time sales of filter brands rose from less than 1.5 per cent to about half of the market.

The health scares of the mid-fifties were not confined to the United States. There were some disturbing reports that transformed medical opinion and spurred the formation of a more vigorous anti-smoking lobby. They had to sweep away past complacency. Arguments in Britain about smoking and health had reached their nadir in May 1947 when Lord Morton of Henryton, self-reformed after heavy smoking for thirty-five years, made some reasonable claims in *The Times* that those who gave up would find health steadily improved, games could be played with less fatigue, enjoyment of food and drink was enhanced, senses were heightened, money was saved and a joyous feeling of independence derived when others were seeking cigarettes and matches.

Alfred H. Dunhill, the famous tobacconist and pipe supplier, promptly sat down and wrote the following letter in reply:

'Sir, Lord Morton's letter on "the smoker" is just another example of the invalidity of the "argument from instances" which is so prevalent in the present controversy on smoking. I do not impugn the honesty of his Lordship's "personal experience". But after all he is only one man and his experience may fairly be set against that of others.

'Englishmen have been "smoking furiously" for three and a half centuries, and the habit has not impaired either their physique or their courage. Roundheads and Cavaliers all smoked and yet all fought bravely and endured incredible hardships. Marlborough's armies smoked and yet won many bloody battles. Clive's men smoked and yet won Plassey against odds of six to one. Wolfe's men—smokers all—climbed the Heights of Abraham and at Quebec won the battle which gave Canada to England. Wellington's "smokers" drove the French from the Spanish peninsula and crushed Napoleon (a non-smoker by the way) at Waterloo.

'To come to modern "instances" the men of El Alamein smoked, but did not suffer from the "tiresome cough" which his Lordship deplores. The men in Normandy, although smokers too, had enough energy to push Jerry across the Rhine. But enough! His Lordship, like many non-smokers, has "proved" too much without really proving anything. Yours faithfully, Alfred H. Dunhill, 30 Duke Street, St James's, S.W.1.'

The standard of discussion, fortunately, would improve markedly in the next few years. Addressing a joint scientific meeting of the Royal Society of Medicine and the British Medical Association, Dr Richard Doll, of the Medical Research Council, reported he had been forced to the conclusion that smoking must be a cause of lung cancer. Together with Professor Bradford Hill, he had carried out a careful statistical investigation which, a year before, led them to the finding that 'smoking is a factor, and an important factor, in the production of carcinoma of the lung'.*

It was twenty-five years since Sir Ernest Kennaway had proved that pyrolysis of many organic materials, within a relatively high temperature range, would give rise to carcinogenic tars. Now, at last, studies into the chemistry of tobacco smoke to determine whether there were constituents capable of producing cancer, would proliferate. Not that there had failed to be some doughty and determined work in the intervening years.

There was the work, for example, of Dr Alton Ochsner, a renowned American thoracic surgeon, who had condemned cigarette smoking before a clinical congress of the American College of Surgeons in 1938, and who in 1951 told an annual conference of the American Medical Association: 'It is frightening to speculate on the possible number of bronchogenic cancers that may develop because of the tremendous numbers of cigarettes consumed in the two decades from 1930 to 1950.'

The flow of reports and papers on smoking and its relationship to cancer came thick and fast in the early fifties. Dr E. A. Graham, Emeritus Professor of Surgery at Washington University School of Medicine, told the American College of Surgeons conference meeting in London at the Royal College of Surgeons of England, Lincoln's Inn Fields, that results of independent studies both sides of the Atlantic 'were so nearly identical that they could almost be superimposed'.

If that was true of medical research, then it was true of some of the responses from manufacturers. Sir Robert (later Lord) Sinclair felt bound to emphasise there was no proof that smoking caused lung cancer and 'in relation to the present state of scientific knowledge there has been much exaggerated comment about this matter—comment that has appeared to ignore the very important reservations contained in official statements'.

In the United States, P. Lorillard's research directors said opinions on the bodily effects of smoking 'are often derived from purely speculative surmises; others are drawn from debatable statistics, while others originate from animal experiments, which have little, if any, bearing on cancer as seen in the lung of man'.

With more smokers showing interest—so many distinguished

* *British Medical Journal*, 30th September 1950 (p. 739).

doctors could not be ignored—and with Governmental agencies showing interest too, the tobacco manufacturers had to recognise some responsibility. In England, the industry in 1954 put up £250,000 for a fund to help the Medical Research Council, and by January 1954 the fourteen leading United States tobacco companies had forced the Council of Tobacco Research, USA, to be led by a scientist of 'unimpeachable integrity and national repute' plus an advisory board of distinguished scientists. Full-page advertisements, however, reassured smokers that recent reports and statements were inconclusive. Their products were not injurious to health, but even a suspicion that cigarette smoking could cause serious disease was a matter of deep concern to them. This was why 'close co-operation would be given to those entrusted with safeguarding public health'.

Soothing words were part of the cigarette manufacturers' stock-in-trade. Many smokers drew comfort from the manufacturers who scorned the evidence of the doctors who unsettled their self-justification for smoking. In February 1953, Sir Robert Sinclair, Imperial's chairman, told his stockholders: 'It has never been our policy to make exaggerated claims for the smoking habit, or to say that it confers upon those who indulge in it benefits other than the pleasure and peace of mind it may bring. If it should ever be proved that there exists something harmful in tobacco, even in the minutest quantities, which could conceivably make smoking one of the causes of this disease, we should, I hope, be the first to take steps to eliminate it.'

The man recruited by the American tobacco industry to be scientific director was Dr Clarence Cook Little, a respected geneticist, once director of an antecedent, the American Cancer Society, but brought in from the Jackson Memorial Laboratory in Maine. Little had written ten years before that 'although no definite evidence exists concerning the relation between the use of tobacco and the incidence of lung cancer, it would seem unwise to fill the lungs repeatedly with a suspension of fine particles of a tobacco product of which smoke consists'.

Just how far the manufacturers had progressed on their research until his appointment was a matter on which Dr Little was too tactful to pronounce. Certainly the behaviour of the tobacco companies was hardly reassuring to scientists interested in finding the facts about health risks. The Federal Trade Commission had already stopped Brown & Williamson, Lorillard, and the Penn Tobacco Company from making misleading claims on the safety of some brands of cigarette. There was open hostility towards the *Reader's Digest* for its regular summaries of medical research. It was true that Liggett & Myers had commissioned and promoted a hard study in 1952 from the Arthur D. Little organisation of the effects of Chesterfields on nose and throat. This showed that there was no harmful result on the organs, hence the heavy promotion to suggest Chesterfields were not harmful. As Susan Wagner has pointed out:* 'This seems from available records to have been the only such test undertaken during this period by a tobacco company.'

Over the years, the manufacturers had shrugged off the periodic alarms of some dedicated scientists—men such as F. H. Müller (the German author of *Tabakmissbrauch und Lungercarcinom*), Dr Morton Levin (director of New York's Bureau of Cancer Control) and Professor Raymond Pearl, of Baltimore, Ochsner, Wynder, Graham—the list is a long one, going back even centuries, blurring into kings and noblemen, who saw tobacco as a curse and not the curative answer to illness that gave tobacco a romantic past.

Professor Alexander Haddow, director of the Chester Beatty Research Institute, went before the sixth International Cancer Congress held in Brazil in August 1954, to declare that the latest research results 'show with practical certainty that a considerable proportion of deaths now recorded as cancer of the lung are due to cigarette smoking'. The American scientist Dr E. Culyer Hammond, of Yale University and the American Cancer Society, elaborated on his own work and theories. Together with Dr Daniel Horn, he suggested that statistical evidence was strong on the connection with the rise in deaths from lung cancer. The team of Hammond and Horn became as respected as the British researchers Doll and Hill. In 1952–3 they conducted a controlled survey that provided striking results, including the fact that the premature death rate of regular cigarette smokers was 68 per cent higher than that of non-smokers. The full report was presented by the American Cancer Society to the American Medical Association in the early summer of 1954—and the battle between Governmental agencies and the tobacco industry on the health issue was

* *Cigarette Country*. Praeger Publishers Incorporated, New York, 1971.

now on in earnest. No longer could the flow of $2,000 million or so in taxes on United States manufactured tobacco restrain Governmental agencies from seeking to curb cigarette smoking in the public interest.

In due course the United States Public Health Service put together a scientific study team to appraise the evidence and research then available by the mid-sixties. By 1957, it was concluded that the causal relationship between lung cancer and excessive smoking was 'adequate for considering the initiation of public health measures'. The response from the American industry was the formation in 1958 of the Tobacco Institute, with a board of fourteen corporate presidents and funds for counter-propaganda on the lines that much more research was needed and the virtue of America's oldest industry could not be sullied.

In Britain, the tobacco manufacturers had been no less quick off the mark. For in August 1956, Imperial, BAT, and the Federation of Home and Export Manufacturers formed the Tobacco Manufacturers' Standing Committee to give formal status to the cooperation in research of those manufacturers who had made the £250,000 donation of 1954 to the Medical Research Council for investigation into the causes of lung cancer. Sir Alexander H. Maxwell, the wartime Whitehall tobacco controller, accepted the chairmanship, and a number of distinguished scientists agreed to act as consultants to the committee.

There was plenty to worry about in Britain. Dr Doll and Professor Hill had made some impact on the medical community, but to nothing like the extent of an official announcement made in February 1954 by the then Minister of Health, Iain Macleod, with full Cabinet approval, that a relationship between smoking and cancer of the lung had been established. His authority was a report, based on three years' work, from his Standing Advisory Committee on Cancer and Radiotherapy. Macleod said he was releasing the report's information at once because of the deep public interest in the disease, and he called a press conference to demonstrate the Government's anxiety not to hide or delay anything.

The British tobacco manufacturers promptly issued a statement: 'Until medical science discovers how the disease is caused, it is impossible to prove or disprove suggestions that smoking or anything else may contribute to it.' Nevertheless, they had already offered £250,000 for research (a trifle compared with the expenditure running to £8 million or so on brand advertising) by the Medical Research Council.

It was enough to finance more damning findings, for by June 1957 the Government was accepting the Council's documented conclusion that a major part of the great increase in deaths from lung cancer among men during the past twenty-five years had been due to smoking tobacco, particularly heavy cigarette smoking. Results of nineteen inquiries into smoking habits and health (undertaken in Britain, the United States, Finland, Germany, Holland, Norway and Switzerland) were cited in outlining the risks. As in the United States, a campaign of public health education was begun, the manufacturers strenuously denying the latest view on the causal connection, via the Tobacco Manufacturers' Standing Committee.

Fresh impetus to the anti-smoking forces was to come in March 1962, when the Royal College of Physicians published a report from a study team of eight doctors led by the president, Sir Robert Platt. They concluded after two and a half years' work, that cigarette smoking was the most likely cause of the world-wide rise in deaths from lung cancer. Those who smoked thirty cigarettes a day had thirty times the chance of dying of the disease than the non-smoker. So perturbed were the team that they recommended action to curb smoking by public education, restriction of smoking in public places, higher taxation, limitations on advertising, the printing of smoke analyses on packets, and the organisation of anti-smoking clinics.

The Tobacco Manufacturers' Standing Committee immediately criticised the Platt report, saying it added little to the Medical Research Council's statements of 1957. The unspoken lesson was the need for more research. This well-rehearsed comment was accompanied by a remark that there had been 'a growing body' of evidence that smoking had pharmacological and psychological effects that were of real value to smokers.

Notwithstanding the ebb and flow of conflicting statements over the evidence of risks, there was one piece of research, concerning smokers in Edinburgh, which showed that two-thirds of those wishing to discontinue the habit gave the expense, rather than the medical evidence, as their reason. It was a point well understood by the British manufacturers who, unlike their counterparts in the United States, where filter tips were actively promoted

to allay health anxieties, sought to counter the widespread desire
to stop the habit of smoking by isolating the motivating factor of
the high cost to the pocket, not the lung.

The search for economy on a heavily taxed product would
drive a substantial number of smokers to smaller cigarettes and
tipped brands. And the proof came when Imperial launched the
Embassy coupon brand, greeted with such wild success not so
long after the Royal College of Physicians report was published.
This did not mean there was no reaction—the health scare did
make many smokers try for a short while to cut down, or to stop
the habit—but consumption was to revive, if at a less rapid growth
than for previous years. A concession to the anti-smoking lobby
by manufacturers, in the form of a voluntary restriction on television advertising before 9 pm (when children were watching),
provided some evidence of the industry's acknowledgement of
the concern among medical experts and some MPs.

Over the next few years the manufacturers would come under
increasing pressures to control their promotional activities. A
change of Government had brought in a determined Minister of
Health, Kenneth Robinson, who went into periodic bouts of
negotiations. These produced a voluntary pact involving an
advertising expenditure ceiling of £10 million for press and poster
promotion, preceded by a statutory ban on television advertising
of cigarettes. The voluntary side of the limitations broke down,
and the cigarette sales battle developed in Britain into new
complexities. These included decisions by Gallaher and Carreras
to market gift coupon brands to combat the onward march of
Embassy, and Player's No. 6. Ronald Plumley, deputy chairman
of Carreras, who despised coupons, was to resign within a year of
his company's offer of coupons with Crown Filter and Guards.
His prediction that the proliferation of coupon trading would bring
down tobacco resale price maintenance was to be proved correct.
Gallaher's similar opposition to gift giving waned as its retaliatory
introduction of coupons on brands other than Kensitas (namely
Sterling, Nelson and Cadets) stopped some of the slide in sales to
Imperial.

By the autumn of 1967, the Government and the industry were
to be locked in dispute. Robinson, the Health Minister, declared,
after a year or so of fruitless talks to try and bring the manufacturers into a new agreement on curbing promotion, he would

introduce legislation to ban coupons and to limit cigarette advertising. Imperial howled that 10,000 jobs would be placed at risk by such action, allowing for the suppliers of the £30 million or more gifts redeemed annually, for the eight coupon brands then on the market. John Partridge, Imperial's chairman, desperately (and curiously) said that the loss of coupons would mean lowering prices with the effect of increasing total cigarette consumption—curious since shareholders might consider that not a bad result. In the event, a ban on coupons—which became redeemable for cash as well as gifts—never came about.

The Labour Government became increasingly preoccupied with the struggle for economic growth, with a sinking pound sterling. To take away smokers' coupons would be a bad psychological blow, and anyway the industry promised some self-restraint, if modest, on an individual company basis. Privately, some Cabinet Ministers were pleased with the way the tobacco manufacturers had smoothly coped with one potentially serious development—the loss of Rhodesian leaf as a consequence of Rhodesia's unilateral declaration of independence in November 1965—shouldering the extra £20 million annual cost without undue complaint and a comparatively modest price rise that did not unduly disrupt taxation estimates. Price inflation moved to the front of the political scene, and the Ministry of Health's campaign to limit smoking was to be disrupted totally as resale price maintenance finally collapsed in the tobacco trade with an orgy, if short-lived, of bulk buying by smokers unable to believe their eyes at some of the resulting price cuts by supermarkets. It would take the Ministry some years to raise again public consciousness of the health risks by the publication of tar content tables, increasingly effective advertising on its own account, and by requiring manufacturers to follow the American example of labelling cigarette packs with a warning that smoking can damage health.

The United States authorities did not obtain that requirement without great struggles. American Tobacco greeted the Surgeon-General's report with a new and untested filter brand called Carlton and announced it was going into tipped cigarettes 'with both feet'. The United States industry mobilised lawyers for a struggle against legislation, starting with the Federal Trade Commission's proposed rules on labelling and descriptions. Manufacturers, lobbyists and Congressmen were to become embroiled in bitter arguments which after delays produced, with Congress approval in 1965, the warning on cigarette packets:

CAUTION: CIGARETTE SMOKING MAY BE
HAZARDOUS TO YOUR HEALTH

This was a compromise and four years later, in 1969, the Congressional opposition to cigarette smoking had been stiffened sufficiently by the American Cancer Society and the United States Public Health Service, among others, for matters to be taken a stage further. Britain (in August 1965), Norway, France, Italy, Denmark, and other countries had banned some or all tobacco advertising. The Cigarette Labelling and Advertising Act (of 1965) was due to expire, and both the Federal Communications Commission and the Federal Trade Commission felt tougher controls could be enforced with wider support. The objective was to halt or to check the expenditure of $225 million on radio-television advertising and sponsorship. The Communications Commission in 1967 had—with some prompting from a young lawyer with a citizen's complaint—ruled that broadcasters give free time under the 'fairness doctrine' to commercials warning of the dangers of smoking, which the Tobacco Institute fiercely opposed. Two prime-time talents, Doris Day and Lawrence Welk, led an exodus of performers from television programmes sponsored by cigarette manufacturers. Film stars and athletes gave their names to American Cancer Society advertisements.

A salient point was that the Act also did something else—it prohibited local, State and federal government agencies, including the Federal Communications Commission and the Federal Trade Commission, the watchdog over product quality and packaging, from *imposing added restrictions on cigarette advertising*. This initially harmless clause now seemed far more important than the caution imprinted on cigarette packets and prompted both sides to reverse their strategy.

The tobacco industry had learned to live with the warning forced upon it by law, and now wanted the Act extended to keep other limitations to a minimum. The anti-smoking forces, convinced that the health hazard warning was inadequate, likewise came full circle. Their strategy today was to let the law expire— and gain a broader field of action by doing so. In a Senate speech in late January 1969, Senator Frank E. Moss of the State of Utah (where no tobacco is grown) said he would oppose extension of the law with all means at his disposal.

The Federal Communications Commission put forward an impressive case: 'We are here faced,' it said, 'with a unique and most serious danger to public health authenticated by official and congressional action. It would thus appear wholly at odds with the public interest for broadcasters to present advertising promoting the consumption of the product [meaning cigarettes] posing this unique danger—a danger measured in terms of an epidemic of death and disabilities.' The Commission's proposal was that packets should state, in no uncertain terms, that cigarette smoking not only endangers health but 'may cause death from cancer and other diseases'.

But the Federal Communications Commission and Federal Trade Commission were not the only formidable opponents of the tobacco industry and its allies. One of the most active government offices was the United States Public Health Service, part of the Department of Health, Education and Welfare. It took an ever more militant stand on smoking since its chief, the Surgeon-General of the United States, in its January 1964 report, officially recognised cigarette smoking as a health hazard 'sufficient to warrant appropriate remedial action'.

Its activities began, as such things usually begin in government agencies, with conferences, reorganisations, meetings with citizens' groups and the like. Yet the outcome was anything but bureaucratic. One of the first moves was to give grants for research on methods that would help smokers to become non-smokers.

Another result was the birth of the National Clearing House on Smoking and Health, organised within the Public Health Service. Its purpose was primarily to obtain and distribute information on smoking and health, to encourage—sometimes with money but mostly to give advice and cooperation—State and local, private and public anti-cigarette drives, and to support research into the psychological and physiological whys of the smoking habit. It was in effect the mother organisation where scores of privately and publicly supported organisations worked together towards their common goal—to ostracise the cigarette.

With Dr E. C. Hammond, for the American Cancer Society,

suggesting that there were now 300,000 cigarette-related deaths
a year, Congressmen and the Federal Communications Commission
joined in a new assault on smoking, centring round the 1965
Labelling Act which forced producers to give a health warning on
packets.

Outside Government, an Inter-Agency Council on Smoking
and Health was by far the most important rallying point of the
anti-smoking forces. Founded by Emerson Foote, an energetic
New York advertising executive, who left his lucrative job as a
protest against cigarette commercials, it became the common meeting ground of civic organisations engaged in battle. Its purpose was
'to raise public awareness of smoking and health problems; and
promote action to reduce smoking and the hazards to national
health'. The council combined national health, education, and
youth agencies, and professional medical organisations, in all but
one or two States of the Union.

From these organisations, individually or in groups came a
flood of publications ranging from detailed medical reports to
pamphlets on how to break the cigarette habit, from statistical
compilations to a listing of films and records available from the
National Clearing House and the Inter-Agency Councils and their
members. A simple placard saying, in white on black, '100,000
doctors have quit smoking, maybe they know something you
don't' was displayed with great effect on Post Office vans, in
hospitals and in public buildings.

A questionnaire used in a one-hour television documentary on
smoking and broadcast nationwide by a network was produced and
distributed millionfold to audiences to check on their knowledge of
the effects of smoking. Nationwide surveys were conducted by the
Public Health Service and many other organisations. Communities,
such as San Diego County, California and the city of Syracuse in
the state of New York made themselves into living laboratories to
experiment and test long-range programmes to reduce cigarette
smoking through individual as well as community action.

Commercial airlines stopped distributing cigarettes to their
passengers. Leading experts on heart, cancer and chest diseases
adopted guidelines for physicians on their own smoking habits
and those of their patients. The American Medical Association
urged its members to play a major role against cigarette smoking
by personal example and advice to patients to discourage smoking

by means of public discussion and educational programmes. Drives were waged against cigarettes among teenagers to prevent them from acquiring the habit.

All these things did, of course, at first, raise questions in the minds of American smokers. In March 1967, it was officially estimated that one million American adults were giving up cigarettes every year. Despite the increase in population, cigarette consumption had recently remained fairly stable, which indicated a lower *per capita* consumption.

Yet, government and non-government experts remained apprehensive. Studies involving over a million people showed that a twenty-five-year-old male who smoked forty cigarettes a day had a life expectancy eight years less than that of his twin-in-age who did not smoke. The twenty-a-day smoker lost five and a half years of his expectable life span.

Such overwhelming evidence has stimulated research on many fronts. The Agriculture Department is searching for non-toxic tobacco strains. The National Institute of Health seeks to pry ever deeper into the connection—as yet not fully understood—between cigarette smoking and various diseases. To its credit, the American tobacco industry has poured larger sums into research than before and the search for a safer cigarette is taking a more determined turn (which had not been so evident when previously the manufacturers had poured out vast sums on counter-propaganda to show cigarettes were harmless and more often beneficial to smokers).

With one hundred brands on the United States markets, the manufacturers fought hard and zealously to retain their independence in selling a legal product. America's oldest industry believed it was fighting for survival on the incomplete evidence of scientists. To have advertising banned from television was a measure not to be contemplated.

The American tobacco economy involved some 600,000 farm families, principally in ten south-eastern States. It involved six large manufacturing complexes with some 35,000 employees. It involved a marketing and advertising industry supplying television with its largest single source of advertising revenues. It involved innumerable retail outlets, which, in addition to cigarettes, sold lighters, cigarette cases, ash trays, and similar items. Consumer expenditures for tobacco products—including taxes accounting for two-fifths of the total—amounted to some $8,000 million a year, of which some $7,000 million went on cigarettes.

Tobacco was the highest value-per-acre crop, yielding something like $1,300 per acre. It was the least mechanised of all farming operations. Government price support—part of a thirty-year-old programme—was available to all types of tobacco. Tobacco is an important source of farm income and vital to the four main cigarette manufacturing States—the Carolinas, Kentucky and Virginia. In North Carolina, tobacco accounted for half the total farm income, in Kentucky for two-fifths, in South Carolina one-quarter, in Virginia (a large cigarette producer but relatively small tobacco grower) one-fifth. More than 80 per cent of the value added to the tobacco leaf by manufacture comes from cigarette production.

Cigarette advertising represented an important income of the advertising industry as a whole and of all communications media. Tobacco manufacturers devoted $217 million, a third of their advertising budgets, to television. This amounted to 8 per cent of all television advertising revenues. Radio advertising accounted for another $17 million. The question then was what a ban on cigarette commercials, widely considered the most potent single antidote to the cigarette habit, would do to tobacco growers and related industries. The broadcasters viewed the cigarette commercials as important but not vital to their operations.

The tobacco interests were summarised in statements carried as full-page newspaper advertisements sponsored by the Tobacco Institute and pointing to the lack of proven clinical links between cigarettes and disease. They detailed the views of Dr Clarence Cook Little, scientific director of the Council for Tobacco Research, USA. The statement said 'There is no demonstrated causal relationship between smoking and any disease. . . . The pure biological evidence is pointing away from, not toward, the causal hypothesis. . . . The genetic set-up of the individual largely determines his susceptibility to cancer, cardiovascular disease and chronic respiratory disease [and] many factors other than smoking are significantly associated with these diseases.'

It was a challenge to researchers to prove in a purely clinical way what medical studies, autopsies, population surveys and animal experiments had shown in a predominantly statistical way.

During 1971, and after several years of wrangling between the

British manufacturers and the two Governments which spanned this period, smokers bought their first packs to bear the following words, printed voluntarily in accordance with an agreed code of practice:

WARNING BY H.M. GOVERNMENT
SMOKING CAN DAMAGE YOUR HEALTH

Some two years later came the publication of the first cigarette tar content league tables, which produced a run on sales of the less dangerous brands and encouraged Imperial to introduce a milder version of its big-selling Embassy coupon cigarettes. The pressure remains on the British Government not to relax a campaign to reduce consumption of a product that yields huge sums for its Exchequer. A vocal band of MPs maintains a barrage of questions in the Commons on progress of the campaign, and from time to time Private Members' Bills appear and fail. British manufacturers were much more discreet in resisting controls. Once an argument was over, they gave the public impression that restricted advertising, or whatever, had resulted from their own initiatives. At one stage, the Governmental smoking and health campaign took a ludicrous turn when resale price maintenance was abandoned and delighted smokers loaded up supermarket baskets with their favourite brands, offered at cut prices. More visible had been the anger of the American tobacco companies. On the New Year's Eve of 1971, when United States cigarette television commercials were to be banned from the following day, Philip Morris spent no less than $1.2 million in half an hour on three networks. Many new brands went on the market and sales forces were strengthened to deal with an increase in store promotion. Sample cigarettes were mailed round the nation and cigarette promotions were stepped up wherever crowds gathered for public events, from race tracks to political meetings. But no longer could American Tobacco's auctioneer cry out over the airwaves 'So-o-o-ld American'.

Only one year after the cigarette advertisers were required to abandon television, the United States industry was still very much intact and apparently unharmed. A record 529 billion cigarettes were consumed, the second year of growth after two years of stagnation. For the first time since 1968, *per capita* adult consumption rose, to 3,989 cigarettes in 1971. Most of the $225 million a year spent on television promotion was to be rechanelled into other media. For example, the spending on magazine advertising went up from 16 per cent in 1970 of total expenditure to 40 per cent. More attention was to be paid to in-store promotion, posters, and newspapers. Premium offers proliferated as Americans were invited to collect hundreds of items from beach balls to cassette tapes. Spending on sponsorship of sporting events soared. Reynolds alone in 1971 was to spend $400,000 on prize monies for events covering car racing, bowling and rodeos. Over forty new brand names were registered during the year and a dozen actually went on the market.

The United States tobacco companies were determined to prove that the role of cigarette advertising was to attract smokers from competitive brands rather than induce the young, or adult non-smoker, to start smoking their brands. Yet, recognising that the health campaign would not abate and the longer-term outlook was uncertain in terms of growth, the big suppliers began to drop the word 'tobacco' from their main corporate files and stepped up the acquisitions of companies outside their industry, or engaged in mergers. The R. J. Reynolds Tobacco Company became R. J. Reynolds Industries, to reflect its substantial diversification. American Tobacco became American Brands.

A similar switch occurred in Britain. Imperial Tobacco, eventually incorporated in the Imperial Group, had as far back as 1960 bought a potato crisp company and deposed the monopoly in crisps of a long-standing concern. In the next ten years, Imperial would buy an educational aids firm, HP Sauce, Smedley's the canners, Ocean Preserving (Epicure pickles), Chipmunk crisps, Ross frozen foods, and Allied Farm Foods, not to mention a big cold storage enterprise, a pulp mill and a plastics moulder. In the early 1970s came more substantial take-overs, such as that of the huge Courage brewing group.

This diversification in both the United States and Britain has been growing larger and more dramatic year by year. It is a recognition that, in spite of the search for a safe cigarette and the still mighty sale of tobacco, the industry feels future growth will be constrained. New generations are being subjected to heavy propaganda about the dangers of smoking. Capital is best deployed in other activities where people will still spend their money.

Statutory decisions to ban advertising on television and to

require health warnings have raised a tangle of moral, economic, and practical issues. Meanwhile, tobacco companies have sought to hold back the rate of decline in consumption (by weight) with some resourcefulness. In Britain, nearly £2 million a year is now being spent on the commercial sponsorship of sport to restore public goodwill towards their industry, besides linking tobacco with the healthy participants of the events staged with this vast sum once spent elsewhere. British athletes were sent to the Munich Olympics with the help of Rothman monies raised by smokers of the king-sized brand over a given period of heavy press advertising.

The clamour for new controls is still strong. The evidence that cigarettes tend to kill those who smoke them heavily is too overwhelming to be seriously doubted any longer. But is that a government's business? Some people would consider that it was definitely not, on the grounds that as a matter of fundamental political philosophy no government can be legitimately concerned with what an individual does to himself (and perhaps to someone else, with their consent). Those who take this view would, perhaps, concede that the individual should be reasonably informed of the consequences of his actions at the time when he makes his decision and that he should be an adult in full possession of his faculties. They might even allow that it could be the Government's business to see that these conditions were fulfilled and that other people or groups did not exploit for their own advantage the ignorance or disability of the citizen. But even with these qualifications, the principle is probably too strong for most people since it must in logic be applied consistently to all activities and could therefore be used to justify untrammelled trade in dangerous drugs provided that they were clearly labelled.

Even if the libertarian objections can be rejected, other points still need to be met. If the Government believe that cigarettes kill and that it is their business to reduce or eliminate suicide of this or any other kind, then surely they should be trying to stop people smoking, whether or not by an absolute ban on sales. It is, no doubt, particularly suitable that such a campaign should start by trying to prevent young people acquiring a habit which is clearly so hard to break. And this, perhaps, makes some sense of the bans on television advertising—to which young people are alleged to be particularly susceptible—and of educational measures to warn people of the danger. It would be even more useful to provide further practical assistance through the health services to those who want to give up smoking, but cannot. But the utility to public health of a ban on coupon gift schemes or commercial sponsorship is less clear, given the evidence that these do not spread the smoking habit, but merely promote switching between brands. Economically wasteful though such nugatory expenditure by the tobacco companies may be, it does not appear to contribute much to the premature death rate.

What really matters is how serious the Government are about curing the nation of the smoking habit. A country in which people neither wanted to smoke cigarettes, nor did so, would certainly be a healthier, wealthier and wiser place. If governments are going to take it upon themselves to move the citizenry in that direction, they should give more evidence that they have the courage of their convictions. They should also show that they have solutions to the serious incidental problems that would arise as cigarette advertising and sales fell off. Huge sums would be lost in Excise duty (even if they proceeded by taxing cigarettes out of existence), to say nothing of the taxes and other contributions paid by the firms and employees who make and sell cigarettes—at least until they found alternative and equally remunerative employment. A number of activities, typically publishing, which depend more or less heavily on revenue from cigarette advertising would also be hit.

The fact is that cigarette sales have become a major mechanism for raising money to finance a great variety of socially beneficial government and private services. If smoking ceased, other ways would have to be found of getting the money from the consumer. Support for any government in cutting down the nation's smoking would be strengthened, if they would demonstrate that they have examined all the economic, cultural, social and financial side-effects and prepared methods of coping with them. More stringent controls will make sense only if followed by more thorough-going measures and only if the Government is able and willing to cope with the consequences.

The few spasmodic sops to political pressure without any real willingness to damage so massive a revenue earner do not add up to a policy. A sincere attempt to cure nations of smoking can be supported; but messing about with the promotional fringes looks like prevarication.

Ironically, the more that the tobacco manufacturing groups widen the base of their business the easier it may one day become to adopt the draconian policies that the industry's critics relentlessly seek. But as diversification proceeds, there is still concentration and rationalisation of ownership to ensure that the supply and production of cigarettes are maintained with customary efficiency, if with less regard to a consequential reduction in competition between the giants. Ownership of a large British cigarette producer, with big cash flows, has always been an objective of American manufacturers ever since Buck Duke was forced to turn tail, fleeing home at the turn of the century. This fact was to be clearly established when Philip Morris and American Tobacco fought for the title to Gallaher. This multi-million dollar promotion staged by Imperial had an ineffectual referee, the City Panel on Take-Overs and Mergers, which was unable to stop some smart fouls.

CHAPTER FIFTEEN

Breaching the City Code

On 13th May 1968, John Murphy, an executive vice-president of Philip Morris International, was passing through London on his way back to the United States from Switzerland. He glanced at a tickertape machine and saw that Imperial Tobacco had boldly decided to sell its large shareholding in its rival Gallaher. He picked up a telephone and put in a transatlantic call to Hugh Cullman, his president. So began a new American invasion of the British tobacco industry.

Prior to that fateful call, Philip Morris had ruled out any idea of trying to buy the second largest British cigarette makers. Its acquisitive ambitions, still secret, were confined to exploratory talks on an offer for the much smaller and more diversified Godfrey Phillips enterprise. The assumption was that control of Gallaher was inevitably blocked by a combined 51 per cent interest held by Imperial and American Tobacco (which had surrendered owner- ship of J. Wix, the Kensitas concern, to Gallaher in return for a minority shareholding). Imperial's decision to offer to the public 25 million Ordinary shares in one gigantic sale, and to use the money to buy its way deeply into the food industry, dramatically changed the situation.

For the next five weeks, Cullman, who as a keen tennis fan had been looking forward to the approaching Wimbledon fortnight (stars such as Emerson, Santana, and Osuna were on the Philip Morris payroll), amassed reports and figures on Gallaher's potential if a successful take-over bid was made. Gallaher had the look of a faded blue chip. Since the Wix-American Tobacco deal, the company's share of the British cigarette market had slipped badly from 37 per cent to around 28 per cent. The export trade was restricted for historical reasons, and, indeed, only a few months earlier, Gallaher had quit the Australian market and sold out to Philip Morris (Australia), ending four years of heavy losses. Devaluation of the pound sterling, the loss of Rhodesian tobacco supplies after UDI, and the heavy costs of meeting Imperial's coupon brand competition seemed to hit confidence. From 1965 profits slumped badly.

Even Gallaher's marketing men did not have their heart in some of their own company's brand strategies, even if most were careful to contain their criticisms when the most senior management was around.

The Morris team decided things could be different in association with a more internationally minded group. With the help of the New York bankers, Lehman Brothers, and S. G. Warburg, the City merchant bank, Cullman and his team established a London campaign headquarters, where a strategy for raising money was worked out and from where permissions were sought from the United States and British Treasuries for transferring $110 million (then £48 million) for an offer. The luckless Gallaher had no inkling that it was being stalked. All the Philip Morris men in town—in early June, Joseph F. Cullman III, Hugh's cousin and the chairman, had booked into the Royal Garden Hotel—had the look of an outing of Wimbledon tennis fans. The truth was that the friendly, good-humoured tobacco men were now talking to the City's newly formed Panel for Take-overs and Mergers to discuss a fair formula for making an offer that did not conflict with the voluntary code for avoiding partial bids.

Philip Morris was not a strong force in the British business community. An English factory had been shut two years before in favour of direct importing of cigarettes. It owned Benson & Hedges in the United States, but this now had no connection with Gallaher's United Kingdom subsidiary of the same name. The brand names Marlboro and Parliament were not well known to English smokers, though there was recognition that Philip Morris was a famous name in tobacco, tracing back to origins in the London merchant trade of the previous century.

While American Tobacco held 11 per cent of Gallaher's stock, the chances of success were good, at least given fair play in any subsequent counter bidding. Imperial's offer to the public of its huge holding of 36¾ per cent (it had been redeemed in 1961 when Gallaher issued some shares for an acquisition) was a flop. *The Economist* had correctly warned that it was 'a task which could prove as difficult as launching a supertanker into Hampstead pond'. Over a third of the shares were left with the offer underwriters.

At 6 pm on 26th June, Philip Morris slapped down with what *The Times* called 'a sensational after hours bid' for the Senior Service and Park Drive enterprise, Gallaher. The offer valued Gallaher at £92 million. It was almost unprecedented for a United States company to make such a substantial bid without a prior approach, but there had been a leak in the previously tight security so there was no opportunity for consultation. Gallaher's managing director was struck dumb, unable to make any comment to the newspapermen who disturbed executives returning to their homes, oblivious on the journey from their offices of the sudden move after the Stock Exchange had closed.

Where Buck Duke had failed nearly seventy years before in buying his way into Britain, Philip Morris now dared to tread again—and over Gallaher's long passive, minority shareholder, American Tobacco, which bore the name of Duke's original trust, if reshaped and reformed in its ways.

There was no doubt that Philip Morris was no mean judge of sales potentials. Its recent home market record showed a climb up the United States industry's rankings only matched by BAT's Brown & Williamson which slipped a place yet raised its American market share from around 10 per cent in 1961 to 16 per cent by 1969. In 1965, Philip Morris sold 53,000 million cigarettes, and the change can be seen in the following table of estimated domestic sales including 1968 and 1969.

Ranking					Sales of cigarettes ('000 million)			
1968	1969	1970	1971		1968	1969	1970	1971
1	1	1	1	R. J. Reynolds	167.7	163.6	165.7	169.9
2	2	2	3	American Tobacco	113.1	108.0	100.5	93.5
3	3	3	4	Brown & Williamson	79.1	81.2	88.2	91.2
4	4	4	2	Philip Morris	72.1	77.1	87.5	96.3
5	5	5	5	P. Lorillard	52.7	47.0	45.1	45.6
6	6	6	6	Liggett & Myers	37.0	35.2	34.0	32.5
				TOTAL	521.7	512.1	521.0	529.0

The importance of Philip Morris was that, like British-American Tobacco, the group was becoming a world-wide operator if on a smaller scale. BAT's growth had been impressive—in forty countries one of its brands was the leading cigarette, proof that an English base and marketing tradition had an international appeal. However, BAT was excluded from the British market even if its headquarters on London's Millbank was the nerve centre. Gallaher was the way into Britain after some years of disappointing effort on Philip Morris's own account and in spite of an increasingly successful invasion of the wider European market from a base in Switzerland. BAT was the largest tobacco manufacturer in the world, with 200,000 employees in seventy countries and sales more than twice those of any other tobacco group, excluding State-owned industries. It had 140 factories in 53 countries besides the United States. Nearly one in five cigarettes—there were 450 brands—smoked in countries where the industry was open to private enterprise came from BAT.

Joseph Cullman saw Philip Morris developing even more rapidly in world markets, where Marlboro was already an internationally recognised brand. By 1972, Philip Morris International would be selling 113,000 million cigarettes in 160 territories, besides the United States, and holding 6.5 per cent of the world cigarette market. The European market was roughly equal to that of the United States and in spite of Philip Morris' development in Switzerland and Holland the ownership of Britain's second largest producer was some prize in the drive for international expansion. To date, the only real success in Britain, and that was limited, had been in the sale of razor blades—through the subsidiary Ever Ready Razor Products (Pal and Personna)—rather than cigarettes. Cullman saw the bid for Gallaher in terms of retaining a British shareholding in accordance with group policy towards other overseas subsidiaries. It was a necessary condition, for the proposal to take control of Gallaher was the largest single American investment in British industry since American Ford bought full control of British Ford ten years earlier, and since Chrysler had joined forces with Rootes in 1962.

Mark Norman, Gallaher's chairman, wasted no time in rejecting the surprise bid. 'Quite inadequate,' he said within the first twenty-four hours. The City felt a fight was brewing, and turned its attention to the silent, shareholding American Tobacco for a reaction. Norman went into a huddle with his advisers, Lazard's, and demanded much more information about Philip Morris's intentions. American Tobacco quietly called in Cazenove and Morgan Grenfell and when it became clear that Philip Morris was determined to press on in spite of Gallaher's board-room opposition matters took a more bitter turn.

Dispatched with instructions from the $350,000 a year chairman of American Tobacco, Barney ('Brand-a-month') Walker, a team of three American Tobacco executives flew into London on Saturday 14th July 1968. Their leader Robert K. Heimann, executive vice-president, announced 'We are here to defend our investment'. So quickly did American Tobacco now move that they set off something of an ethical crisis in the City as well as stirring memories of the swashbuckling deeds of Buck Duke whatever the poise and polish of the modern American tobacco executives who trooped in and out of their London merchant banks.

Until three or four years before American Tobacco was something of a sleeping giant. It missed the boat in the switch to filters. Wall Street wags, reading the famous nostalgic advertisement showing the soldier in the German cornfield ('Remember how great cigarettes used to taste? Luckies still do') quipped 'Remember how great American Tobacco used to be? Stop.' In recent years, however, American Tobacco had made significant advances. Tareyton, a cigarette with an activated charcoal filter, is claimed as America's fastest-growing filter brand. According to American Tobacco it is the only 'scientifically advanced' cigarette in the top ten. Three years ago American Tobacco was first to introduce the 100-millimetre cigarette, a category which now accounts for 15 per cent of United States sales.

With Lucky Strike, Pall Mall, Tareyton and Silva Thins, the company was now well represented across the board in the cigarette market. It was also a powerful factor in cigars.

American Tobacco had also joined the world-wide trend of tobacco companies to diversify into other products. Of its $1,493 million total sales some $333 million was accounted for by the sales of two new subsidiaries, Sunshine Biscuits and James B. Beam Distilleries. Sunshine is one of the leaders in biscuits, crackers and snacks. It has 20 per cent of the American market for specially baked goods and also sells sweets and dog food. Jim Beam is America's biggest selling bourbon. In addition the Duffy-Mott subsidiary markets such exotic-sounding products as Sunsweet prune juice and Mott Apple brands.

Morgan Grenfell's Lord Harcourt said: 'I am totally confident that the purchases are in full conformity with the City code.' Only a few hours before, Robert Heimann had sought to allay possible anxieties by declaring 'We believe we have been a good corporate citizen of the United Kingdom for 41 years.'* From the United States, Barney Walker, president and chairman of American Tobacco, wrote to Gallaher shareholders: 'We are familiar both with the tobacco business in the United Kingdom and with the way business in general is conducted there. I believe the record shows that we can expect to continue to be a responsible member of the British business community.' American Tobacco was guaranteeing continued operational autonomy for Gallaher and the maintenance of an all-British executive team. There was 'no intention of changing the present management's policies with regard to production and marketing in the United Kingdom and leaf buying.'

Barney Walker was seen by Gallaher's Mark Norman as Sir Gallahad, flying to rescue his flagging business from the clutches of Philip Morris. 'Independence is sweet, but there is a time when matrimony is attractive, too,' he said, thereby blessing a hurriedly prepared counter offer approved in basic detail only by the watch-dog panel administering the City's take-over code. On the morning of 16th July, the Gallaher board recommended an outline offer from American Tobacco for at least 50 per cent of its equity, valuing Gallaher at £130 million against the £92 million value put on by Philip Morris's earlier offer. The news was hardly on news-agency tapes before American Tobacco's brokers, Cazenove, moved into the London stock market and in a massive £20 million plus operation gained within one hour 12 million Gallaher shares to give their client a dominating 28 per cent stake instead of the previous 13 per cent. The Take-Over Panel had not been told of the intended market raid during which institutional shareholders sold on undisclosed terms before Gallaher's smaller investors ever knew or could complain about a partial bid that would deprive some of their gain in share value. A Board of Trade approved rise in

* Heimann tactfully only went back to 1927, ignoring the Tobacco Trust affair of earlier years.

tobacco product prices, announced on 15th July, had confused the outlook for profits and judgements on Philip Morris's offer, which might have been raised.

Well behaved or not, there came a storm of protest over the action of American Tobacco and its City advisers in snapping up a decisive block of shares, mainly from institutions, before the general shareholders either had heard news of the bid or had time to consider the terms. Such a move trampled right across recently introduced rules for fair play in take-over deals. Public concern about the City's behaviour in various merger situations and contested bids was already bothering the Establishment. Only that March the Take-Over Panel had been set up voluntarily, with Bank of England and other institutional backing, to counter the increasing pressures for the Labour Government to set up an American-style Securities and Exchange Commission. The Panel, under Sir Humphrey Mynors, a serving director of Imperial Tobacco, met hurriedly on 8th July and issued a statement censuring the blue-blood brokers Cazenove and bankers Morgan Grenfell for breaching Article 7 of the general principles of the code administered by the Panel. The tactics had cut right through the rule that no offer should be made that was more favourable than that to other shareholders.

The general Gallaher shareholder was left with the choice of selling only half his holding to American Tobacco, or staying in with Gallaher, while he who was party to the market coup sold at a better price.

The City, where their word is their bond, shook at the sight of two respected institutions being lambasted in public for their behaviour. Newspapers condemned the parties. Morgan Grenfell and Cazenove even declined to be contrite, pleading their innocence and continued support for the voluntary code. Nevertheless, the market operation was too blatant to escape further censures. The Stock Exchange Council and the Issuing Houses Association duly issued their own criticisms. The Governor of the Bank of England seized the opportunity to warn the City to put its house in better order. He was looking over his shoulder at the Labour Government which was contemplating the case for statutory controls and a tightening of merger discipline.

For the next few years, the American Tobacco-Gallaher affair became a City bogey, an often quoted case when the arguments for statutory regulations were put by critics of the Square Mile's so-called feudal barons of finance. All American Tobacco could do, its name sullied yet again, if only by accepting advice, was to keep quiet in its victory over Philip Morris, and keep out of any other trouble. Unfortunately, Gallaher was to feature in another big row early in 1973 when American Brands, as it became known, proposed to buy up more shares to raise its 67 per cent investment to just over 80 per cent. This time American Brands' advisers were a little more cautious, consulting the Panel on Take-Overs. But they were not cautious enough, for the institutions were hopping mad over the price being offered.

There were three reasons for the bid: (a) American Brands would get a handy tax bonus, since United States tax provisions were more generous for foreign subsidiaries that were 80 per cent or more owned; (b) the existing holding in Gallaher had been very profitable in comparative terms to American Brands' performance back home; and (c) the current stock market slump allowed Gallaher shares to be picked up relatively cheaply.

The institutions felt the price was inadequate and objected to another partial bid that made the remaining equity less marketable and so less valuable. There was a row in the Gallaher board room—some of the directors were also on the board of American Brands, and faced a conflict of interests in advising shareholders. The merchant bankers Baring Brothers were called in, at the City Panel's request, for an independent opinion. It was unfavourable. Bewildered shareholders called it another farce. Matters were not helped by reports showing that American Brands' shares on Wall Street were on a price/earnings ratio of 10.5, whereas Philip Morris (reflecting its rapid growth by clever marketing) had quadrupled its sales in ten years, and shares were on a spectacular, for tobacco, p/e ratio of 30.4. Confidence in the Gallaher board's choice of partner could hardly have been lower for minority shareholders. Fortunately the offer was in cash, and many decided that, at least, they could hope to get out, if partially, and invest the money elsewhere.

The board of Gallaher chose to ignore Philip Morris's growth over the past five years. Naturally all the unwanted suitor's brands were filters, whereas American Tobacco's leading Pall Mall brand was plain and had been eased from top of the best selling United

States lists by Winston. Philip Morris had promoted with the Benson & Hedges 100, a big rise in sales of 100-millimetre cigarettes, even though American Tobacco had actually been the first in this field and Liggett & Myers had recently gone one better with 101-millimetre Chesterfields. In the five years to 1967, Philip Morris's compounded sales growth rate was 9.5 per cent and its earnings increased 13.5 per cent. American Tobacco's sales were growing at only 4.4 per cent and earnings by 4.1 per cent. Reynolds, Liggett & Myers and Lorillard lagged behind. Only BAT's Brown & Williamson understood the Philip Morris strategy and came close to matching its international rival's performance.

By the end of July 1968, Philip Morris had withdrawn from the tussle, letting its 25s a share offer lapse against 35s from American Tobacco for 27,325,000 of the 51,944,236 outstanding which it did not own. On 27th August, American Tobacco had won control and controlled 67 per cent of Gallaher's equity.

Far from retiring hurt and angry from Britain, Philip Morris's team sought a consolation prize. In a matter of weeks, the dejected suitor had acquired Godfrey Phillips, the producers of speciality Virginia and Turkish cigarettes, and importers of high quality cigars. The group had raised a huge Eurodollar loan to finance European operations, and they would now help to shut Gallaher out of export markets into which American Tobacco hoped to take their new subsidiary. R. J. Reynolds, then American's biggest cigarette exporter, was making a big sales effort in Continental Europe, and building factories in Germany and Switzerland, appointing enthusiastic licensees elsewhere.

BAT, export agents for Imperial's British brands, obviously had cause to worry about American activity in Europe. Philip Morris was bent on making Marlboro the Continent's second leading filter brand (it had been closing up fast in the United States market on Reynold's Winston, the number one brand) and European sales of the company's cigarettes were rising more than 20 per cent a year. Back in the United States, the average growth in sales of BAT's Brown & Williamson had fallen from 9.7 per cent per annum between 1961 and 1965 to 5.2 per cent per annum between 1965 and 1970. It was a good performance in a relatively unstable overall market that fell from around 540,000 million to 515,000 million cigarettes between 1968 and 1970 (in 1961 the total was some 490,000 million), yet the real growth had to be fought for in non-American, non-British markets. Philip Morris International, the main overseas corporation of Incorporated, was engaged on a comprehensive programme of internationalisation to secure bigger sales abroad than at home. Deals were struck with the state tobacco monopolies in France (Regie Tabac), Yugoslavia, Austria, Spain, and Italy as well as the former Swedish state monopoly in obtaining at least 7 per cent of the entire European market from Finland to Ireland.

The advent of Europeanism was soon to bring new structural changes. Imperial Tobacco and BAT were under stronger attack and the historic role of the former looking after the home market and the latter the world markets was in need of reappraisal. The prospect of British entry into an enlarged European Community, with new taxation policies and rules on market and trade-mark sharing, looked like requiring a mass merger into a trust that neither Europe nor the United States could possibly permit. The alternative was to negotiate a new understanding suited to the changing times. Gallaher was now American-owned and Philip Morris had stormed into Europe from another direction. Even as Imperial's directors began to contemplate tentatively future structure, the much smaller Carreras was being drawn into a unique response to the pressures for forming, or refashioning, alliances.

The cosy days of each combine to his own market were over. The Anglo-American understanding of separate development was being broken. New groupings and new agreements were vital to expand international operations. This explained the speed with which Philip Morris had acted after failing to buy up a controlling holding in Gallaher. On 18th August 1968, their agreed offer of £11.5 million for Godfrey Phillips, earning 87 per cent of its profits outside Britain, was announced. Derrick Littlejohn, managing director of the 124-year-old British concern, said his board was accepting because Godfrey Phillips was 'bound to face growing problems in the international tobacco trade as a small firm combatting large companies with limitless funds'. Carreras would take a different course of action, avoiding the waiting arms of American companies.

A formidable collection of business minds gathered at 114 Old Broad Street on 18th April 1972 in the City of London. There were accountants and lawyers, management consultants and merchant bankers, tax specialists and industrialists. The scene of the meeting was the board room of Samuel Montagu, the merchant bankers. The object: to set in train the whole complicated process that eventually led to the creation of what is now the fifth largest tobacco company in the world. Mergers and take-overs in the normal course of events are the very stuff of merchant banking. This one, the formation of Rothmans International, was fraught with a peculiar set of complications.

In the first place, it was to be a merger on a truly European scale. Its basic corporate ingredients: Carreras, the smallest of the three major United Kingdom tobacco companies; Martin Brinckmann, West Germany's 159-year-old tobacco manufacturer; the Belgian Tabacofina, the leading cigarette supplier to Holland and Belgium; and the Dutch Turmac company, another major force in the Low Countries' tobacco market. Also included in the package were two substantial stakes in a New Zealand and an Australian tobacco company; and United Kingdom and European export rights to four internationally established brands of cigarettes (Rothmans King Size Filter, Consulate, Peter Stuyvesant and Rothmans Pall Mall).

Secondly, the merger was to be effected in such a way that the newly formed company would have its shareholders widely spread within the major countries in which it operated. Different national preferences for different forms of security had to be catered for—the British, for example, have a predeliction for equities; Continentals prefer bonds. A wide variety of investment tastes had to be satisfied.

Thirdly, there was the sheer scale of the merger. It meant creating a major multinational company, with 44 factories in seventeen countries, with a work force of 25,000 employees, with a monthly output of 9,000 million cigarettes, an annual turnover of well over £600 million and profits before tax of nearly £40 million.

This then was to be no run-of-the-mill merger. The merging of two companies across European frontiers is a rare enough phenomenon. Putting four companies together at one time from different countries seemed a daunting prospect, to say the least.

The central figure in the whole affair was Dr Anton Rupert, the former chemistry lecturer at the University of Pretoria in South Africa who turned his mind at an early age to the world of commerce and industry. The most remarkable monument to his achievements was the world-wide Rembrandt group of companies, a tobacco empire which he built up on the basic concept of co-existence through industrial partnership—'he who covets all will lose all' is his often quoted maxim. An essential ingredient of Rupert's industrial philosophy is that the local people in the numerous countries in which the Rembrandt group operates are offered a half-interest in his industrial ventures. Dr Rupert's involvement in the European tobacco industry had developed by a process of gradual evolution. Just before the creation of Rothmans International he had, through his various holding companies, 100 per cent stakes in Turmac (and its Swiss subsidiary, Sullana) and Martin Brinckmann (which in turn owned 60 per cent of Tabacofina); and, by an eccentric equity voting structure, 29 per cent of the equity of Carreras and 50 per cent of its voting power. His 'partnership' with Carreras began in 1958 when Rembrandt acquired a minor stake in the company, this was intensified three years later when he sold to Carreras the Rothmans of Pall Mall business in Britain in return for a controlling interest in the former. Since then Carreras' share of the United Kingdom cigarette market had grown in fits and starts from around 2 per cent to nearly 8 per cent.

Concern about the *status quo* of the Rupert interests in Europe began to emerge around two years ago. The question that Rupert, the team of experts close to him and the managers of the European operating companies asked themselves was this: did it make sense for each of the four companies in Europe to go their own, largely independent ways? There were a number of factors militating against the continued separate development of the Rupert companies in Europe. In the first place, there was an awareness that lack of coordination was leading to unnecessary and possibly harmful duplication of resources and effort. In Italy, for example, the group had three separate competing distribution forces. In the Benelux countries, there was a triplication of sales organisations. In Switzerland, the Carreras cigarette brands were competing head on with Tabacofina's Laurens brand. And throughout Europe the group had no fewer than twenty-five different factories. 'One of the troubles in this group,' commented one close observer, 'is that the constituent European companies are all falling over each other's feet.'

A second factor that had to be considered was the modern-day logic of the tobacco industry which seemed to point inexorably in the direction of large-scale operations. Each of the European companies was dwarfed by the giants of the industry—British-American Tobacco, Imperial Tobacco, Philip Morris, American Brands and Reynolds. Carreras had long been the junior member of Britain's tobacco industry—an industry effectively dominated by Imperial Tobacco and Gallaher. There seemed to be compelling reasons why tobacco companies should look beyond their traditional national frontiers in the future—not least the imminent enlargement and integration of the European Economic Community. Yet activity on this scale required massive resources.

Thirdly, there was the uncertainty whether the existing relationships between the Rupert companies in Europe would stand the increasing militancy of the EEC anti-trust authorities. Would the competition officials in the Common Market Commission in Brussels turn a blind eye towards closer collaboration between four ostensibly independent companies? Recent policy of the EEC anti-trust experts suggested that closer alignment could invoke a strong reaction from Brussels.

Then there was the question of trade-marks. Carreras, for example, owned the Rothmans King Size brand in Britain: Turmac in the Netherlands. Could this and other similar arrangements be continued once Britain joined the EEC? The right for a company to assert territorial control of a brand name in one EEC country and not in others had been called into question by recent Community litigation (the Sirena case). The Rupert group trade-mark arrangements in Europe seemed unlikely to stand the test of time and litigation. A similar view was being taken by Imperial Tobacco and British-American Tobacco of their trade-mark situation in Europe.

Tobacco duties in Europe were another complicating factor. The process of fiscal harmonisation in the EEC was bound to lead eventually to a common basis for a levying tax on tobacco products, with the duty almost certainly levied per cigarette rather than according to the weight of tobacco (the basis for levying duties in the United Kingdom). This would have the effect of narrowing the price gap between cheap and expensive cigarettes and benefit manufacturers, like the Rupert companies, whose strength rested in the higher priced sector of the market. But the full benefit could have been lost if each of the European companies continued an independent existence.

These were the main causes of concern among the top management of the Rupert companies in Europe as the prospects of an enlarged EEC became clearer. The response within the Rupert organisation was to establish a Committee for Europe, comprising the chief executives of all the main European operating companies and chaired by Dr Rupert himself. In the summer of 1971, the Committee called in McKinsey, the American management consultants, to make an assessment of the benefits of closer co-operation and to recommend how such benefits might be achieved. The McKinsey team saw themselves very much as independent brokers, examining the prospects of each company in isolation and seeing how its future would fit into a more closely co-ordinated group structure. The answer that McKinsey came up with at the beginning of 1972 was quite unequivocal. 'Our conclusion,' says John Beard, the consultant who headed the McKinsey team, 'was that any form of co-operation that didn't resolve the shareholding problem would not achieve the benefits.' In short, a single financial holding company for the different European interests was the McKinsey verdict.

The multi-million pound question from then on was: *how?* In January, John Chown, a City-based leading expert on international tax problems, received what he calls 'a cryptic telephone call' from McKinsey. They wanted him to discuss with them the possibility of merging what was then an anonymous group of companies—the consultants did not disclose the identity of their client till later. Without a lot of detailed thought, Chown was able to outline a variety of problems, which without a solution would act as a severe constraint on any merger plan. There was the problem of profit flows across national frontiers—double taxation agreements between different countries in practice have their limitations resulting in larger chunks of tax being lopped off than if profits remained within a single set of national boundaries. There were exchange control problems, capital gains tax problems, stamp duty problems and, finally and not least, the difficulties of finding the right mix of securities for the merger transaction which would allow the optimal solution to all these problems and would satisfy the different preferences for marketable assets among the wide range of investors who would end up as stakeholders in the new merged company.

The search for solutions was widened to include the joint merchant bank advisers to Carreras, Samuel Montagu and N. M. Rothschild. The first three months of the year saw a diffuse assortment of financial brain power working towards the solution of the problem. Volumes of memoranda were generated. The overriding question was what corporate structure would be the most desirable. At first sight, there seemed no obvious answer. There were numerous logical possibilities. Historical precedent pointed in the direction of a two holding companies solution on the lines of Dunlop/Pirelli, Agfa/Gevaert, Unilever or Royal Dutch/Shell. The permutation on this formula alone seemed almost inexhaustible. The alternative was the single holding company approach. But where should this master company be based? Holland, Switzerland, Luxembourg, West Germany or the United Kingdom? The decision to opt for the United Kingdom solution had a number of causes. In the first place, there was an apparent tax saving of £4 million to £5 million a year in the foreseeable future compared with other solutions. Secondly, the greater sophistication of United Kingdom capital markets would clearly stand a United Kingdom-based holding company in good stead. Finally, when the choice was narrowed down within realistic limits, the United Kingdom and the Netherlands emerged as the strongest contenders as the base for the new company. And as the British Carreras was larger than the Dutch Turmac, the former seemed the obvious candidate. It is unlikely that the management of Carreras would have been happy in a position of formal subordination to their Dutch partners.

By the time the participants in the merger plan converged on the City headquarters of Samuel Montagu in April, the outline design of the new company had been agreed. Carreras was to be the vehicle into which almost all the Rupert tobacco interests outside North America and South Africa would be drawn together. The vehicle was to be modelled according to the principles of Dr Rupert's industrial philosophy. In other words, he would end up controlling 50 per cent of the new company, with the remaining control spread locally among the principal countries, in which the group operated. For a variety of reasons—tax, investment preferences among different nationalities of shareholders and exchange control—the main currency in which the deal would be transacted was to be convertible bonds. In conceptual terms, the vehicle at this stage was hardly even a chassis. The bodywork had still to be designed and added.

It is worth pointing out at this stage who the *dramatis personae* in the merger deal were. The negotiants were effectively two separate parties, but they were closely interlinked. The role of Dr Rupert was essentially that of a vendor—he was selling the continental companies in which he had complete control (remembering that Rupert's direct stake in Tabacofina was only 60 per cent, but that he had a 100 per cent interest in Tabacofina's parent company, Martin Brinckmann) to Carreras. Insofar as Dr Rupert controlled half of Carreras, the South African would in effect be sitting on both sides of the negotiating table at the same time. It was therefore of paramount importance from the outset that the interests of the other Carreras shareholders should be scrupulously taken into account.

The negotiants had as their advisers some of the most irreproachable patrician names in the professional world of high finance. Advising Carreras were Cooper Brothers, the accountants, and the merchant banking houses of N. M. Rothschild and Samuel Montagu, who essentially saw their role as being to safeguard the interests of the main body of that company's shareholders—in practice they were on the opposite side of the negotiating table to Dr Rupert. The Rupert Group was advised by Peat, Marwick, Mitchell & Company, another leading chartered accounting firm. Then there were the solicitors: Linklaters & Paines acting for Carreras; Slaughter & May for the Rupert group; and Ashurst Morris Crisp for the merchant banks. 'There were a lot of cooks involved in the broth,' says David Montagu, chairman of Samuel Montagu. The scale of activity can be gauged from the fact that the bill for putting the new company together came to the grand total of £850,000. Right from the outset, there was a great urgency to complete the deal. When the forty or so participants arrived at Samuel Montagu's in mid-April, they were told that everything had to be tied up by the end of May. A more realistic deadline of 31st July was suggested. The whole deal was in fact announced to the press and shareholders on 1st August 1972.

In broad terms, there were two critical issues that had to be resolved in this time: the overall price for the deal; and the mix of securities which was to make up the price. Subordinate to these overriding issues was a whole complex of other problems. In the first place, there was the question of exchange control regulations which have usually required United Kingdom companies to finance foreign acquisitions either by foreign currency borrowing or by paying the dollar premium. Issuing convertible bonds to foreign investors—and over £100 million worth of them to boot—clearly would not fit into the traditional scheme of exchange control.

The bonds were to be issued to foreign investors who could then exercise their rights at the appropriate moment to convert into the equity of a United Kingdom company. The point is that those same investors could then sell their United Kingdom equity to British investors and in the whole process no dollar premium would have been paid.

Secondly, there was taxation. The interest on the bonds had to be paid without any tax deductions (otherwise they would have had limited attractions to foreign investors) and had to be allowable against United Kingdom corporation tax. This again would involve some flexibility of treatment on the part of the authorities.

Thirdly, the decision to issue a large extra chunk of subordinated loan stock meant that a quite separate set of negotiations would have to be conducted with Carreras' existing loan stockholders. The financial gearing requirements of Carreras meant that nearly £10 million worth of unsecured loan stock had to be repaid. This would involve detailed negotiations with the investment protection committees representing loan stockholders among the pension funds, insurance companies, and investment trusts.

Fourthly, there were accounting problems. Accounting periods among the various constituent companies of the new group differed. Different levels of disclosure in the various companies were an added problem. The accountants, therefore, had to set to work establishing a common accountancy base for the merger constituents.

Fifthly, the mechanics of the bond issue itself were by no means straightforward. This, after all, was an untried way of financing a United Kingdom-based multinational merger. How could the bonds be made sufficiently attractive to foreign investors?

These were the principal obstacles which the participants saw ahead of them as the starting pistol was fired for the £200 million merger. It was a formidable course to run by any standards. 'The tax complications,' says David Montagu, 'the complications over

the Treasury and the Bank of England, and the time scale in which
we had to operate, made me believe that it was an astonishing feat
of co-ordination. This is where we have pioneered something. It
looked impossible when we started to do it within the time scale.
It looked impossible to do the scheme at all. And we knew that the
negotiations would be terribly tough with the vendor.' Inevitably,
some of the obstacles proved more easily surmountable than others.
It is fair to say that the whole merger deal would have been impossible had not the British Government authorities (the Treasury
and the Bank of England) taken a liberal approach to it from the
point of view of taxation and exchange control. 'There has been a
sea change in the attitude of the authorities,' says Samuel Montagu
director, David Bucks, 'since we have decided to go into Europe.
Had that sea change not taken place this transaction would not
have taken place.' The authorities clearly foresaw what the consequences of a negative attitude might have been. If Rothmans
International had not been encouraged to make the United
Kingdom its base, could they realistically expect other European
multinational companies in future to become domiciled in Britain?

Some of the obstacles were quite unforeseeable at the start.
Like the details of the British Government's new corporation tax,
which only emerged in the Finance Bill in May. Or the United
Kingdom decision in June to float the pound, which sent back on
to the drawing board the details of the sterling/Deutsche Mark
convertible bonds. The most unpredictable element in the whole
deal turned out to be the vendor himself.

Dr Rupert has a fearsome reputation as a negotiator and his
behaviour in this deal proved to be no exception. Stanley Berwin,
a director of Rothschild's, remembers the hot summer day in
July when the whole merger nearly fell through. The scene was a
conference room in St Swithin's Lane at Rothschild's City office.
The two negotiating teams were gathered, Hoogenhuit representing
Dr Rupert, who was in South Africa. 'They asked for another
£x million and other conditions,' says Berwin, 'and we offered
£y million. They then went out of the room to consider our offer
and when they came back we had put on our coats, had got up
from the table and were all ready to leave the room and call it off.'
The Rupert team instantly agreed to the latest offer. The negotiating strength of Dr Rupert lay all along in the possibility that he
could have merged the Continental companies together leaving

Carreras to find its own solution independently. 'There were several moments between April and July,' says David Montagu, 'when we assumed that things wouldn't come off for one reason or another, whether it was floating exchange rates or the negative attitude of the German Bundesbank (whose permission had to be obtained for the bond issue) or whether the vendor wouldn't accept our term.' The brinkmanship was unnerving.

As an intellectual exercise in financial problem solving, the Rothmans International merger was without precedent. Much has been said of the City's likely role in the enlarged financial structure of the European Economic Community. There are as many doubters who wonder whether the City's future role in the wider EEC has been overstated as there are optimists who believe that the City will become increasingly the focal point of the Community's financial activity. The Rothmans International merger in isolation could only strengthen the case of the optimists.

CHAPTER SIXTEEN

The European Dimension

Richard P. Dobson, son of a Professor of Greek at Bristol University, smokes a pipe and speaks softly. A product of classical scholarship at King's College, Cambridge, Dobson has the deceptive ease in manner of many English industrialists that American businessmen have learned is a cover for confident perception. The tie is often striped and the hair carefully parted. Hobbies are golf and fishing. His war record is impeccable, a Spitfire pilot who served in the Middle East, Italy and Burma. But there were the years of hard work in China, Rhodesia and in tobacco markets elsewhere round the world that qualified him to assume from 1st July 1970 the chairmanship of British-American Tobacco, the world's biggest free enterprise tobacco business, which first took him on the payroll at twenty-two in 1935.

His predecessor, Denzil Clarke, once said, 'We used to be known as the dumb Colossus.' Under Dobson, BAT has shed its previous enigmatic image and proclaimed many of the secrets of its size from its museum-like headquarters within the shadow of the Houses of Parliament along London's Thames-side embankment road, Millbank. That Dobson bestrides a Colossus cannot be doubted.

BAT is a British company, with almost 99 per cent of its equity currently held by British stockholders, and it is listed by *The Times* as the third largest industrial group based in the United Kingdom. The turnover for the year ended 30th September 1972 was £2,037 million. The increase in group profit before taxation and net assets over the past ten years had been 131 per cent and 144 per cent respectively.

Group products are manufactured in seventy countries. Taking the subsidiaries together with companies in which there is a substantial minority investment, BAT has over 200,000 employees throughout the world and the 158,000 shareholders in the parent company in the United Kingdom are considerably outnumbered by those holding shares in group companies in many different countries.

On its formation in London in 1902, BAT acquired from Imperial Tobacco and the American Tobacco Company (now called American Brands Incorporated) the ownership of their trade-marks and brands throughout most of the world outside Great Britain, the Republic of Ireland, and the United States of America. Since then BAT has developed or acquired many other brands. Its sales are more than twice those of any other tobacco group, excluding state-owned industries, and it has one hundred and forty factories manufacturing tobacco products in fifty-four countries. Brown & Williamson Tobacco Corporation, a member company of the group, is one of the largest tobacco companies in the United States market. Although BAT does not at present sell any tobacco products on the domestic market in the United Kingdom, nearly one cigarette in five smoked in the countries where the industry is open to private enterprise is a BAT product. Nearly four hundred and fifty of the group's cigarette brands are currently on sale in the world, together with some three hundred brands of tobacco and two hundred cigar and cigarillo brands. In forty countries the leading cigarette brand is a BAT product.

Some 95 per cent of the group's tobacco products are manufactured in overseas countries for their domestic markets, but direct exports from factories in the United Kingdom, United States and other countries make a substantial contribution to BAT's total business. Cigarettes are exported to over one hundred and seventy countries, and supplied to practically every international shipping line and air line in the world, as well as to British and United States Forces overseas. These exports are mainly from the United Kingdom which include Wills' Embassy, Three Castles, Benson & Hedges, John Player Special, Player's Gold Leaf, Player's Medium Navy Cut, Senior Service, State Express 555 and du Maurier, and from the United States, which include Pall Mall, Lucky Strike, Viceroy and Kool.

Smoking tobaccos are exported to nearly one hundred and forty countries; they include State Express, Three Nuns, Capstan, Gold Block, Player's and St Bruno from the United Kingdom, Hollandia and Taconis from Holland and Sir Walter Raleigh from the United States. Cigars are exported to over one hundred and thirty countries, from Holland, Belgium, Switzerland, Jamaica and Canada. Every size from high-grade Coronas to small cigarillos is included in this range under such names as Henri Wintermans, Velasques, Castella, Vautier, La Tropical de Luxe, Old Port and Reas.

With some two-thirds of its net assets still concerned with tobacco, this remains BAT''s principal business. But the group had however for many years been involved in paper manufacture, printing and packaging as ancillary activities to its tobacco business. Now a policy of planned investment in these industries irrespective of their relationship to tobacco has been adopted. Wiggins Teape, since 1970 a wholly-owned subsidiary which BAT purchased for some £80 million, manufactures high-grade printing and writing papers in addition to a wide range of speciality industrial papers. Mills and factories are established in the United Kingdom, Belgium, Latin America, Africa and Asia.

Mardon Packaging International Limited, formed in 1962, is jointly owned by BAT and the Imperial Group, each having invested over £20 million. Mardon Packaging International has a number of companies in the United Kingdom undertaking the production of cartons, cases, tins, and plastic bottles and packs. Recent developments in Europe have been the acquisition in Belgium of a plastics company and in France three companies manufacturing cartons, labels and expanded polystyrene.

Dobson and his board have not been content with such multinational power and the consequential profits. There were management mistakes in a policy of diversification—such as the unhappy acquisition of the Tonibell ice cream business, and initial difficulties in entering the cosmetics trade on a sound footing. Dobson has continued to build up the original investment in cosmetics to £50 million, with the interests spanning Yardley, Lenthéric, Morny, Germaine Monteil, Scandia and Tuvaché, selling in more than one hundred and forty countries, with local manufacture in thirty-four countries. Companies overseas have also acquired interests outside tobacco in local industries such as food, soft drinks and farming.

The policy of rapid diversification has its roots, of course, in the problem of smoking and health. 'It's hard to argue that filling your lungs with smoke can be actually good for you,' Dobson said soon after taking on the chairmanship of BAT.* 'But surely it is a question of moderation, and I do sincerely believe that the tobacco industry, in total, does more good than harm. I know more people who have had liquor problems than have had tobacco problems, and I know of more people of all ages who have been killed in motor accidents. . . .' Meanwhile, he feels the industry must 'press on looking at other, alternative areas'.

'We are thinking all the time in very large dimensions—the big and powerful concerns. We're quite convinced it's no good buying any little companies; they take up just as much management time, and the rewards are too small.'

The record shows Dobson was making no idle statement. Perhaps the best illustration of the huge expenditures BAT is ready to make can be given by the invasion of retailing. In the United Kingdom, International Stores, which BAT purchased for £68 million in 1972, is a wholesale and multiple retail grocery and provisions company. It has some 934 stores in the United Kingdom, of which the great majority are either supermarkets or self-service and over four hundred are licensed to sell wines and spirits. It also owns the Ridgways tea business. In 1973 came a £10 million takeover of the Pricerite supermarket chain.

In West Germany, Horten AG, of which BAT's German subsidiary Interversa purchased 25.6 per cent of the equity for £32 million in 1971, has over fifty department stores covering most of the larger towns in the Federal Republic. In Brazil, Supermercados Peg-Pag SA, of which BAT's subsidiary, Cia. de Cigarros Souza Cruz, purchased 60 per cent of the equity for £3 million in 1973, operates a chain of thirty-six supermarkets. In the United States of America, the Kohl Corporation, of which BAT's United States subsidiary, Brown & Williamson, purchased 80 per cent of the equity capital for £30 million in 1972, operates a chain of seventy supermarkets, department stores and drug stores in Wisconsin and Illinois. This was to be followed by the purchase in July 1973 of 93 per cent of America's famous Gimbel Brothers Incorporated, including the 20 per cent interest previously held by the Loews Corporation. It was a consolation prize for an abortive

* *The Director*, September 1971.

attempt to buy Green Giant and a frustrated plan to acquire H. J. Heinz, the food canners, in the wake of the purchase in 1969 of Vita Food Products Incorporated, Aleutian King Crab and Sea Pass Corporation.

It is in discussion of such extensions of multinational power that Dobson becomes animated. He worries about the power and the anxieties of critics of the untrammelled influence of international business. 'There is more bloody nonsense talked on this subject than on any other business topic... it has become the oh-so-fashionable subject . . . there's an avalanche of books and conferences on the subject, but little common sense . . . we have to be better behaved than anyone else . . . we are put upon in all sorts of outrageous ways . . . you can fall over backwards to be a good citizen of the countries where you operate, and then find yourself denounced as exploiters . . . something sinister seems to have attached itself to the title "multinational corporation"; well, whatever you call it governments have killed a hell of a lot more people than companies... governments tend to make the world companies their scapegoats, partly because they don't realise the limitations of their own power.'*

In spite of his and other protestations, the critics are continuing to grow in number. Tobacco companies have enormous cash flows which make them potentially the most powerful adversaries for effecting mergers and take-overs. They are already treading across other industries and sectors of national economies. R. J. Reynolds Industries, owners of the largest United States tobacco group, has even appointed a former president of Federated Department Stores and ex-Campbell Soups, J. Paul Sticht, as president and chief operating officer. Reynolds formed its holding company in 1970 to drive into food and transportation. A merger with McLean Industries took Reynolds into containerised freight alongside food, aluminium sheet packaging and industrial corn products. Liggett & Myers' diversification has embraced pet foods (Allen Products' Alpo, Perk Foods' Vet, and Liv-A-Snaps), Paddington Corporation (importers of J. & B. Scotch), Carillon (Grand Marnier, Bombay gin), Austin Nichols (Wild Turkey Bourbon), National Oats (cereals and popcorn), Brite Industries (watch straps), Earl Grissmer (Blue Lustre cleaning compounds), and Mercury Mills (rugs and carpets), among others.

* *The Director*, September 1971.

In Britain, Gallaher has gone into valves and pumps, tile panelling, cash-and-carry grocery warehousing, toys, and the optical trade, though not all the ventures have been too successful, and a few disastrous. More impressive, of course, have been Imperial Tobacco's steady take-overs in the food manufacturing and brewing industries. So large is the presence in other sectors that the name of the parent holding company has now been changed to the Imperial Group and the tobacco interests restructured into a wholly-owned subsidiary, Imperial Tobacco.

And it is at this point in time that this narrative takes its most breathtaking twist, given the history of Duke's notorious Tobacco Trust, and the formation of both Imperial and BAT at the turn of the century to pursue their policies of separate development in the British and overseas markets respectively, scrupulously observing an agreement for BAT to act as exporter of Imperial brands outside the United Kingdom and Ireland. The British Monopolies Commission virtually avoided comment in 1961 on the relationship between the two mighty tobacco enterprises, though describing the trading and financial agreements with the Molins tobacco machinery group. The two groups jointly control Mardon Packaging and are associated with the Tobacco Securities Trust Company, formed in 1928 and holding various investments round the world, such as a large holding in the Canadian tobacco, food and wine concern Imasco. There have been numerous working arrangements of a confidential character, some covering the obscure world of filter rods supply where Bunzl Pulp & Paper has nearly 14 per cent of its shares held by Imperial. Much research work has been shared, too. Above all, Imperial holds 28 per cent of the equity shares of BAT, an investment worth over £220 million and providing a number of seats on the board, including a place reserved for the prevailing chairman of Imperial.

This holding in BAT has always been regarded with suspicion outside Britain. In the United States the Justice Department has always treated the two combines as one, placing some constraints on the pace of Brown & Williamson's expansion outside tobacco as well as ensuring sensitivity to the public interest in Anglo-American leaf-buying policies. Yet it was the historic agreement on trade-marks that brought new anti-trust problems, and not in the United States but in Europe. Curiously, a somewhat minor brand of American shaving cream called Prep brought the two mighty groups face to face with the restrictive relationship that divided the world between them. In 1972, it took BAT and Imperial to the brink of a total merger into a world combine with over 3,000 million annual sales, making it one of the three largest companies outside the United States.

From 1971 and into 1972—even as Imperial was bidding successfully for the huge British brewing group Courage Barclay— their boards wrestled with the question of their future relationship, a very necessary exercise in view of the United Kingdom's entry from 1st January 1973 into the European Community.

Enlargement of the EEC created a new domestic market, the prospect of new competition from Continental exporters, new regulations, tax disadvantages (the EEC followed a system of duty concerned with value rather than weight and quality of tobacco leaf) and preferential subsidies on leaf grown within the Community. More traumatic were the implications of Articles 85 and 86 of the Treaty of Rome, which are concerned with intra-Community competition. Until 1971, it was not too clear just what those implications might be for the Imperial-BAT market sharing pact, for no trade-mark cases had been taken before the European Court under the two Articles to help shape Community competition policy. But then came the Sirena case, already mentioned in the last chapter in the background to the Rothmans International deal.

The background to this case was that back in 1937 the Mark Allen Company, of the United States, licensed an Italian company, Sirena, to make a shaving cream, known as Prep. A few years later Allen made a similar arrangement with a German manufacturer for that market. By 1970, the Germany company had started selling its Prep on the Italian market through a local importer at lower prices than Sirena charged for the same brand. Sirena took the importer to a Milan court for infringement of trade-mark. The Milan authorities promptly referred two fundamental questions arising from the case to the European Court. Did Articles 85 and 86 apply to agreements entered into before the Treaty of Rome 1958? How did the Articles affect intra-Community trade in terms of legally registered trade-marks in individual member states?

Eventually the European Court held that pre-dating the Treaty did not matter. While the Treaty did not overrule national legislation on industrial property, such law could not be used to justify restraint of trade and unfair competition between member states. So, though the right to industrial property was allowed, the exercise of rights to carve up Community markets was not. The German company was within its rights to undercut Sirena in Italy. For BAT and Imperial's legal advisers it meant the worst—that the territorial arrangements between the two companies would not stand up under the Community's Treaty and operational rules for promoting competition across national boundaries.

There was a certain irony in the way seventy years of the market agreement between BAT and Imperial were threatened. For the urbane chairman of Imperial, Sir John Partridge, newly knighted for his services to the business community, had done more than most industrialists to champion the case for British entry into the EEC. Like Dobson of BAT, he was an ardent European and had just completed a strenuous term of office as president of Britain's premier industrial organisation, the Confederation of British Industry. His tanned (Fleet Street photographers called him 'Nick Nicotine'), puckish face, faultlessly combed hair and studded collar were as familiar on television as the deep brown voice, always putting the case for his fellow industrialists on issues of the day, was to radio listeners. During his CBI presidency, Britain negotiated the terms for entry and Sir John enthusiastically proclaimed the prospective benefits for industry, while reserving some more cautious comments on tobacco taxation and leaf supplies for Imperial's shareholders and employees.

By 10th August 1973, both groups were admitting publicly that their relationship was under careful review—and a merger of two vast enterprises with a combined stock market capitalisation of £1,460 million could not be ruled out.

Six days later, Sir John was announcing the outcome, and why a merger with BAT—25 per cent of whose profits came from £300 million worth of European assets—had to be rejected, with some reluctance. He said:

'Over the past year and more we have separately and jointly examined in depth a variety of options as to our future relationship. Broadly there were three: first, a total merger; second, some form of merger of our European interests; and third, continued independent development but with no territorial barriers.

'There were powerful arguments in favour of the first option. It would have produced an immense international group with a strong United Kingdom base. There were some possibilities of rationalisation, though not very material in the total context. The organisational problems were not so formidable as to defy a fairly quick solution, particularly as the two companies have enjoyed a close and friendly relationship over many years.

'The second option also had much to commend it, in that a combination of the Imperial Tobacco Group's tobacco interests in the United Kingdom and BAT's Continental interests would have produced in volume terms the strongest tobacco force in Europe.

'There was however a danger in each of these options which the more we examined it the more serious it appeared to both companies to be. It was this. Both companies have historically depended very greatly on one trading area—tobacco. While each of us firmly believes in the future of the tobacco business we have each thought it right in recent years to take active steps to broaden our trading base; and certainly we in Imperial believe that, while continuing to put every effort behind our tobacco business, our policy in the years to come must also include a substantial development of other interests.

'A close survey of the regulations under the Treaty of Rome and of the anti-trust rules in other parts of the world (in particular, the United States) convinced us both that joined together (a) we would be vulnerable to attack on grounds of size, especially in relation to future acquisition, and (b) we would therefore run a much greater risk of our development plans being thwarted than if we pursued them separately.

'Needless to say, between us we considered a variety of possible ways of resolving this dilemma but none of them satisfied us. At the end of the day the balance of probability in every case pointed to the likelihood of a joint enterprise—either world-wide or in Europe—finding itself with more limited freedom of development than if we went our separate ways.

'The Board of each company finally concluded that this objection to either a total merger or a European merger was an overriding one, and that the long-term interests of its company would best be served by the third option of independent development—coupled, however, with continuing close liaison on matters of mutual concern, such as our joint interest in Mardon Packaging International, tobacco leaf supplies, production machinery development, and scientific and technical research including that relating to smoking and health.

'From this decision there flow certain corollaries, in particular:
(a) the territorial arrangement between us has been terminated;
and (b) a number of problems affecting ownership and use of
trade-marks are being examined between us.'

And so this was how the biggest issue ever to cross the board-
room tables of Britain's major tobacco companies was resolved, in
amity. The partners in defence and attack against the Americans
ever since the repelling of James Buchanan Duke had decided to
go their own ways, engaging in competition once the ownership
of trade-marks could be revised to meet the European Community's
laws against restrictive practices. Not that the break is yet total, for
Imperial at the time of writing is still faced with pressures to
divest itself of the large shareholding in its new rival in world
markets. But the European Commission's watchdogs on competitive behaviour have been reassured by the formation in July
1973 of Imperial Tobacco International to develop trade in
European and other markets, supported by several of the world's
newest, largest and most advanced factories under completion at
Nottingham and Bristol.

The exchange back of brand names has begun so that each giant
will have complete ownership of its brand rights throughout
Western Europe. But BAT's ownership of the existing trade-marks
and house names of Imperial brands registered in countries outside Europe continues unchanged. BAT has given Imperial rights
in Europe to Player's Medium Navy Cut, Gold Leaf, Special and
No. 6, Wills' Embassy, Three Castles and Woodbine. Imperial's
marks in Britain and Ireland that go to BAT are H. B., Gladstone,
Belair, Viceroy, Matinee, Kool and Wintermans.

Clearly, the European market is destined to become a much more
obvious battleground between British and American producers
and the few surviving independent producers. Early in 1974,
Lorillard of the United States signed a deal with Imperial for the
latter to market Kent cigarettes in Britain. Kenneth McAllister,
president of Liggett & Myers cigarette division, reports that his
European headquarters in Brussels has been greatly strengthened
by top-flight managers and marketeers. The Swiss subsidiary has
begun exporting Chesterfield and L & M brands into Britain and
building up a sales organisation to cope with future growth. 'The
international cigarette market is several times the size of the United
States market and continues to grow at a faster rate, especially in

the more affluent countries and in the developing nations. Consequently, there are good opportunities for United States manufacturers to increase sales and earnings in overseas markets.'

A progressive running down of the French and Italian state tobacco monopolies is envisaged from 1976 and already foreign companies are seeking new licensing arrangements for their brands ahead of firm decisions in line with the competition policies which the European Community is seeking to promote. Consumption of cigarettes in France is about 70,500 million units annually and that of Italy 60,400 million. Since only 5 per cent or so of sales comes from imports and the combined market to be decontrolled is larger than either Germany or Britain, the opportunities for expansion are obvious.

Total consumption in West Germany is about 120,000 million units, with filter brands commanding 85 per cent of the market. Although thirteen concerns operate in the Federal Republic, the top six cover 97 per cent of sales (Reemtsma 33, BAT 28, Brinckmann 20, Roth-Handle 10, Neuerberg 5, Philip Morris 1). Exports total around 6,500 million units a year.

In Belgium, consumption is amounting to 18,000 million units a year, of which 2,000 million are imported. Filters account for 65 per cent of sales. There are seven manufacturers (Tabacofina 39 per cent, Gosset 21, Cinta 11, Odon Warland 11, Weltab 8, Van Landewijck 5, and Rembrandt 5).

Some 19,000 million units are sold in the Netherlands cigarette market. Exports account for another 5,000 million units. Filters represent about 40 per cent of total home consumption. There are five main manufacturers (Laurens 34 per cent, BAT 27, Turmac 21, Niemeyer 9, Crescent 5).

The concentration of manufacturing and distributive power is already evident in the United States and Britain, but the tentacles are stretching into Europe. Philip Morris's growth has already been described, as have been the moves by the Rembrandt organisation* to create the multinational cigarette combine Rothmans International out of Martin Brinckmann, Turmac, Tabacofina, and Carreras Rothman. Some other connections are Lorillard's association with Van Landewijck in Belgium, where Odon Warland is a subsidiary of BAT, already number two in the

* At the time of writing, this group was building up a shareholding in Liggett & Myers.

Netherlands and West Germany. Cinta of Belgium is under the wing of Reemtsma of Germany. Laurens of the Netherlands is part of Brinckmann (Rothmans International group, which also includes Turmac). Niemeyer of the Netherlands comes under Gallaher (American Brands, who control Ritmeester), while Crescent has links with Philip Morris. In Germany, Reynolds has a large holding in Neuerberg. The web grows more complex if the situation elsewhere round Europe is examined. The threads are intricate, with trade-marks not always owned by home producers outside their domestic markets by reason of take-overs of third-party licences or historical assignments of rights.

Struggle as everyone may for the European markets, the owners of the great Anglo-American tobacco enterprises are not solely concerned with profits from tobacco. Huge sums are being earmarked for acquisitions in other industries and new combinations will be formed before 1980. Initially, the emphasis of take-overs has been on consumer products and retailing, where the tobacco barons' skills of marketing and distributive organisation are proven, or in the paper, board, packaging and machinery industries with whom there has always been a close relationship for the supply of raw materials and manufacturing know-how. Where will the giant tobacco corporations strike next in an era when the British Match Corporation can merge happily with a razor blade producer, Wilkinson Sword, or BAT can joyfully swallow some of Manhattan's departmental stores, and Loews Theatres can operate alongside a United States tobacco manufacturer? With the great oil and motor vehicle corporations running into a variety of problems, it is not a wild forecast that the tobacco groups of Britain and the United States may become the new leviathans of the 1980s, vast conglomerates channelling their cash flows in new directions and across national boundaries.

One industry that may move closer to tobacco is chemicals, especially as the search for a safe cigarette, necessary to protect the huge cash flow from tobacco production, reaches a more critical stage now that all governments recognise their responsibilities in emphasising the dangers to health from smoking cured leaf. The Imperial Group is already linked in a £13 million-plus venture with Imperial Chemical Industries to produce and market a new smoking material, which soon will be blended in new and existing brands of cigarette. Celanese and Courtaulds have rival materials.

Other research is producing other alternatives. In the United States an army of chemists and biologists is experimenting with tobacco, from plant cross-breeding to new methods of filtration of tars. Milder, tar-reduced brands are beginning to sell with some success in Britain ahead of the introduction of substitutes to cigarette recipes. Eastman Kodak, with its historic grip on patents for materials used in filter rod production round the world, is deeply engaged in new research to improve protection of the smoker.

Just what might happen if the search for a safer cigarette is successful must be almost beyond the comprehension of business analysts. A resumption of rapid growth in smoking, coupled with diversification, is not, however, an unlikely event (nor, of course, is the possibility that chemists might find a cure for the habit). While the huge tobacco manufacturing organisations hedge against their future by reducing their dependence on the mystical leaf, the planters of North America are beginning to feel leaner times, in spite of Government support programmes and help to meet competition from growers elsewhere in the world. More and more United States tobacco farmers and workers are leaving the land each year, or turning to cultivating other crops. Those who stay either get bigger, or go under.

The fragrant weed has been smoked, chewed, sniffed, and burned ever since primitive man first became enslaved to its mystic properties. Kings and prelates have variously sought to stifle its usage, or to build nations on its revenues. The eternal leaf has provided the United States with its oldest industry and the earliest source of mass employment for the colonists of what proved to be the richest territory on earth.

Perhaps the romantic past, which tobacco antiquarians still seek to recall, has been made even more misty by one hundred years of progressive industrialisation. It took the late Compton Mackenzie, a convinced smoker, more than 100,000 words to compile his scholarly explanation, in *Sublime Tobacco*, of man's addiction, fatal or otherwise. This narrative has taken his story on to the age of capital and giant corporations. Yet tobacco is still an enigma for the scientists, who have yet fully to understand both its chemical properties and why people fill their lungs with the smoke of 2,270,000,000,000 cigarettes round the world every year. And sales are still growing at the rate of 200,000 million units a year.

A Short Guide to Tobacco Cultivation

WHERE IT COMES FROM

Bright and semi bright
flue-cured tobacco   Flue-cured tobacco is the principal type used in the United Kingdom and North America, forming almost the whole content of cigarettes and a large part of the ingredients of pipe tobaccos. Only shade grown cigar wrapper leaf is more intensively cultivated. There are many grades. The flue-curing process, which yields leaf ranging from light lemon to dark mahogany in colour, was developed in the early 19th century. There is production in the states of Florida, Georgia, North and South Carolina and Virginia. Production of this type of tobacco is also undertaken in Rhodesia, Canada, India, Zambia and Malawi. Efforts to expand output are being made within Europe, though little is used in British manufacture.

Dark-fired tobacco   This is a large, heavy kind of leaf grown in heavier soil than flue-cured. Main use is for Roll and Shag tobaccos and gives off a strong smoke. First grown in Virginia and Kentucky, but output is now supplemented by Tennessee and very successful growing in Malawi.

Burley and other
air-cured tobaccos   Grown in naturally fertile limestone soil. Chief sources are the USA, mainly Kentucky, Canada, India, and Malawi. The seed varies from that used in flue-cured tobacco production. Air-curing gives

the leaves a reddish-brown colour. Burley is widely used in the USA, both for cigarettes and pipe mixtures. It has not obtained quite the same popularity elsewhere.

Oriental tobaccos
These have a distinctive aromatic flavour. Smaller leafed plants than Virginia-type tobaccos. Mainly grown in the Balkans and countries bordering the Black Sea. Greece and Turkey are important suppliers of high-quality Oriental leaf.

Latakia
Latakia is the smallest of all the tobacco plants, originating from Latakia, Syria. A very heavily-fired tobacco, dark in colour when cured, it is mostly used for pipe smoking mixtures. Cyprus is a main supplier.

Cigar tobaccos
Once virtually all cigars were made from West Indian and Cuban leaf. Main sources today are Cuba (Havana), Jamaica, Brazil, Indonesia, USA (Connecticut) and Cameroun. All cigar tobacco is air-cured and the closest attention is given to cultivation of a uniform leaf, which is strictly graded for size, colour and texture.

Perique
An air-cured tobacco, Perique is cultivated on the banks of the Mississippi near New Orleans. It is a very strong tobacco, with a marked smell and flavour. Mostly used for seasoning pipe tobaccos.

CULTIVATION OF THE LEAF

The cultivation and harvesting of tobacco leaf can vary from region to region, from country to country. Broadly, in the Northern Hemisphere a sheltered spot with a southern aspect is usually selected for the bed in which seedlings are grown. The soil has to be porous and well drained, with the beds sterilised to destroy weeds, insects and disease, and treated with fertilizers. Tobacco seeds are so minute—from 300,000 to 400,000 per ounce—that one tablespoonful can sow 100 square yards. These are sown and covered by cheesecloth in February and March in the southern states of America, in May in Canada, and in September and October in Zambia, Rhodesia, and Malawi. The strongest seedlings are transplanted when five or six inches high. Close attention is paid to hoeing and protection during the main cultivation period. About two months after transplanting, flower buds and top leaves are removed to produce new shoots at the axil, which are also taken off to encourage healthy and uniform growth. Harvesting takes place when the leaves ripen, and these are taken to curing barns. Tobacco is very much a smallholder's crop, and much expert help is available to them in controlling yields and quality. In the United States some 700 miles separates the northern and southernmost parts of the flue-cured tobacco belt. Florida starts growing first and Virginia last in the annual cycle.

CURING

When it is harvested, tobacco leaf is not suitable for smoking, for it is full of moisture and quickly becomes mouldy unless cured. There are four main methods of curing:

Flue-curing This gives leaf a bright golden appearance and is the most widely used method. Almost all British cigarettes are made with this tobacco and much goes into pipe mixtures and tobaccos. Generally, curing barns are made of wood or brick, containing racks on which sticks are placed to hold the tobacco while a heating system, usually consisting of sheet iron flues running across the floor (connected to an outside furnace), dries the green leaves. Fresh air ventilators control the drying and great care is taken to ensure that no smoke comes into contact with the leaves.

Individual farmers use their own judgement, but generally there are three principal stages in the curing process: 1. Yellowing the leaf, taking about 24 to 36 hours at temperatures rising from 80°F to 120°F. 2. Fixing the colour by raising the heat gradually to 140°F, with plenty of ventilation, over 10 to 18 hours. 3. Drying the stems, with ventilators closed, by raising the temperature further by 5 degrees an hour to 170°F.

Air-curing Tobacco is suspended on lathes in barns for about five weeks, exposed to a flow of air. The leaves turn a light reddish-brown.

Sun-curing Producing a tobacco similar in look to air-cured leaf, the sun-curing method involves racking the leaves in the sunshine for set daily periods over four weeks, depending on the weather. Additionally, there is air-curing in a barn.

Fire-curing This method takes from one to six weeks. Plants are hung in barns, cured by wood fires lit in trenches across the floor so smoke comes into direct contact with the leaf, turning it dark brown.

Production of leaf tobacco in the principal producing countries
(million lb, wet weight)

	Average 1960–64	1966	1967	1968	1969	1970	1971	1972
Commonwealth								
Bangladesh	63	60	84	87	89	90	85	60
India *a*	739	656	779	813	796	743	798	902
Australia *a*	27	27	28	25	34	38	38	35
New Zealand *a*	8	7	6	6	8	7	9	9
Malawi *a*	44	41	39	32	26	49	58	67
Zambia *a*	19	17	12	15	12	11	14	13
Tanzania	5*a*	12	18	23	26	28	34	27
Uganda	4	6	9	10	8	11	8	10
Canada	196	234	213	219	247	222	224	182
Total c	1,105	1,060	1,188	1,230	1,246	1,199	1,268	1,305
Foreign								
United States	2,178	1,887	1,968	1,710	1,804	1,907	1,708	1,751
Argentina *a*	106	99	139	137	118	146	136	162
Brazil	412	503	535	569	552	539	540*e*	530
Colombia	80	114	95	96	98	93*e*	84*e*	80
Cuba	107	113	113	102	80	88	60*e*	120
Dominican Republic	52	45	41	36	46	48	51*e*	54
Mexico	151	152	153	104	159	175*e*	183*e*	176*e*
Paraguay	31	19	30	49	53	40	39	41

Burma a	87	73	91	150	125	134	91	114
Indonesia	229	194	149	152	152	159	164e	154
Japan	333	435	460	426	383	331	330	314
South Korea	77	159	146	154	131	124	140e	207e
Pakistan	149	243	308	287	276	252	249	192
Philippines	144	128	113	143	125	135	123e	124
Taiwan	38	33	39	46	45	46	37e	35
Thailand	123	195	172	188	176	205	209	218
France	91	104	105	114	98	103	21	105
West Germany	23	21	19	16	17	19	94	23
Italy	130	161	192	163	175	162	175	170
Greece	220	217	254	194	174	198	197	187
Turkey	289	362	417	359	323	324	370	388
Spain	68	47	69	58	43	55	61e	66
Yugoslavia	86	119	120	97	103	107	96	128e
Bulgaria	211	291	261	251	212	269	264e	313
Hungary	48	43	53	58	60	39	36e	38
Poland	128	106	171	183	200	187	154e	187
Rumania	62	89	76	72	52	50	67	66
Soviet Union b	375	518	573	575	516	569	560	530
South Africa a	61	61	49	60	84	75	71e	66
Total	6,089	6,531	6,911	6,549	6,380	6,579	6,310	6,539
Total above countries	7,194	7,591	8,099	7,779	7,626	7,778	7,578	7,844
Estimated world total	10,200	10,200	10,500	10,200	10,000	10,200	10,100	10,400e

a Seasons ending in year shown. b Including Mahorka. c Excluding Rhodesia and small producers. d Average 1962–64. e Revised. f Forecast.
Source: Commonwealth Tobacco Seretariat.

Sale and Manufacture

After sorting and preliminary grading by the planter, the leaf, which has been allowed to absorb some moisture after curing, is tied in bundles of 20 to 30 leaves ready for sale. Most tobacco is sold by auction in special warehouses where farmers have their bales or baskets laid out for official grading and rapid sale by auctioneers to skilled buyers acting for the big tobacco manufacturers or merchants. Tobacco is subsequently transferred to leaf-packing plant for examination, a check on grading and stemming. Hydraulic rams are often used to compress the tobacco tightly into casks, known as hogsheads, weighing from 725 to 950 lb each. Excess moisture has been removed. In Britain, shipments of leaf are deposited in bonded warehouses until required for use—an operation supervised by the Customs and Excise, with duty being required to be paid before the leaf is drawn for factory manufacturing.

There are eight main types of cigarette and pipe tobacco produced from the basic cured leaf. These are Shag (light and dark), Honeydew and Fancy Scented, Mixture, Flake and Cut Plug, Navy Cut, Plug and Bar, Roll and Pigtail (also known as Twist), and Fancy. The Plug and Bar and the Roll and Pigtail are often referred to as hard tobaccos, mainly used for pipe smoking or chewing.

The art of making pipe tobaccos is an amalgam of years of long patient experience in the skills of blending various grades and types of leaf. Modern equipment is now used to maintain a consistent quality that cultivates the loyalty of smokers of their selected brand. Experts prepare mixtures of cut blended leaf, flakes, and spun products. Strict manufacturing controls ensure the right moisture content and freedom from moulding.

Snuffs are often produced from secret recipes handed down over the years. Blends of tobacco are pulverized and the processing for flavour, pungency, colour and texture varies considerably over the industry. The practice of snuff-taking was once more common than smoking. British-made snuff is widely sold round the world. The United States is the largest consumer, using around 40 million lb annually. Snuff is not made from waste but specially selected leaf.

Cigars comprise a filler, a binder and a wrapper. Again skilled selection and blending of leaf based on many years of experience is involved. Machines are increasingly used to produce standard qualities. The cigar is a direct descendant of the roll of tobacco leaves that the Mayas of Central America smoked 2,000 years ago, and of the thick bundles of tobacco wrapped in dried palm or maize leaves that the West Indians were smoking when Christopher Columbus came upon them in the fifteenth century. The design and constituents, therefore, epitomise the history of smoking. There is a variety of romantic sounding names for sizes, such as Corona Grandee, Panatella, Cheroot, Whiff and the more modern cigarette style Cigarillo, involving a wrapper of reconstituted leaf. Much effort goes into making cigars, some made by hand rolling for the connoisseurs.

Cigarette factories are complex industrial plants that vary in their layout and technology. Automation has provided production lines that carry leaf rapidly from preliminary leaf processing stages after withdrawal from bond, through threshing and the bulking of the resulting lamina, and onto cutting and shredding. Controlled temperatures and humidity are no less important than the recipes for blending different tobaccos for a particular brand. High-speed machines produce filled rods, cut into cigarettes of required length and dimensions, including filter tips. Complex packing, parcelling and packaging machinery dovetails with cigarette makers. Production is always carried out in conditions of tight security as cigarettes are a high value product. Quality control standards are stringent as smokers have a choice of many brands offered by a producer's competitors. There is little romance in contemporary cigarette making, but smokers have their illusions, often stimulated by the brand names and the marketing skills of the salesmen. Computers control distribution to wholesalers and retailers, whose stocks and orders are reflected in the pace of production on the factory machine room floor. The length, size and dimensions of cigarettes vary from market to market, and from one country of manufacture to another.

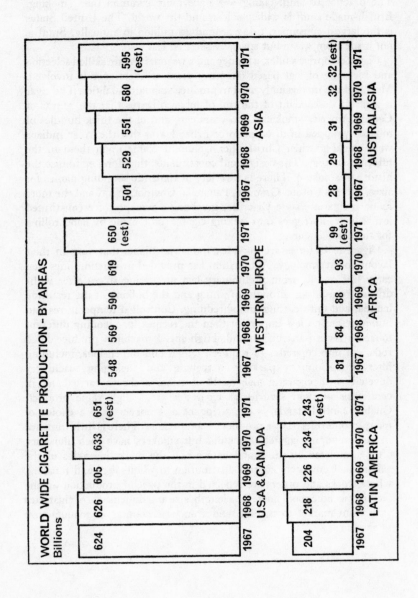

WORLD WIDE CIGARETTE PRODUCTION - BY AREAS
Billions

ASIA
1967: 501
1968: 529
1969: 551
1970: 580
1971: 595 (est)

AUSTRALASIA
1967: 28
1968: 29
1969: 31
1970: 32
1971: 32 (est)

WESTERN EUROPE
1967: 548
1968: 569
1969: 590
1970: 619
1971: 650 (est)

AFRICA
1967: 81
1968: 84
1969: 88
1970: 93
1971: 99 (est)

U.S.A & CANADA
1967: 624
1968: 626
1969: 605
1970: 633
1971: 651 (est)

LATIN AMERICA
1967: 204
1968: 218
1969: 226
1970: 234
1971: 243 (est)

The Statistics of Cigarette Production and Consumption

UNITED KINGDOM

Consumption (million cigarettes)		Consumption (million cigarettes)	
1961	113,400	1967	119,100
1962	109,900(a)	1968	121,800
1963	115,200	1969	124,900
1964	114,400(b)	1970	127,900
1965	112,000	1971	122,400(c)
1966	117,600		

(a) First Royal College of Physicians health report
(b) United States Surgeon-General's report 'Smoking and Health'
(c) Second Royal College of Physicians report
Source: Tobacco Research Council

	Estimated market shares % (1971)	Advertising Expenditure £m (1971)
Imperial Tobacco	67.0	6.5
Gallaher	24.0	5.3
Carreras	8.0	2.9
Others	1.0	–

Total consumer expenditure on tobacco products (1972), including cigarettes, was £1,808 million.

Total value of United Kingdom manufacturers' output, including direct exports, but deducting duties, margins for distributors, and imports was about £465 million in 1971 for all tobacco goods. Direct exports were worth about £45 million.

		% of market (1972)
Sales by type		
Plain	Standard	8
	Small	11
Filter	King Size	6
	Medium	38
	Small	37

Coupon and trading stamp brands account for an estimated 65 per cent of all cigarettes sold.

Imports of Unmanufactured Tobacco (lbs '000)

	From All Sources	From United States of America
1900	98,349	88,805
1910	111,258	98,951
1920	219,043	117,508
1930	237,028	197,765
1940	141,430	59,060
1950	305,804	143,699
1955	343,705	178,496
1966	262,093	132,693
1967	279,573	132,560
1968	328,431	164,600
1969	305,487	134,643
1970	283,557	116,850
1971	268,587	97,676
1972	297,700	115,100

The leading Commonwealth sources of unmanufactured tobacco in 1971 (lbs '000) were: Canada—51,558; India—37,774; Malawi—18,082; Tanzania—7,836; Pakistan—2,791; and Zambia—2,672. Prior to UDI, Rhodesia in 1966 supplied 15,206 out of a total 110,334 purchased from Commonwealth sources.

Appendix Three

Consumption (1973)   *'000 m units*

	1972	1973	% of market
Ordinary tipped	297.40	310.22	54.0 ⎫
Mentholated tipped	135.30	146.42	25.5 ⎬ Total tipped
Charcoal tipped	29.27	29.89	5.2 ⎭ 84.7
Regular plain	40.74	38.79	6.7
King size plain	51.45	49.65	8.6
Total consumption:	554.16	574.97	

Production by manufacturers (1973) '000 m units

	Home	Export	Total	% of home market
R. J. Reynolds	179.08	14.30	193.38	31.2
Philip Morris	121.95	15.50	137.45	21.2
Brown & Williamson	100.65	7.70	108.35	17.5
American Brands	93.93	4.00	97.93	16.4
P. Lorillard	49.06	8.60	57.66	8.5
Liggett & Myers	29.50	8.50	38.00	5.1
Others	.80	.20	1.00	0.1

The Top Ten Brands (1973) '000 m units
(estimates only)

1. Winston 87
2. Marlboro 78
3. Kool 56
4. Pall Mall 53
5. Salem 48
6. Kent 30
7. Camel 24
8. Benson & Hedges 23
9. Tareyton 19
10. Viceroy 18

* Maxwell Report. By permission of J. C. Maxwell Jr, director of the Maxwell division, Wheat, First Securities, Inc., Richmond, Va.

The Giants

R. J. Reynolds Industries Inc. (Headquarters: Winston-Salem, North Carolina)
Holding company owning R. J. Reynolds Tobacco Co., world's third-largest cigarette producer with sale of over 200 billion units in 1972.

Interests include:
RJR Foods (products include Hawaiian Punch, Chun King, College Inn, My-T Fine, Vermont Maid, Brer Rabbit Filler, Patio and Davis)
RJR Archer Inc. (maker of aluminium foil products and packaging)
Filmco Inc. (maker of vinyl packaging)
Sea-Land Service Inc. (containerised freight transport)
American Independent Oil Co. (oil producer and refiner)

Total sales $2,957,630,000 (1972)
Tobacco sales $2,168,242,000 (1972, world-wide)
$1,914,147,000 (1971, North America only)

Main brands in United States:
Cigarettes   Winston, Salem, Doral, Camel, Vantage, Tempo
Pipe tobacco Prince Albert, Carter Hall, Madeira Gold, Apple Pie
Chewing plug Days Work, Apple

Additional information:
R. J. Reynolds tobacco sells in over 100 markets round the world. Brands used include Winston, Salem, Camel. Has been leading United States exporter, but Philip Morris now claims to have overtaken Reynolds, which is the largest United States manufacturer.

American Brands Inc. (Headquarters: Park Avenue, New York)
Holding company owning the American Tobacco Company and
Gallaher of the United Kingdom.

Interests include:
  James B. Beam Distilling Co. (liquor suppliers)
  Swingline Inc. (office equipment and fasteners)
  Andrew Jergens Co. (hand care products)
  Master Lock Co. (lock makers)
  Sunshine Biscuits Inc. (biscuit and snack food producers)
  Acme Visible Records Inc. (information retrieval systems)
  Duffy-Mott Co. Inc. (branded food processors)

Total sales $2,998,900,000 (1972)
  Tobacco sales $972,700,000 (1972, United States)
          $1,165,900,000 (1972, international)

Main brands in United States:
Cigarettes   Tareyton, Pall Mall, Silva Thins, Carlton, Lucky Strike,
       Maryland, Montclair, Half and Half, Iceberg, Bull
       Durham, Lemon Twist
Pipe tobacco Half & Half, Bull Durham, Paladin, Black Cherry
Cigars   La Corona, Antonio y Cleopatra, Roi-Tan, Bock y Ca,
       Tipton, Trumps, Golfers, Cabanas, Cigarillos

Additional information
The United Kingdon subsidiary, Gallaher, is the second largest
British domestic market tobacco producer. Also owns Niemeyer of
Holland, among other European tobacco interests. Cigarette brands
include Park Drive, Sovereign, Kensitas, Senior Service, and Benson &
Hedges. Cigars include Hamlet and Manikin. Smoking tobaccos
include Condor, Old Holborn, and Benson & Hedges' Mellor. Gallaher
has group sales of £543 million. Its non-tobacco interests include
Dolland & Aitchison (Britain's largest opticians), Warriner & Mason
(cash and carry wholesalers), Sanders Valve, Mono Pumps, and
Fourbuoys (newsagents).

Philip Morris Inc. (Headquarters: Park Avenue, New York)
Holding company for multinational organisation that includes Philip
Morris USA, Philip Morris International, Philip Morris Europe and
Philip Morris & Co. (UK). Owns Godfrey Phillips among the tobacco
interests round the world. Group is world's second-largest publicly
held cigarette producer after BAT, and sells 225 billion units of
cigarettes.

Interests include:
   American Safety Razor Co. (Personna shaving products and hospital
   equipment)
   Miller Brewing Co. (brewers)
   Milprint (packaging materials)
   Clark Gum Co. (confectionery and gum maker)
   Nicolet Paper Co. (speciality paper manufacturer)
   Polymer Industries (speciality chemicals)
   Mission Viejo Co. (house building and developers)
   Kaye Cards (greeting cards)

Total sales $2,131,224,000 (1972)
   Tobacco sales not available

Main brands in United States:

Cigarettes	Marlboro, Benson & Hedges Premium, Parliament, Virginia Slims, Philip Morris, Alpine, English Ovals, Galaxy, New Leaf, Muratti Ambassador
Pipe tobacco	Bond Street, Player's Navy Cut, Revelation, Country Doctor, Wakefield, Handsome Dan, Barking Dog, Puritan, Lyons Own
Cigars	Benson & Hedges

Additional information:
Philip Morris International sells over 113 billion units of cigarettes
annually and holds about 7 per cent of world-wide cigarette market.
Brands marketed in 160 countries through export and local manufacture
by affiliates and licensees. Marlboro and Philip Morris are among
world's leading brands, but other example names include Target
(Nigeria), Alpine (Australia), and Lido and Astor (Venezuela). For the
five years from 1972, some $500 million is to be spent on expanding
factories in United States and overseas.

Liggett & Myers Inc. (Headquarters: Fifth Avenue, New York)
Holding company operating tobacco division under the same name
(includes Pinkerton Tobacco).

Interests include:
   The Paddington Corporation (branded liquor suppliers)
   Austin, Nichols & Co. (liquor suppliers and importers)
   Carillon Importers (liquor importers)
   Allen Products (pet food manufacturers)
   Alpo Canned Dog Foods (pet food manufacturers)
   Pet Food Treats (pet food manufacturers)
   Perk Food Inc. (pet food manufacturers)
   Vets (pet food manufacturers)

Mercury Mills (rugs and carpets)
Earl Grissmer (household cleaners)
National Oats Co. (cereals and animal foods)
Brite Industries (watch straps and fashion accessories)

Total sales $753,627,611 (1972)
  Tobacco sales $371,118,000 (1972, world-wide)

Additional information:
Rothman of Canada holds at time of writing 10 per cent interest in
Liggett & Myers besides its own sales of 143,000 million units of
cigarettes.

Main brands in United States:

Cigarettes	L & M, Lark, Chesterfield, Eve, Fatima, Home Run, Oasis, Picayune, Piedmont
Pipe tobacco	Granger, Masterpiece, Velvet, Duke's, Buckhorn, Buffalo, Country Gentleman, Harmony Mixture, King Bee, Plow Boy, S & M, Sterling, Summertime, Sweet Tip, Virginia Extra
Chewing plug	Red Man, Red Horse, Union Standard, Pay Car, Drummond, Horse Shoe, Masterpiece, Pick, Spark Plug, Star, Tinsley's Thick, W.N.T.

Additional information:
Since 1965, diversified non-tobacco operation income has risen to 60
per cent of total.
The tobacco division exports to over 100 countries, and a considerable
proportion are made under licence in many countries. Equity share-
holdings are held in tobacco companies in Argentina, Brazil, Mexico,
Peru, Switzerland and West Germany. Losses have been sustained in
Europe. In 1973, the Rembrandt Organisation began buying a share-
holding in Liggett & Myers following abortive talks between Cavenham
Foods of the United Kingdom and Liggett on an exchange of interests.

Loews Corporation (Headquarters: New York)
Conglomerate holding company for group of interests in leisure and
tobacco industries, operating through 130 main, wholly or partly
owned, subsidiaries spanning theatres, hotels, bowling alleys and candy
stands. A main division of Loews Theatres is P. J. Lorillard, acquired in
1968.

Total sales $761,067,000 (1972)
  Tobacco sales $600,000,000 (1972 world-wide, income estimate only)

Main brands in United States:
Cigarettes   Kent, True, Old Gold, Newport, Spring
Pipe tobacco   Briggs, Union Leader, Burgundy, India House, Friends
Cigars   Between-the-Acts, Madison, Omega, Erik, Stagg
Chewing plug   Beech Nut, Bag Pipe, Havana Blossom, Big Red

British-American Tobacco (Headquarters: Westminster, London)
The world's largest tobacco manufacturer, registered in the United
Kingdom (a large shareholder is the Imperial Group). The largest single
subsidiary is Brown & Williamson, the major United States tobacco
producer. Owns numerous tobacco companies round the world and
has major holding with Imperial in Tobacco Securities Trust, Mardon
Packaging International, Molins.

Interests include:
  Gimbel Bros (departmental stores)
  Saks Fifth Avenue (fashion shops)
  Kohl Stores Inc. (retail group)
  International Stores UK (food retailers)
  Pricerite UK (supermarket chain)
  Wiggins Teape (paper manufacturers)
  Horten AG, Germany (departmental stores)
  Vita Foods Inc. (food processors)
  British-American Cosmetics (Yardley, Lenthéric, Morny, Germaine
  Monteil)

Total sales £2,807,740,000 (1973, world-wide)
  Tobacco sales £2,162,100,000 (1973, world-wide)

Brown & Williamson: Main Brands in United States:
Cigarettes   Kool, Viceroy, Raleigh, Belair, du Maurier, Life
Smoking tobacco Sir Walter Raleigh, Taconis, Long Cuts, Laredo,
                 Bugler, Kite, Target
Chewing plug   Bloodhound, Sun Cured, Red Juice
Snuff   Tube Rose

Additional information:
The BAT world organization markets 400 brands of cigarettes, 250
brands of pipe tobacco, and 190 cigar and cigarillo brands. Operates
140 factories in 54 countries and sells in 130 countries. Cigarette output estimated at 460,000 million units. Brands exported from England*
have been Player's, Embassy, Gold Leaf, Senior Service, State Express
555, Woodbine, Three Castles, du Maurier and Benson & Hedges

  * At the time of writing, Imperial and BAT were exchanging brand
ownerships in Western Europe.

(outside the Americas). BAT has 12,000 trade-marks registered throughout the world, though not all are in use. Examples of brands sold in various markets are Durbar (Ghana), Bicycle and Galleon (Nigeria), Pacific (Fiji), Lulu (Jordan), Tom-Tom (Malawi), Gladstone (Holland), Continental (Brazil), Charminar (India), HB Kronen Filter (Germany). Exports from the United States include Lucky Strike, Pall Mall, Viceroy, and Kool. In 40 countries, a BAT brand is the market leader.

Imperial Group (Headquarters: Grosvenor Place, London)
Holding company for group of companies, including Imperial Tobacco and the newly-formed Imperial International. Largest domestic United Kingdom tobacco manufacturer and until 1973 had not engaged in export trade under historic agreement with British-American Tobacco in which it held 26 per cent of the Ordinary Stock at March 1974.

Interests and associates include:
    Finlay & Co. (retailers)
    Robert Fletcher (paper manufacturer)
    St Anne's Board Mill Co. (board maker)
    Creators (Holdings) (plastics manufacturer)
    Albion Bottle Co. (glass manufacturer)
    E.S.L. (Bristol) (educational equipment)
    Golden Wonder (potato crisps)
    Nitrovit (feeding stuffs)
    Ross Companies (food processors and catering)
    Young's Seafoods (fish products)
    Lowland Bulb Co. (mail-order horticulturalists)
    S.P. Commercials (commercial vehicle suppliers)
    British United Trawlers (fishing vessels)
    Mardon Packaging International (packaging group)
    Courage Ltd (brewing, 6,000 public houses)
    Beecham-Imperial Aviation (air charter hire)
    British Sidac (film manufacturers)
    Cantrell & Cochrane (soft drinks)
    Harp Lager (brewers)
    Taunton Cider Co.
    Wine Traders Consortium
    Bunzl Pulp and Paper
    Glenlivet Distillers
    Tobacco Securities Trust
    Anchor Hotels and Taverns
    Smedley HP Foods (canned foods, pickles and sauces)
    Lea & Perrins Inc.
    United Carlo Gatti (cold store operators)

Total sales £1,573,100,000 (1973)
  Tobacco sales £1,991,500,000 (1973, United Kingdom)

Main brands in United Kingdom: (Wills, Player, and Ogden marks)

Cigarettes	Embassy, Three Castles, Capstan, Sothebys, Slim Kings, Woodbine, Solent, Passing Clouds, Carlton, No. 6, John Player Special, Player's No. 10, York, Gold Leaf, Kool, Special Mild, Perfectos, Milford
Smoking tobaccos	Golden Virginia, Digger, Sun Valley, Hearts of Oak, Whiskey Flake, Capstan, Three Nuns, Navy Cut, 'No Name', Malvern, Aintree, Royal Navy, Sweet Briar, St Bruno, Gold Block, Ogden's No. 6, Royal Hunt, Grand Cut, Weaver, Four Square, A1, Exmoor Hunt, Walnut, Cragman, St Julien
Cigars	Embassy, Castella, Wills' Whiffs, Doncella, El Sol, Finos, Napoleon, La Tropical, Hoyo de Monterrey, Panter, Tom Thumb, Grandee, Imperial, Henri Wintermans (through BAT)
Snuffs	Wilson range, including SP (No. 1), Wallflower, Jockey Club, Otto de Rose, Menthol, Top Mill, Aniseed

Rothmans International
A unique European amalgamation of tobacco manufacturing interests with 200 brands and links to the Rembrandt Group of South Africa (founded by Dr Anton Rupert). Members are: Carreras-Rothmans, United Kingdom; Brinkmann, Germany; Tabacofina, Belgium; Turmac, Netherlands. Their associates include Muratti, Alfred Dunhill, Vander Elst, Ed. Laurens, P. J. Carroll, Murrays, and Sullana.

Total sales £940,000,000 (year to June, 1973)

Main brands in Europe:

Cigarettes	Rothmans King Size, Dunhill International, Craven A, Consulate, Piccadilly, Ransom, Peter Stuyvesant, St Moritz, Belga, Caballero, Laurens, Stella, Tivoli, Golden American, Lord, Lux, Peer
Pipe tobaccos	Erinmore, M.B., Stanwell, Batavia, Lincoln, Craven Mixture
Cigars	Schimmelpenninck

Additional information:
The group operates through 44 factories in 17 countries, and markets 200 brands. Carreras-Rothmans has up to 1973 accounted for 60 per cent of Britain's direct tobacco exports.

Note on Sources

The most daunting task facing any author of a work on tobacco is the division of his time between typewriter and research. It took some years of concentrated reading of the many excellent general and specialist books and pile upon pile of documents, reports, cuttings—besides the interviewing, investigation, and correspondence—before the writer could dare compile a selective narrative on the development of the Anglo-American tobacco industry. Every author hopes his work will make a new contribution, supplementing the devoted research undertaken by others over so many years. The tobacco industry is unusually well-endowed with many fine books and most manufacturers, too, are to be commended for their archives, which have helped so many historians. Just a selection of the works, which are recommended for further reading, as well as requiring acknowledgement, can be mentioned in the Bibliography. They are mentioned here because of their special value to the author, but the exclusion of others does not imply either ignorance of their existence, or any lack of appreciation of their merits.

It is also necessary to acknowledge the helpful resources, records, and cuttings of a variety of publications. These include *Tobacco*, *The Economist*, *The Times*, *The New York Times*, *The Financial Times*, *The Wall Street Journal*, *The Guardian*, *Business Week*, *Richmond News Leader*, *Richmond Times-Dispatch*, and journals of individual tobacco companies. Further help has been given by the United States Information Service.

Bibliography

Alford, B. W. E., *W. D. & H. O. Wills and the Development of the United Kingdom Tobacco Industry 1786–1965*. Methuen & Company, London, 1973.

Barr, A. G., *Tobacco from the Grower to Smoker*. Pitman, London, 1950.

Boyd, W. K., *The Story of Durham*. Duke University Press, 1927.

Clements, F. and Harben, Edward, *Leaf of Gold*. Methuen & Company, London, 1962.

Cox, Reavis, *Competition in the American Tobacco Industry 1911–1932*. Columbia University Press, New York, 1933.

Dickinson, Sue V., *The First Sixty Years*. American Leaf Organisation and Imperial Tobacco, 1963.

Dobson, R. P., *China Cycle*. Macmillan, London, 1946.

Dunhill, A. H., *The Gentle Art of Smoking*. Max Reinhardt, London, 1954.

Heimann, Robert K., *Tobacco and Americans*. McGraw-Hill, New York, 1960.

Koskowski, W., *The Habit of Tobacco Smoking*. Staples Press, 1955.

Mackenzie, Compton, *Sublime Tobacco*. Chatto & Windus, London, 1957.

Scott, A. B., *A Short History of Smoking*. Imperial Tobacco publication, 1950.

Tennant, R. B., *The American Cigarette Industry*. Yale University Press, 1950.

Tilley, Nannie May, *The Bright Tobacco Industry*. University of North Carolina Press, 1948.

Wagner, Susan, *Cigarette Country*. Praeger Publishers, New York, 1971.

Winkler, John K., *Tobacco Tycoon*. Random House, New York, 1941.

The Arents Tobacco Collection. New York Public Library.

Bibliography

Sold American, The First Fifty Years. American Tobacco publication, 1954.

Tobacco: Its History, Culture and Manufacture. W. D. & H. O. Wills, 1962.

The American Tobacco Company and the Imperial Tobacco Company: Federal Trade Commission Report. United States Government Printing Office, Washington DC, 1926.

A History of the Tobacco Trade, and other Imperial Tobacco information brochures, 1972.

Federal Trade Commission Report on the Tobacco Industry. United States Government Printing Office, Washington DC, 1921.

Monopolies Commission Report on the Supply of Cigarettes and Tobacco and of Cigarette and Tobacco Machinery. Her Majesty's Stationery Office, London, 1961.

Smoking and Health: Royal College of Physicians. Pitman, London, 1962.

Smoking and Health: United States Surgeon-General's Advisory Committee Report. Department of Health, Education and Welfare, Washington DC, 1964.

Index

Index

313

Index

Index